Adobe®
Edge Animate
onDemand

Steve Johnson, Perspection, Inc.

Que Publishing, 800 East 96th Street, Indianapolis, IN 46240 USA

Adobe® Edge Animate on Demand

Library of Congress Cataloging-in-Publication Data is on file

ISBN-13: 978-0-7897-4936-9
ISBN-10: 0-7897-4936-X

Printed and bound in the United States of America
First Printing: December 2012
15 14 13 12   4 3 2 1

Que Publishing offers excellent discounts on this book when ordered in quantity for bulk purchases or special sales.

For information, please contact: U.S. Corporate and Government Sales

1-800-382-3419 or corpsales@pearsontechgroup.com

For sales outside the U.S., please contact: International Sales

1-317-428-3341 or International@pearsontechgroup.com

Trademarks

Warning and Disclaimer

Publisher
Paul Boger

Associate Publisher
Greg Wiegand

Acquisitions Editor
Laura Norman

Managing Editor
Steve Johnson

Author
Steve Johnson

Page Layout
James Teyler

Interior Designers
Steve Johnson
Marian Hartsough

Indexer
Kristina Zeller

Proofreader
Beth Teyler

Team Coordinator
Cindy Teeters

Acknowledgments

Perspection, Inc.

Adobe Edge Animate on Demand has been created by the professional trainers and writers at Perspection, Inc. to the standards you've come to expect from Que publishing. Together, we are pleased to present this training book.

Perspection, Inc. is a software training company committed to providing information and training to help people use software more effectively in order to communicate, make decisions, and solve problems. Perspection writes and produces software training books, and develops multimedia and web-based training. Since 1991, we have written more than 120 computer books, with several bestsellers to our credit, and sold over 5 million books.

This book incorporates Perspection's training expertise to ensure that you'll receive the maximum return on your time. You'll focus on the tasks and skills that increase productivity while working at your own pace and convenience.

We invite you to visit the Perspection web site at:

www.perspection.com

Acknowledgments

The task of creating any book requires the talents of many hard-working people pulling together to meet impossible deadlines and untold stresses. We'd like to thank the outstanding team responsible for making this book possible: the writer, Steve Johnson; the production editor, James Teyler; proofreader, Beth Teyler; and the indexer, Kristina Zeller.

At Que publishing, we'd like to thank Greg Wiegand and Laura Norman for the opportunity to undertake this project, Cindy Teeters for administrative support, and Sandra Schroeder for your production expertise and support.

Perspection

About the Author

Steve Johnson has written more than 80 books on a variety of computer software, including Adobe Photoshop CS6, Adobe Dreamweaver CS6, Adobe InDesign CS6, Adobe Illustrator CS6, Adobe Flash Professional CS5, Microsoft Windows 8, Microsoft Office 2010 and 2007, Microsoft Office 2008 for the Macintosh, and Apple OS X Mountain Lion. In 1991, after working for Apple Computer and Microsoft, Steve founded Perspection, Inc., which writes and produces software training. When he is not staying up late writing, he enjoys coaching baseball, playing golf, gardening, and spending time with his wife, Holly, and three children, JP, Brett, and Hannah. Steve and his family live in Northern California, but can also be found visiting family all over the western United States.

We Want to Hear from You!

As the reader of this book, *you* are our most important critic and commentator. We value your opinion and want to know what we're doing right, what we could do better, what areas you'd like to see us publish in, and any other words of wisdom you're willing to pass our way.

As an associate publisher for Que, I welcome your comments. You can email or write me directly to let me know what you did or didn't like about this book—as well as what we can do to make our books better.

Please note that I cannot help you with technical problems related to the topic of this book. We do have a User Services group, however, where I will forward specific technical questions related to the book.

When you write, please be sure to include this book's title and author as well as your name, email address, and phone number. I will carefully review your comments and share them with the author and editors who worked on the book.

Email: feedback@quepublishing.com

Mail: Greg Wiegand
         Que Publishing
         800 East 96th Street
         Indianapolis, IN 46240 USA

For more information about this book or another Que title, visit our web site at *www.quepublishing.com.* Type the ISBN (excluding hyphens) or the title of a book in the Search field to find the page you're looking for.

Contents

Introduction

Welcome to *Adobe Edge Animate on Demand*, a visual quick reference book that shows you how to work efficiently with Edge Animate. This book provides complete coverage of basic to advanced Edge Animate skills.

How This Book Works

You don't have to read this book in any particular order. We've designed the book so that you can jump in, get the information you need, and jump out. However, the book does follow a logical progression from simple tasks to more complex ones. Each task is presented on no more than two facing pages, which lets you focus on a single task without having to turn the page. To find the information that you need, just look up the task in the table of contents or index, and turn to the page listed. Read the task introduction, follow the step-by-step instructions in the left column along with screen illustrations in the right column, and you're done.

What's New

Adobe Edge Animate 1.0 is the debut version of the product, so everything in the product is **New!** You can look forward to many more new features in the next version of the product.

Keyboard Shortcuts

Most menu commands have a keyboard equivalent, such as Ctrl+I (Win) or ⌘+I (Mac), as a quicker alternative to using the mouse. A complete list of keyboard shortcuts is available in the back of this book.

How You'll Learn

How This Book Works

What's New

Keyboard Shortcuts

Step-by-Step Instructions

Real World Examples

Project Examples

Workshops

Get More on the Web

Step-by-Step Instructions

This book provides concise step-by-step instructions that show you "how" to accomplish a task. Each set of instructions includes illustrations that directly correspond to the easy-to-read steps. Also included in the text are time-savers, tables, and sidebars to help you work more efficiently or to teach you more in-depth information. A "Did You Know?" provides tips and techniques to help you work smarter, while a "See Also" leads you to other parts of the book containing related information about the task.

Real World Examples

This book uses real world example files to give you a context in which to use the task. By using the example files, you won't waste time looking for or creating sample files. You get a sample file to see how a feature works and apply what you have learned. Not every topic needs an example file, such as changing options. The example files that you need for project tasks are available on the web at *www.queondemand.com* or *www.perspection.com*.

Easy-to-follow introductions focus on a single concept.

Illustrations match the numbered steps.

Numbered steps guide you through each task.

See Also points you to related information in the book.

Did You Know? alerts you to tips, techniques and related information.

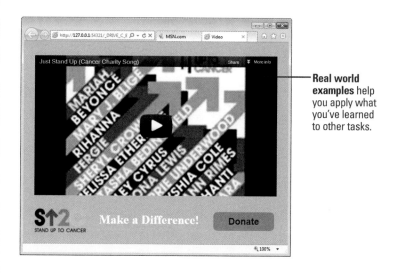

Real world examples help you apply what you've learned to other tasks.

Project Examples

For some topics, this book includes project examples that provide step-by-step tasks with specific end results. They are like mini-workshops. You start each project with a sample file, work through the steps, and then compare your results with a project results file at the end. The project example files are available on the web at *www.queondemand.com* or *www.perspection.com.* Look for the icon: **PrEx**. The icon appears in the table of contents so you can quickly and easily identify them.

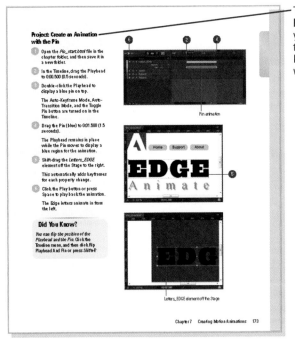

The **Project Examples** walk you through tasks to help you put Edge Animate to work.

Workshops

This book shows you how to put together the individual step-by-step tasks into in-depth projects with the Workshops. You start each project with a sample file, work through the steps, and then compare with a results file at the end. The Workshops and associated files are available on the web at *www.queondemand.com* or *www.perspection.com.*

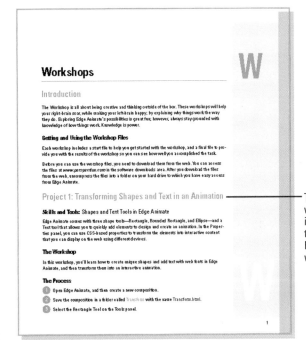

The **Workshops** walk you through in-depth projects to help you put Edge Animate to work.

Get More on the Web

In addition to the information in this book, you can also get more information on the web to help you get up-to-speed faster with Edge Animate. Some of the information includes:

Productivity Tools

◆ **Keyboard Shortcuts.** Download a list of keyboard shortcuts to learn faster ways to get the job done.

More Content

◆ **More Content.** Download new content developed after publication.

You can access these additional resources on the web at *www.queondemand.com* or *www.perspection.com*.

Keyboard Shortcuts

Adobe Edge Animate 1.0

If a command on a menu includes a keyboard reference, known as a keyboard short-cut, to the right of the command name, you can perform the action by pressing and holding the first key, and then pressing the second key to perform the command quickly. In some cases, a keyboard shortcut uses three keys. Simply press and hold the first two keys, and then press the third key. Keyboard shortcuts provide an alternative to using the mouse and make it easy to perform repetitive commands.

Edge Animate operates virtually the same on both Macintosh and Windows versions, except for a few keyboard commands that have equivalent functions. You use the [Ctrl] and [Alt] keys in Windows, and the ⌘ and [Option] keys on a Macintosh computer. Also, the term *popup* on the Macintosh and *list arrow* in Windows refer to the same type of option.

If you don't see a keyboard shortcut for a command or want to change an existing one to another keyboard combination, you can define your own in Edge Animate. For detailed steps and instructions, see "Defining Keyboard Shortcuts" on page 52 in this book.

Keyboard Shortcuts

Menu Command	Windows	Macintosh
Edge Animate (Mac)		
Quit Edge Animate	Ctrl+Q	⌘+Q
File		
New	Ctrl+N	⌘+N
Open	Ctrl+O	⌘+O
Close	Ctrl+W	⌘+W
Close All	Ctrl+Shift+W	⌘+Shift+W
Save	Ctrl+S	⌘+S
Save As	Ctrl+Shift+S	⌘+Shift+S
Publish	Ctrl+Alt+S	⌘+Option+S

289

Additional content is available on the web.

Getting Started with Edge Animate

Introduction

Adobe Edge Animate 1.0 is a web motion and interaction design tool that allows you to bring animated content to websites using standards like HTML5, CSS3, and JavaScript/jQuery. You can use Edge Animate to create motion content that runs on desktop browsers, such as Firefox, Chrome, Safari, and Internet Explorer 9 or later, and mobile devices, such as Apple iOS and Android.

Edge Animate is a standalone program that you can use independently or along side other Edge tools and services, such as Edge Inspect or Edge Web Fonts. However, you do use other tools to create assets and content for use in Edge Animate. For example, you can use Adobe Illustrator, Fireworks or Photoshop to create graphics and artwork, which you can import into your project in Edge Animate. In Edge Animate, you can create new projects, known as **compositions**, from scratch using HTML (Hyper Text Markup Language) building blocks, text, and imported web graphics—JPG/JPEG, PNG, SVG, and GIF files—and adding animation and interactivity. You create responsive compositions that adjust to different screen sizes. In addition to creating new compositions, you can also open existing HTML documents created in other programs, such as Adobe Dreamweaver, and add animation to it in Edge Animate. Edge Animate makes minimal, non-intrusive changes to existing HTML code in order to reference its own JavaScript files.

Edge Animate uses a familiar user-interface based on a stage, timeline, and panels for elements and properties similar to those used in Adobe After Effects and Flash Professional. So, if you're familiar with these Adobe programs, then you're one step ahead. However, if you're new, Edge Animate is an easy program to learn and use.

What You'll Do

Find Out What You Can Do with Edge Animate

Explore Edge Animate and Edge Tools

Start Edge Animate

Use the Welcome Screen

View the Edge Animate Window

Create a Project Plan

Build an Edge Animate Project

Create a New Animation

Get Sample Animations

Open an Existing Animation

Work with Multiple Animations

Preview an Animation in a Browser

Save an Animation

Get Online Support

Finish Up

Finding Out What You Can Do with Edge Animate

Where Does Edge Animate Fit In?

Adobe Edge Animate is a new addition to the existing set of Adobe web tools, such as Dreamweaver, Flash Professional, and Flash Builder. Each tool has strengths for their respective use.

Adobe Edge Animate

Adobe Edge Animate is best used for creating advertising, simple animations and motion design for new compositions or using existing CSS-based page layouts. Edge Animate uses the following technologies: JavaScript, JSON (JavaScript Object Notation), HTML/HTML5, CSS, web graphics including SVG, jQuery-based animation framework. Edge Animate works natively with HTML along with related JavaScript files, so you can run it in your web browser.

Adobe Dreamweaver

Adobe Dreamweaver is best used for creating websites and web application for desktops, smartphones, and other devices. Dreamweaver uses the following technologies: HTML/HTML5, CSS, JavaScript, PhoneGap, site management, FTP, CMS frameworks, and SVN (Subversion). The HTML documents you create in Dreamweaver can be opened and modified natively in Edge Animate. This means you can create HTML web pages in Dreamweaver, and add animations to them in Edge Animate, while still preserving the integrity of CSS-based layouts.

Adobe Flash Professional

Adobe Flash Professional is best used for creating full-featured interactive experiences, mobile application, gaming, premium video,

or complex advertising. Flash uses the following technologies: ActionScript, Flash Player, AIR for desktop and mobile devices.

Adobe Flash Builder

Adobe Flash Builder is best used for creating Rich Internet applications (RIAs) and mobile applications. Flash Builder uses the following technologies: Professional ActionScript IDE, Flex, Flash Player, AIR for desktop and mobile devices.

Adobe Illustrator, Adobe Fireworks, and Adobe Photoshop

Adobe Illustrator, Adobe Fireworks, and Adobe Photoshop are best used for creating and modifying vector and bitmap graphics for website and print-based projects. The web graphics—including JPG/JPEG, PNG, SVG, and GIF files—you create using these Adobe programs can be added to your compositions in Edge Animate.

Understanding Animations in Edge Animate

Animation is simply change over time. You can create an animation by making one or more property changes for an element over time. A composition is the framework for an animation. Each composition has its own timeline. A typical composition includes multiple layers that represent elements, such as shapes, text, and graphics. You add elements to a composition by creating an animated layer. You can arrange layers within a composition in space and time. Layers are the elements that make up a composition. Each layer has properties, which you can modify and animate.

Exploring Edge Animate and Edge Tools

What Can I Do with Edge Tools?

Along with Edge Animate, there are other tools and services you can use to develop content for the web. These tools and services include Edge Reflow, Edge Code, Edge Inspect, Edge Web Fonts, Typekit, and PhoneGap Build.

Edge Animate

With Edge Animate, you can create interactive and animated content using HTML and JavaScript.

Edge Reflow

With Edge Reflow, you can create responsive layouts and visuals with standards-based CSS. This program allows you to use the power of CSS to create designs simultaneously for all screen sizes without sacrificing your design look, quality, or capability.

Edge Code

With Edge Code, you can view and work with code content and program with HTML, CSS, and JavaScript. This program allows you to preview CSS, edit code, and use integrated visual design tools to help speed up the development process.

Edge Inspect

With Edge Inspect, you can preview and inspect your web designs on mobile devices. This program allows you to synchronize browsing in Chrome for wirelessly paired iOS and Android devices, update a device with remote inspection, and capture screenshots from all connected devices.

Edge Web Fonts

With Edge Web Fonts, you can get access to a free web font library from Adobe and Google for use in your site designs.

Adobe Typekit

With Typekit, you can browse commercial fonts by classification, properties, or recommended use, and add them to your site designs.

PhoneGap Build

With PhoneGap Build, you can build mobile apps with HTML, CSS, and JavaScript by reusing existing skills, frameworks, and tools and package mobile apps in the cloud.

Getting Edge Animate and Edge Tools & Services

Adobe Edge Animate and Edge Tools & Services are available for download on the web using Adobe Creative Cloud services at *create.adobe.com or html.adobe.com/edge*. After you sign up for a membership, you'll have access to Edge Animate and other Adobe Edge Tools & Services. You can download Edge Animate and its related tools on either the Apple OS X or Windows platforms as separate programs from the site to your hard drive before you install each one on your system. Some tools may be still in the development or preview process, so check with Adobe for the latest version available.

You can get specific instructions on preparing for, downloading, and installing Edge Animate and Edge Tools & Services in Appendix A, "*Installing Edge Animate and Tools*" in the back of the book.

Starting Edge Animate

You can start Edge Animate in several ways, depending on the platform you are using. When you start Edge Animate, your system displays a splash screen and then the Edge Animate window. When you start a new Edge Animate session or close all documents, a Welcome screen appears, providing easy access links to create new documents, open existing documents, and open recent items to help you get started with the product. You can also use links to access websites to learn more about the product and download sample documents.

Start Edge Animate in Windows

1. Start Windows, if necessary, and then use the method for your Windows version.

   ◆ **Windows 7.** Click **Start** on the taskbar, and then point to **All Programs** (which changes to Back).

   ◆ **Windows 8.** Display the Start screen; click or tap the **Start** button on the Charm bar.

2. Click **Adobe Edge Animate**.

   The Edge Animate window opens, displaying the Welcome screen.

Did You Know?

You can find out the version number. Click Edge Animate (Mac) or Help (Win) menu, and then click About Edge Animate. The version number appears along with a scrolling list of information about the product. Click the screen to exit it.

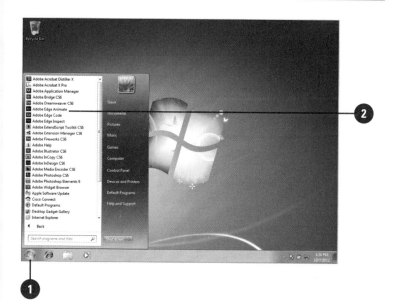

Welcome screen
Provides easy access links to create and open Edge Animate documents, take In-App lessons, view key features, and get online resources.

Start Edge Animate in Macintosh

1 In the Finder, open the Applications folder.

◆ **Mac OS X Lion and OS X Mountain Lion.** You can click the **Launchpad** icon on the Dock, and then click the **Edge Animate** icon.

2 Double-click the **Adobe Edge Animate** folder.

3 Double-click the **Edge Animate** application icon.

The Edge Animate window opens, displaying the Welcome screen.

Did You Know?

You can create a shortcut on the Macintosh. Drag and drop the Edge Animate program to the bottom of the monitor screen, and then add it to the dock.

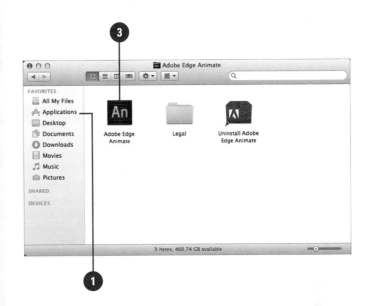

Shortcut for Adobe Edge Animate

For Your Information

Launching Edge Animate and Opening a File

You can also start Edge Animate and open an Edge Animate file at the same time. Double-click the Edge Animate file icon in Windows Explorer (Win) or in a Finder folder (Mac). You can identify an Edge Animate file by the file icon or AN file extension. A file extension is a three or four-letter suffix at the end of a filename that identifies the file type for the operating system. The Macintosh doesn't need to use file extensions, but added the feature to promote cross platform use. In the Mac Operating System (OS) 10.6 or later, you have the option to show or hide file extensions. When you are working on both platforms, using file extensions on the Macintosh allows Windows and Edge Animate to recognize and open the files.

Using the Welcome Screen

When you start Edge Animate, the program displays a Welcome screen, which provides a place to get started with Edge Animate. You can create a new composition, open existing or recent files, or learn Edge Animate using In-App Lessons to help you get started with the project. The In-App Lessons provide seven step-by step topics with the aid of the Lessons panel to walk you through the process of creating animations with Edge Animate. The lessons include *Quick Start* to help you get going, *Create* to teach you how to work with shapes, text and images, *Animate I* and *II* to show you how to use keyframes and pins, *Resize* to learn how to respond to size changes, *Extend* to learn how to loop and handle user interaction, and *Reuse* to show you how to create reusable objects with symbols. You can also use links to access a list of key features and product release notes, and helpful resources from online content, including Help and Tutorials, videos on Adobe TV, community forums, and sample projects. In addition, you can access social media, Facebook and Twitter, to get more information about Edge Animate.

Use the Welcome Screen

1. Start Adobe Edge Animate, or close all open documents (click the **File** menu, and then click **Close All**).

2. To work with Edge Animate projects, use the **Create New**, **Open File**, or **Recent Files** links to create or open projects.

3. To access social media for Edge Animate, click the **Facebook** or **Twitter** icon.

4. Click a link to access training, information, and resources.

   ◆ **Getting Started.** An area to start an In-App Lesson.

   ◆ **Key Features.** An area to review the main features of Edge Animate and access product release notes.

   ◆ **Resources.** An area to access links to Help and Tutorials, Adobe TV, Community forums, view and download samples, and JavaScript reference material.

   ◆ **Quiet.** A blank area reserved for future content.

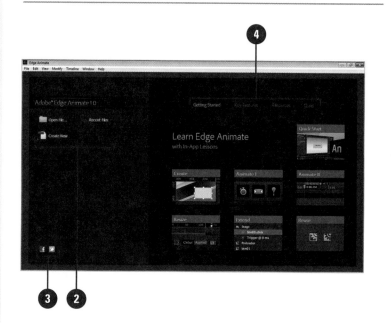

Use an In-App Lesson

① Start Adobe Edge Animate, or close all open documents (click the **File** menu, and then click **Close All**).

◆ When the Welcome screen is closed, you can also click the **Window** menu, and then click **Lessons** to open the Lessons panel.

② Click **Getting Started**, if necessary.

③ Point to a lesson tile to view a brief description, and then click a lesson tile to start it.

The Welcome screen closes, Edge Animate creates a new Untitled project, and the Lessons panel opens with the selected lesson.

④ Read and perform the lesson steps in the Edge Animate window as indicated in the Lessons panel; be sure to scroll down as needed to complete all the steps.

⑤ At the bottom of the Lessons panel, click the **Next Step** link.

⑥ Follow the additional steps or click links to start other lessons.

After you complete the lesson, you can save or close the Untitled project.

⑦ To close the Lessons panel, click the **Window** menu, and then click **Lessons**.

See Also

See "Saving an Animation" on page 20 for more information on saving an Edge Animate composition.

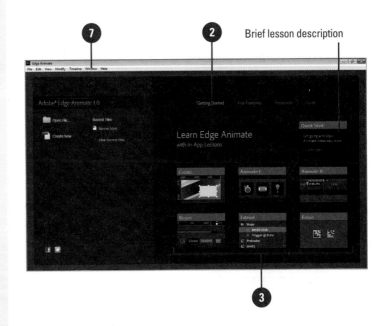

Brief lesson description

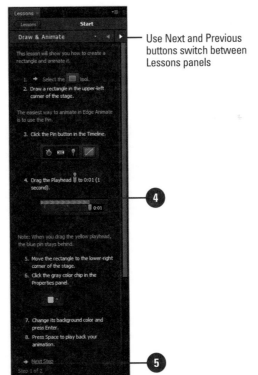

Use Next and Previous buttons switch between Lessons panels

Viewing the Edge Animate Window

Tools Panel
Contains tools to create and work with shape, text, and graphic elements.

Document tab
Displays/switches to open composition or HTML files on the Stage.

Elements Panel
Displays a list of elements used in the file. Contains options to work with individual or multiple elements.

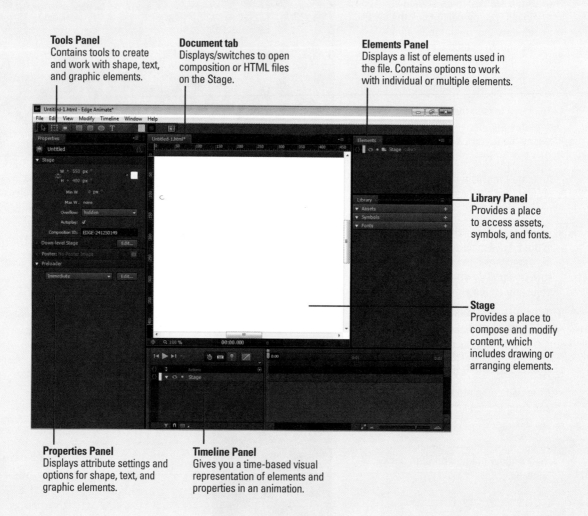

Library Panel
Provides a place to access assets, symbols, and fonts.

Stage
Provides a place to compose and modify content, which includes drawing or arranging elements.

Properties Panel
Displays attribute settings and options for shape, text, and graphic elements.

Timeline Panel
Gives you a time-based visual representation of elements and properties in an animation.

Preparing for a Project

As you prepare for a project in Edge Animate, you need to create work folders. The work folders should contain all the elements of the project. You first start with a main folder for the project. The **main folder** contains all the elements of the project; every single piece of the project is included within this folder.

Creating a main folder will help you in the creation and the moving of the project. If everything involving the construction of your project is contained within a single folder, it helps to keep you organized and in control.

It's critical that you save a new Edge Animate composition in the main folder, because the program saves multiple files needed to display Edge Animate content. It saves a composition as an Edge Animate AN file and as an HTML file. In addition, it also saves related files—JS (JavaScript) and Edge Animate includes—and creates an empty images folder, where it places a copy of the graphics you import into a composition. If any of these files are renamed, deleted, or moved, the Edge Animate composition will not run properly, if at all. Within the main folder, you can also set up other folders based on your own needs. See "Examining Edge Animate Files," on page 242 for more information on the composition files.

Create a Project Folder

1. Right-click on the desktop or in a folder, point to **New**, and then click the **Folder** button from the context menu (Win) or control-click on the desktop or in a folder, and then click **New Folder** from the popup menu (Mac).

2. Name the main folder according to your project (in this example, *Banner*).

3. Double-click to open the folder, and then add additional subfolders to the main folder as desired to meet your needs.

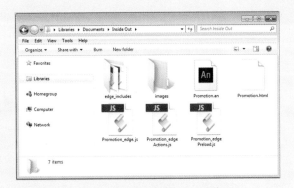

Preparing for Project Management

An Edge Animate project starts with a project plan, which provides the client, developers, and other team members with a plan to complete the overall design, development, and implementation of the animation. A project plan should include the following phases: (1) Define, (2) Structure, (3) Design, and (4) Build and publish. The project plan becomes the roadmap for assigning project management tasks and responsibilities, and determining schedules and due dates.

The **Define phase** consists of a project overview, goals and target audience, content and style information, content collection, and delivery requirements. The **Structure phase** consists of text scripts and schematic flow-charts. The **Design phase** consists of design comps, design review and redesign, and production storyboard. The cycle of client review, feedback, and redesign continues until the client approves the design. Upon approval, you combine the flowcharts and final designs into production storyboards with a detailed visual look at page layouts and navigation links. The **Build and publish phase** consists of Edge Animate production, technical testing against storyboards and bug list, usability testing, revision, revision testing, and final publishing based on delivery requirements.

Creating a Project Plan

Before you begin to create an animation in Edge Animate, it's important to develop a project plan first. The project plan provides a roadmap for you to follow as you build your project in Edge Animate. Without a project plan, you'll inevitably hit road blocks, which will cause you to waste time redesigning all or portions of the animation. Planning a project involves (1) defining its purpose and identifying the audience, (2) logically developing content and organizing the structure of the content, (3) developing the layout and design, and (4) building and publishing the project. With a project plan in place, you'll be ready to create an animation.

Plan an Animation

Creating an animation can take a long time; it's worth the effort to plan carefully. The tendency for most first-time developers is to start creating an animation without carefully planning the project. Before you begin, you need to develop and follow a plan. Otherwise, you might end up spending a lot of time fixing or completely changing parts of the animation, which you could have avoided from the beginning. You need to figure out the goal of the project, the look and feel of your production, its length and size, how it will interact with the viewer, and how and for whom it will be distributed. When planning an animation, it's important to accomplish the following:

Define the purpose and audience

Is it for training? Sales? Entertainment? Informing? The answer will determine the types of features you may want to include or exclude in your design. If the purpose is to create a training site, you might want to include easy-to-use instructional material, simple navigation, and a help system. On the other hand, if the purpose is to create a sales promotion, you might want to include eye-catching graphics to get users' attention and draw them into the animation.

How you create your animation will depend on how you classify the target audience. If the intended audience consists of novice computer users, you will have to concentrate on making the navigational controls and layout as simple to use as possible. If the users are experienced computer users, you can include more advanced interactions.

Develop the content and structure

The most beneficial planning tools for the multimedia developer are the script and schematic flowchart. The script tells the story of your production in text form. Just like in the movies, a script is used to describe each section, to list media elements, and to provide a basis for the text that will appear onscreen. Schematic flowcharts are the best way to sketch the navigational structure of an animation and make sure that each of the sections is properly connected. After you have the script and schematic flowchart mapped out on paper, you will quickly see the correlation between what you have developed and what you will begin to set up in Edge Animate.

Develop the layout and design

The storyboard tells the story of your animation in visual form. It helps you design the layout of each screen in your animation. The storyboard follows the script and develops a visual perspective of the animation's main transitional points, which help you develop the media elements you will use to create your animation. A storyboard can take a long time to develop, but the media elements you assemble and create in the process will shorten the overall development time. As you develop your layout and design, be sure to keep consistency and usability in mind:

◆ **Navigation and layout.** Create similar and consistent controls (bars, menus, buttons, and graphics) and layout on every page for ease-of-use.

◆ **Color.** Create a consistent look and feel and layout for the audience; and use a limited color palette for simplicity.

◆ **Text and fonts.** Create easy to read text; use scroll bars similar to the desktop software; and use a limited group of fonts (typically 2 or 3).

◆ **Transitions.** Use similar and consistent transitions between pages.

◆ **Size.** Keep the main folder size as small as possible for faster downloads and playback. Optimize and compress graphic images to reduce file sizes.

Build and publish the animation

Now, you can work in Edge Animate to implement your layout and design based on the storyboards. As you build the animation, you need to include technical testing against storyboards and bug list, usability testing, revision, and revision testing based on delivery requirements before you publish the product.

Some computers are more up-to-date than others. You need to determine the minimum computer and server hardware and software requirements in which your animation will be delivered. Some hardware requirements you need to consider for the delivery computer are (1) CPU (central processing unit), which determines the speed with which your computer can compute data; (2) RAM (system memory), which determines how fast files load and how smoothly they run; (3) Sound hardware, which determine if you can use any related sound files; (4) Video hardware, which determine the quality and speed of the graphic and video display, and (5) Monitor resolution, which determines the color display (number of available colors), size, and overall look of your animation. Some software requirements you need to consider are the operating system version and supported web browser type and version. See "Preparing for Edge Animate and Tools" on page 280 for specific details about these requirements.

Sample storyboard and script

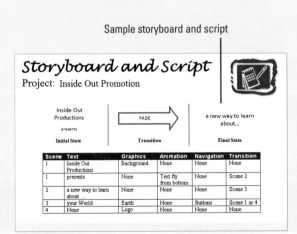

Sample flowchart

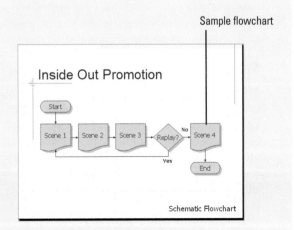

Building an Edge Animate Project

After you develop a project plan, you can use Edge Animate to create an animation based on it. Creating an animation in Edge Animate involves six main steps: (1) setting up Stage properties, (2) assembling media elements, (3) positioning the elements on the Stage and sequencing them in the Timeline, (4) adding custom functionality and interactive elements, (5) previewing and testing the animation, and (6) publishing it for distribution.

Build an Animation

Before you start creating an animation using Edge Animate, it's important to understand the process of development. The basic steps for developing web motion and interaction with Edge Animate are listed below.

Step 1: Set up Stage properties

You can open and work on an existing web composition or create a new one from scratch. Before you start a new composition in Edge Animate, you need to set up initial Stage properties—such as the user's screen size and background color—for how your animation looks and operates. It's important to specify these property settings, especially the user's screen size, that affect the entire animation at the beginning of the project, so you don't have to redesign the animation later.

Step 2: Create or import media elements

Media elements include shapes, graphics, and text. You can create new media elements in Edge Animate or import ones that have already been developed. Edge Animate provides shape and text creation tools for creating new media elements. You can import other media elements, such as buttons and photographs. As you import graphics, it's important to size and compress them before-hand to reduce file sizes and Internet download times. Media elements are either static or dynamic. Static media is an element, such as text or graphics, created or imported into an animation that doesn't change unless the author makes the change and republishes it. Dynamic media is an element, such as data, stored outside of the animation and loaded when needed or changed by scripting, which makes updating easy and provides information to the user.

Step 3: Position the elements on the Stage and sequence them in the Timeline

A composition is the framework for an animation. A typical composition includes layers that represent media elements, such as shapes, text, and graphics. Each composition has its own Stage and Timeline. The Stage is the viewing area you use to display where elements appear in an animation, and the Timeline is the area you use to organize what you want to occur with the elements (layers) at the time and duration you specify. You use the Stage and Timeline together to add and sequence elements within a composition to create animated layers in space and time. The Stage represents the elements' position in space (where) and the Timeline represents the elements' position in time (when).

Step 4: Add navigation, interactivity, and motion effects

After you add media elements and sequence them in the Timeline, you can use scripts to add functionality to the elements to make them perform actions. Scripting allows you to add custom functionality to your animation, such as moving elements on the Stage and controlling the animation in response to specific conditions and events, such as a mouse click. In Edge Animate, scripts are written as

Actions. To help you get started scripting and save you some time, Edge Animate comes with built-in scripts known as snippets. For example, Edge Animate includes snippets to play or stop the timeline, open URL, and change text. In addition, you can use built-in Timeline effects to add motion to elements.

Step 5: Preview and test the animation

After you create your project, you use the Publish In Browser command to preview and test the animation to make sure it runs the way you want it to in your web browser. It's important to test the technical functionality and visitor usability of your animation; check to make sure all buttons and links work properly, according to the flowchart, and all text (including spelling and grammar), layout, graphics, and animation work property according to the storyboard.

Step 6: Publish the animation

When the animation runs the way you want it to, you can publish your production three different ways. You can publish your animation as a web HTML file for display on a web page using a web browser, as a Deployment Package (.oam) for use in other Adobe programs, such as Adobe InDesign, or to Apple iBooks Author as an iBooks/OS X Dashboard Widget (.wdgt). You can publish your animation by using the Publish Settings and Publish commands. For use on the web, you use an FTP (File Transfer Protocol) program or one with those capabilities, such as Adobe Dreamweaver, to transfer all the files in your main folder to your web server. It's critical that you keep all the files together using the same file and folder structure, otherwise the animation will not run properly, if at all.

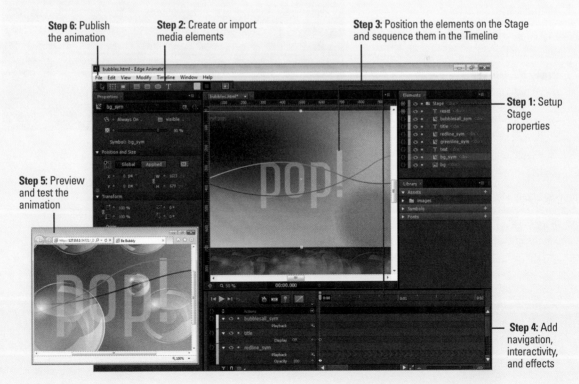

Step 6: Publish the animation

Step 2: Create or import media elements

Step 3: Position the elements on the Stage and sequence them in the Timeline

Step 1: Setup Stage properties

Step 5: Preview and test the animation

Step 4: Add navigation, interactivity, and effects

Creating a New Animation

You can create new animations in Edge Animate by using the New command on the File menu or the Create New link in the Welcome screen. When you create a new animation in Edge Animate, it creates a blank HTML file, ready for you to create or insert shapes, graphics, and text. By default, the first HTML file in Edge Animate is titled *Untitled-1.html*, which appears on the Document tab and Window menu in Edge Animate. Edge Animate numbers new HTML files consecutively. You can create and work on as many new HTML files as you have memory (RAM) for, which is typically as many as you want. Each new animation contains its own Stage, Timeline, Elements, and Library panel. When you save a new HTML file, Edge Animate also creates an Edge Animate file with the AN filename extension and other related JavaScript files, so you can run it in your web browser. The AN file contains information that points to and uses the HTML and JavaScript files created by Edge Animate.

Create a New Blank Composition

◆ **Welcome screen.** Start Adobe Edge Animate or close all open files, and then click **Create New**.

   ◆ To close all open files, click the **File** menu, and then click **Close All**.

◆ **File menu.** Click the **File** menu, and then click **New**.

   TIMESAVER *Press Ctrl+N (Win) or ⌒⌘+N (Mac).*

   Edge Animate creates a blank Untitled HTML file.

See Also

See "Working with Multiple Animations" on page 18 for more information on working with multiple documents at the same time.

File menu   Welcome screen

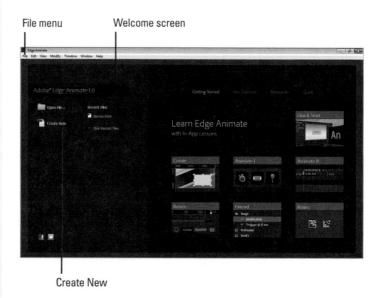

Create New

Getting Sample Animations

If you're not sure where to start, you can download and view sample Edge Animate projects to see how they work. They say a picture is worth a thousand words. Well, they are right. Opening and viewing sample animations can help you see what's happening in an Edge Animate project from a time-based perspective. So, it's a good idea to take the time to download some sample documents and experiment with them. You can quickly access samples on the web from Adobe Creative Cloud by using the Welcome screen.

Download Sample Animations

1 Start Adobe Edge Animate, or close all open files (click the **File** menu, and then click **Close All**).

2 In the Welcome screen, click **Resources**.

3 Click the **View and download samples** link.

Your default web browser opens, displaying a web page with Adobe Edge Animate showcase sample files.

4 Locate the link to the download the sample files.

5 Scroll through the page, locate the sample you want, and then click the **Download** link associated with the sample you want.

 ◆ If prompted (Win), click **Save** or **Save as**, select a destination folder, and then click **Save**.

The sample files are typically compressed in a ZIP file, which you need to uncompress before you can use it with Edge Animate.

6 When you're done, close your web web browser.

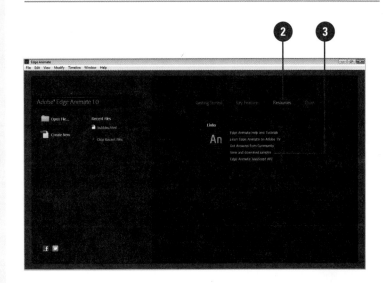

> ### See Also
>
> *See "Previewing an Animation in a Browser" on page 19 for more information on viewing an Edge Animate animation.*

Opening an Existing Animation

In Edge Animate, you can use the Welcome screen or Open commands on the File menu to open existing Edge Animate compositions or web pages. You can open web pages with the HTML or HTM file format, which you can create in Edge Animate or another web design program, such as Adobe Dreamweaver, and then add an animation to it. A composition is made up of multiple files, including an Edge Animate file with the AN filename extension. When you open an HTML or AN file in Edge Animate, the HTML file for the composition opens in the Document tab and on the Stage. You can open multiple HTML files during a session, which you can switch between using the Window menu or the Document tab. After you've opened an HTML file in Edge Animate, you can quickly re-open it by using the Open Recent list on the File menu or the Recent Files list in the Welcome screen. Since a composition in Edge Animate is made up of multiple files, it's critical that you keep all the files together for the project using the same file and folder structure, otherwise the animation will not run properly, if at all.

Open an Existing Composition or HTML Web Page File

1. Click the **File** menu, and then click **Open**.

   TIMESAVER *Press Ctrl+O (Win) or ⌘+O (Mac).*

   TIMESAVER *Click Open File in the Welcome screen.*

2. To open a specific type of file, click the **File as type** list arrow (Win), or the **File type** popup (Mac), and then select the file format you want.

   ◆ **All Formats.** Displays all valid formats (.html, .htm, .an, .edge).

   ◆ **HTML File.** Displays all .html files.

   ◆ **HTM File.** Displays all .htm files.

   ◆ **Edge Animate File.** Displays all .an or .edge files; .an is the default file format for Adobe Edge Animate; .edge is the old default file format.

3. Navigate to the drive and folder where the file is located.

4. Click the file you want to open.

5. Click **Open**.

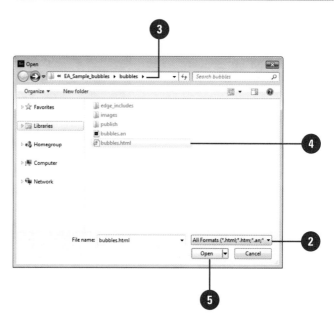

Open a Recently Opened File Using the Welcome Screen

1. Start Adobe Edge Animate, or close all open documents (click the **File** menu, and then click **Close All**.

2. In the Welcome screen, click the HTML file you want to open.

Did You Know?

You can open a recent file quickly from the Start menu (Win7). Click the Start button, point to Adobe Edge Animate, and then click the file name you want to open.

Clear Recent Files

Open a Recently Opened File Using the File Menu

1. Click the **File** menu, and then point to **Open Recent**.

2. Click the HTML file you want to open.

Did You Know?

You can clear the Open Recent list. Click the File menu, point to Open Recent, and then click Clear Recent or click Clear Recent Files in the Welcome screen.

You can open an Edge Animate file from Windows/File Explorer or the Finder. In Windows/File Explorer (Win) or the Finder (Mac), double-click the Edge Animate file with the .an extension.

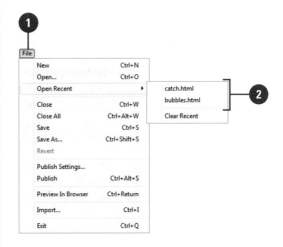

Working with Multiple Animations

When you open multiple composition or HTML files, you can use the Window menu or the down arrow on the Document tab to switch between them. You click the Document tab arrow next to the active HTML file name, and then click a file name to switch and activate the already opened HTML file. By default, the tab list is displayed in the order in which you open or create files. When you want to move or copy information between files, it's easier to display several files on the screen at the same time and move them around. However, you must make the window active to work in it. The Document tab also includes a Close button to quickly close the active HTML file.

Switch Between Multiple Animations

1. Open more than one composition or HTML file.

2. Click the **Document tab** arrow, and then click the file name to switch to the file.

    ◆ You can also click the **Window** menu, and then click a file name at the bottom of the menu.

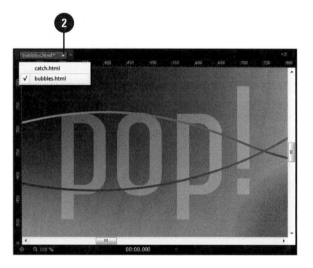

Previewing an Animation in a Browser

As you work on the development of an Edge Animate project, you will probably want to occasionally stop and see what it looks like when previewed within a web browser. One of the most used features for testing your documents is the Preview In Browser command on the File menu. This is one of the most used when working in Edge Animate. It lets you see what your animation will look like in your default browser. When testing an animation on a web page, it's a good idea to check it out in more than one browser, and in more than one version of the browser on different operating systems. For example, it may look great in Safari on the Macintosh, and not even work in Internet Explorer on Windows. Edge Animate works with Firefox, Chrome, Safari, and Internet Explorer 9. If you don't have access to other browsers and operating systems, you can use Adobe Browser- Labs, an online service that you can use from within Adobe Dreamweaver, to view your web pages.

Preview an Animation in a Web Page

1. Open the HTML file with the animation you want to view.

2. Click the **File** menu, and then click **Preview In Browser**.

   TIMESAVER *Press Ctrl+Enter (Win) or ⌘+Return (Mac).*

3. If prompted, save your Edge Animate composition.

   Your default web browser opens, displaying your content on a web page.

   TROUBLE? *If the web page doesn't open, your web browser, such as Internet Explorer 8 or lower, is not compatible.*

4. When you're done, close the web browser.

Did You Know?

You can check HTML5 compatibility. You can test your browser to make sure it's compatible with HTML5. Go go *http://html5test.com*. You can also get information at *http://html5please.com*.

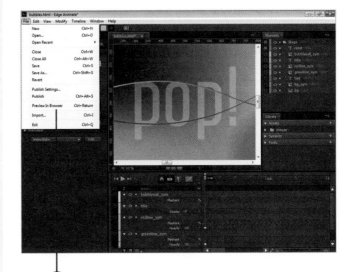

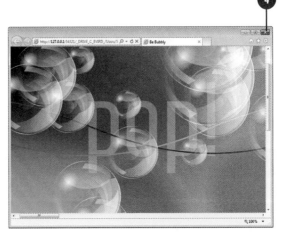

Saving an Animation

When you save a project in Edge Animate, the program saves an HTML file and an AN file along with other related files—JS (JavaScript) and Edge Animate includes—needed to display Edge Animate content. When you save a new composition, you should select or create a folder location in which to save all the files and give it a name. Name your project clearly so you can easily locate it later. Edge Animate uses the name in all its file naming conventions. It's critical that you keep all the files together for an Edge Animate project using the same file and folder structure, otherwise the animation will not run properly, if at all. An unsaved Edge Animate composition displays an asterisk (*) after the name in the title bar or Document tab. If you don't want to keep currently unsaved content, you can revert to the most recently saved version of the composition by using the Revert command on the File menu. To keep interim versions of an Edge Animate composition and all its related files as you make changes, you need to use the Save As command and give each version a new name, such as project1, project2 and so forth, and save it in a new folder.

Save an Edge Animate Composition

1. Click the **File** menu, and then click **Save**.

    TIMESAVER *Press Ctrl+S (Win) or ⌘+S (Mac).*

    If you are saving a composition for the first time, continue. Otherwise, Edge Animate saves the current one.

2. Type the new file name.

3. Navigate to the drive and folder location where you want to save the composition.

    ◆ To create a new folder, click the **New Folder** button, type a folder name, and then press Enter (Win) or click **Create** (Mac).

4. Click the **Format** popup (Mac) or **Save As Type** list arrow (Win), and then click **Html File (*.html)** or **Htm File (*.htm)**.

5. Click **Save**.

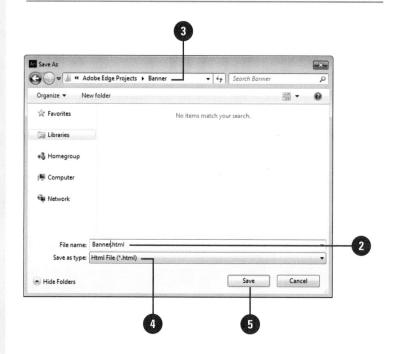

Save an Edge Animate Composition in a Different Folder and Name

1 Click the **File** menu, and then click **Save As**.

TIMESAVER *Press Ctrl+Shift+S (Win) or ⌘+Shift+S (Mac).*

2 Type the new file name.

3 Navigate to the drive and folder location where you want to save the composition.

4 To create a new folder, click the **New Folder** button, type a folder name, and then press Enter (Win) or click **Create** (Mac).

5 Click the **Format** popup (Mac) or **Save As Type** list arrow (Win), and then click **Html File (*.html)** or **Htm File (*.htm)**.

6 Click **Save**.

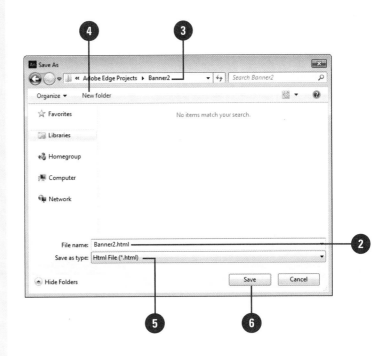

Did You Know?

You can revert to the most recently saved version. Click the File menu, click Revert, and then click Revert. All your unsaved changes are lost and the most recently saved version of your project is opened.

There is a difference between Save and Save As. When you save an existing composition using the Save command, Edge Animate performs a quick save, which appends new content to the existing files. When you save a new composition using the Save As command, Edge Animate performs a complete save, which includes all the related content files.

Edge Animate Composition Files

Format	Description
filename.an	A file that points to and uses HTML and JavaScript files for an Edge Animate composition, not published.
filename.html	A file that stores HTML code used to execute an Edge Animate composition animation in a web browser.
*filename*_edge.js	A separate file with JavaScript that defines the Stage, Timeline, and elements used in an Edge Animate composition.
*filename*_edgePreload.js	A separate file with JavaScript that loads the resources and scripts used in an Edge Animate composition.
*filename*_edgeActions.js	A separate file with JavaScript that executes actions and triggers used in an Edge Animate composition.
edge_includes folder	A folder that contains standard JavaScript and jQuery files to display Edge Animate content in JavaScript.

Getting Online Support

If you need more detailed information about Edge Animate or want to find out about available resources, you can find out on the web from Edge Animate Help, Edge Animate JavaScript API, and Edge Animate Community Forum websites. Edge Animate Help provides access to information and tutorials for beginner and advanced users to help you develop and design web-based content in Edge Animate. Edge Animate JavaScript API provides information on how Edge Animate uses JavaScript and how you can too. Edge Animate Community Forum provides a place to ask questions and get answers from other Edge Animate users. You can access the online resources by using the Help menu or links under Resources in the Welcome screen.

Get Edge Animate Help

1. Click the **Help** menu, and then click **Edge Animate Help**.

   Your web browser opens, displaying the Edge Animate Help and tutorials website.

2. Scroll through the web page to access software help.

   ◆ **Getting Started.** Provides introductory topics to help you get started with Edge Animate.

   ◆ **Advanced animation.** Provides more advanced topics to help you take Edge Animate to the next level.

3. Click a link to the topic you want to find out more about.

   NOTE *Some topics take you to third-party web sites.*

   ◆ Click the **Back** button in your web browser to return back to the main page as needed.

4. When you're done, close your web browser.

Back button

For Your Information

Participating in Adobe Product Improvement

You can participate in the Adobe Product Improvement Program. Click the Help menu, click Adobe Product Improvement Program, and then follow the on-screen instructions. This is an opt-in program that allows you to test Adobe products and make suggestions for future products. This program enables Adobe to collect product usage data from customers while maintaining their privacy.

Get Help from the Edge Animate Community Forum

1. Click the **Help** menu, and then click **Edge Animate Community Forums**.

   Your web web browser opens, displaying the Adobe Community Forum for Edge Animate website.

2. To ask a question, click in the What can we help you with? text box, type a question, and then press Enter.

3. To browse through Frequently Asked Questions or Get Started With Edge Animate, click a link to the topic to find out more.

   ◆ Click the **Back** button in your web browser to return back to the forum as needed.

4. When you're done, close your web web browser.

Get Help from the Edge Animate JavaScript API

1. Click the **Help** menu, and then click **Edge Animate JavaScript API**.

   Your web browser opens, displaying the Adobe Edge Animate JavaScript API website.

2. Click a link to the topic you want to find out more about.

   ◆ Adobe Edge Animate overview.

   ◆ Triggers, events and actions.

   ◆ Work with symbols.

   ◆ JavaScript API.

   ◆ Advanced topics.

3. When you're done, close your web browser.

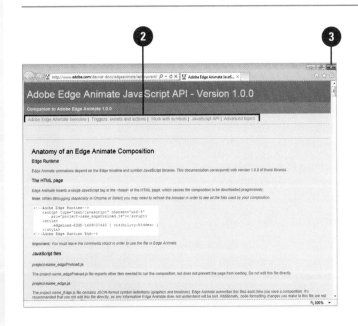

Finishing Up

When you finish working on a composition, you can close it to keep Edge Animate open and work on another project or exit Edge Animate. Exiting Edge Animate closes the current composition and the Edge Animate program and returns you to the desktop. Before you close a composition or exit Edge Animate, you should save your work. A composition that needs to be saved displays an asterisk (*) after the name in the title bar or Document tab. As a safe guard, if you try to close a composition or exit Edge Animate without saving your changes, a dialog box opens, asking if you want to do so.

Close a Composition

1. Click the **Close** button on the Document tab, or click the **File** menu, and then click **Close**.

   TIMESAVER *Press Ctrl+W (Win) or ⌘+W (Mac).*

   TIMESAVER *Click the File menu, and then click Close All to close all open documents.*

2. If necessary, click **Yes** (Win) or **Save** (Mac) to save any changes you made to your open composition before it closes.

Exit Edge Animate

1. Choose one of the following:

   ◆ Click the **Edge Animate** menu, and then click **Quit Edge Animate** (Mac).

   ◆ Click the **Close** button, or click the **File** menu, and then click **Exit** (Win).

   TIMESAVER *Press Ctrl+Q (Win) or ⌘+Q (Mac).*

2. If necessary, click **Yes** (Win) or **Save** (Mac) to save any changes you made to your open compositions before the program quits.

1 Close button on Document tab

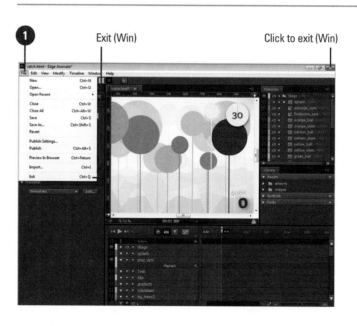

Exit (Win)   Click to exit (Win)

Working Within the Edge Animate Window

2

Introduction

Getting to know the Edge Animate authoring environment makes you more effective and efficient as you create movies. You'll get to know the parts of the Edge Animate window, which include a group of panels: Tools, Stage, Elements, Timeline, Properties, Library, Code, and Lessons. Panels are windows that allow you to view, organize, and change elements and related options in a document.

The Tools panel contains tools that you can use to draw, select, and modify artwork and text on the Stage. The Stage is a blank canvas where you can compose and arrange the content for an animation in Edge Animate. As you create and import content, the Elements panel provides a centralized place to view, manage, and organize it. The Timeline represents the overall structure of an animation and controls the content. The Timeline is time, not frame-based. The Timeline consists of keyframes that make up an animation. The order in which content appears in the Timeline determines the order in which it appears on the Stage. As you play an animation, the Playhead moves through the Timeline displaying the current content at that specific moment on the Stage. The Properties panel is a specialized panel that allows you to change element-specific attributes and options, and add keyframes to the Timeline.

As you work with Edge Animate, you'll open, close, and move around panels to meet your individual needs. As you do, you can create custom workspaces, or use the default workspace provided by Edge Animate.

What You'll Do

Examine the Edge Animate Window

Change Stage Properties

Work with the Stage

Change the Stage View

Use the Tools Panel

Use the Properties Panel

Use the Elements Panel

Use the Library Panel

Use the Timeline Panel

Work with Timeline Panel Controls

Use the Code Panel

Work with Panels

Dock and Undock Panels

Create and Use Workspaces

Define Keyboard Shortcuts

Change the Language

Undo and Redo Changes

Examining the Edge Animate Window

When you start Edge Animate, the program window displays several windows you can use to create an animation. These windows, known as panels, include the Tools, Stage, Timeline, Elements, Library, Properties, Code, and Lessons. You'll do the bulk of your work in Edge Animate with these windows.

The program window displays a title bar at the top along with resizing buttons and a Close button on the right side. Below the title bar is the the menu bar, which provide individual menus—including File, Edit, View,

Modify, Timeline, Window, and Help. A **menu** is a list of commands that you use to accomplish specific tasks. A **command** is a directive that accesses a feature of a program. On a menu, a check mark identifies a feature that is currently selected (that is, the feature is enabled or on). To disable (turn off) the feature, you click the command again to remove the check mark. A menu can contain several check-marked features. A bullet (Win) or diamond (Mac) also indicates that an option is enabled, but a menu can contain only one

Tools Panel
Contains tools to create and work with shape, text, and graphic elements.

Stage
Provides a place to compose and modify content, which includes drawing or arranging elements.

Elements Panel
Displays a list of elements used in the file. Contains options to work with individual or multiple elements.

Library Panel
Provides a place to access assets, symbols, and fonts.

Properties Panel
Displays attribute settings and options for shape, text, and graphic elements.

Timeline Panel
Gives you a time-based visual representation of elements and properties in an animation.

Code Panel
Provides a place to view and edit actions and triggers in a separate window.

bullet-or diamond-marked feature per menu section. To disable a command with a bullet or diamond next to it, you must select a different option in the section on the menu.

When you perform a command frequently, it's faster, and more convenient, to use a shortcut key, which is a keyboard alternative to using the mouse. When a shortcut key is available, it is listed beside the command on the menu, such as ⌘+I (Mac) or Ctrl+I (Win) for the Import command on the File menu.

Below the menu bar is a set of panels. A **panel** is a window you can open, close, move, and group with other panels, known as a panel group, to improve accessibility and workflow. A panel appears with a header bar, which includes a title tab, close button, and additional options. A panel group consists of a separate window with individual panels organized together with tabs to navigate from one panel to another.

The **Tools panel** contains a set of tools you can use to select and create shapes, such as rectangles, rounded rectangles, ellipses, and text. You can fill shapes with a color, pattern, or custom tile. The shapes and text you create in Edge Animate are saved as media elements in the Elements panel. When you position the pointer over a button on the Tools panel, a tooltip appears, displaying the button name.

The Document tab displays one or more open compositions or HTML documents in Edge Animate. The panel displays the Stage for the active document. When you have more than one document open, you can use the panel tab to switch back and forth between them. The **Stage** is the rectangle canvas area in the Document panel where you place media elements—including vector shapes, text boxes, and imported graphics—to create an animation. You can define the

properties of the Stage, such as its size and color, and the work area around it.

The **Timeline panel** organizes and controls media elements along with their properties over time in a linear sequence to create animations using layers and keyframes. As you play an animation, the Playhead moves through the Timeline displaying the current content on the Stage.

The **Properties panel** provides an easy way to view and change attributes of elements on the Stage. After you select an element, relevant commands and attributes for it appear in the Properties panel. You can set attributes—such as name, HTML tag, location, size, opacity, overflow, transform, rotate, skew, and scale—for shapes, graphics, and text.

The **Elements panel** provides a convenient way to view and organize all media elements within an animation in a structured list. The panel includes controls that allow you to quickly hide, show, lock, or unlock elements, and access element scripts. The Elements panel uses the HTML DOM standard, which defines how to get, change, add, or delete HTML elements, for compatibility on the web.

The **Library panel** provides a convenient way to view, add, and use assets, such as artwork and images, symbols, and web fonts. Assets are media elements in an animation, symbols are reusable elements, and web fonts are web stored fonts.

The **Code panel** allows you to view and edit all the actions and Timeline triggers in a separate window as an undocked panel for ease of use.

The **Lessons panel** provides seven In-App lessons you can take within Edge Animate. Each lesson provides step-by-step instructions you can follow to complete a task.

Changing Stage Properties

When you create a new composition in Edge Animate, it's important to set up Stage properties at the beginning of the project, so you don't have to recreate how your animation looks and operates when properties change. You use the Properties panel to specify Stage property settings that affect the animation, including the size, background color, and overflow area outside of the Stage, and browser display, including the title, preload resources, and autoplay for the animation. You can set the Stage width and height units property to pixels (fixed position) or percentage (relative position). The percentage option allows you to create a responsive, or adjustable, layout based on the screen size. You can set a minimum and maximum width to maintain your design layout.

Change Stage Properties

1. Click the **Selection** tool on the Tools panel.

2. Click the **Window** menu, and then click **Properties** to open the Properties panel, if necessary.

3. Click the **Stage** element in the Elements panel.

4. View and change settings in the Properties panel:

   ◆ Title. The title in your browser. The default name is *Untitled*.

   ◆ Open Actions. Displays scripts associated with the Stage.

   ◆ Width and Height Size. The current size of the Stage. Point to the width (w) and height (h) and drag the scrub or click and enter a size in pixels (px) (fixed position) or percentage (%) (relative position).

      ◆ Link Width and Height Size. Click the **Link** icon to toggle on or off.

      ◆ Change Width and Height Units. Point to the current unit, and then drag the slider to switch between pixels (px) or percentage (%).

   ◆ Background Color. The color of the Stage background. Click the **Background** color box, and then select a color.

Title   Open Actions

Background color

Width and Height size & Min W and Max W

◆ **Min W and Max W.** The settings specify the CSS minimum and maximum width for the Stage when the screen size changes.

◆ **Overflow.** The area outside of the Stage. Click the **Overflow** list arrow, and then select an option: **visible**, **hidden**, **scroll** (adds right and bottom scroll bars), or **auto** (adds scroll bars as needed).

◆ **Autoplay.** Select to start playing the animation when it is ready in your browser. If deselected, you need to use a JavaScript trigger to run the animation.

◆ **Composition ID.** The class name in HTML for the composition. The name is set randomly to avoid conflicts.

◆ **Down-level Stage and Poster.** Create a display for browsers that aren't HTML5 compliant.

   ◆ Click the **Camera** icon to capture the Stage and use it as the poster image.

   ◆ Click **Edit** to edit properties for the poster image.

   ◆ Click the **View** menu, and then click **Down-level Stage** to open and close it.

◆ **Preloader Stage.** Display a loader image as resources, including JavaScript libraries and images, load to display the composition in a browser.

   ◆ Select the Preloader Treatment as **Immediate** or **Polite** (takes a little longer).

   ◆ Click **Edit** to select a loader template and edit properties for the preloader.

   ◆ Click the **View** menu, and then click **Preloader Stage** to open and close it.

Autoplay   Overflow

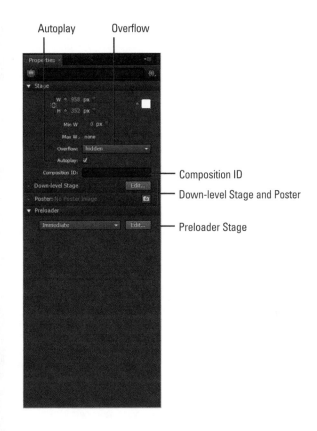

Composition ID

Down-level Stage and Poster

Preloader Stage

Click to exit Preloader Stage   Edit the Preloader Stage

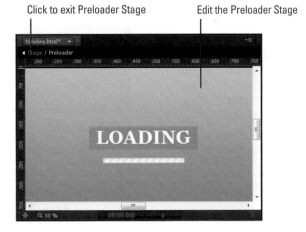

Working with the Stage

When you create or open a composition or HTML document, the Stage appears by default with a vertical and horizontal ruler at the top and on the left, persistent scroll bars on the right and bottom, and controls below the scroll bars. The rulers are useful add guides and align elements on the Stage. The ruler displays the size of the Stage in pixels, starting from (0, 0) in the upper-left corner. You can set the Stage width and height units property to pixels (fixed position) or percentage (relative position). When you set it to percentage, an adjustable pin and non-adjustable marker appear on the right (width) or bottom (height) Stage edge of the ruler, where you can reposition the pin to preview how the design layout responds to Stage size changes. The marker (small down arrow) remains in place to indicate the original width and height. Below the persistent scroll bars that are always available, you can use controls to center the Stage in view, change the view percentage, adjust the timeline, and display code and script notifications and errors.

Work with the Stage

◆ **Rulers.** Click the **View** menu, and then click **Rulers** to show or hide them.

   TIMESAVER *Press Ctrl+R (Win) or ⌘+R (Mac).*

◆ **Relativity Pin/Marker.** Available when the Stage width or height units are set to percentage (%). An adjustable pin appears on the ruler at the width or height edge.

   Drag the pin to preview the responsive design on the Stage based on the relative value set. A marker (small down arrow) is set above the pin to indicate the original width or height.

◆ **Center Stage.** Click the **Center the Stage** icon to display the center of the Stage.

◆ **Time Code.** Point to the time code, and then drag the scrub or click and enter to adjust the time code and play head in the Timeline panel.

◆ **Notifications.** Click the **Notification** icon (Error, Warning, or Info) to notify and display code or script notification and errors. If the icon is grayed out, no problems are detected.

Ruler   Marker

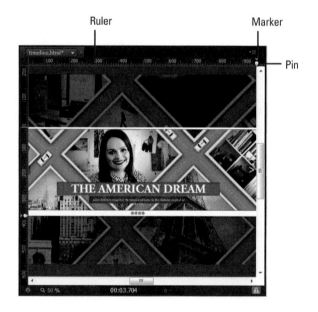

Pin

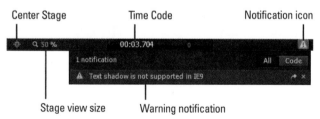

Center Stage   Time Code   Notification icon

Stage view size   Warning notification

Changing the Stage View

Because the Stage and overflow area in Edge Animate share the same space, it's often necessary to change the magnification level. You can use the Zoom commands on the View menu or the View scrub at the bottom of the Stage to zoom out and see the entire piece or zoom in to do more detailed work on a small portion. After using the Zoom commands, you can use the Actual Size command to go back to 100% view. You can speed up of zooming in and out and getting back to actual size by using keyboard shortcuts.

Zoom In and Out

◆ **View menu.** Click the **View** menu, and then click a zoom command:

> ◆ **Zoom In.** Zooms in the Stage to work on individual elements.

> **TIMESAVER** *Press Ctrl+=
(equal) (Win) or ⌘+= (equal)
(Mac) to Zoom In.*

> ◆ **Zoom Out.** Zooms out the Stage to work on the entire piece.

> **TIMESAVER** *Press Ctrl+-
(minus) (Win) or ⌘+- (minus)
(Mac) to Zoom Out.*

> ◆ **Actual Size.** Resizes the Stage to 100%, the actual size.

> **TIMESAVER** *Press Ctrl+1 (Win)
or ⌘+1 (Mac) to display the
actual size.*

◆ **View scrub.** Point to the View percentage at the bottom of the Stage, and then drag the scrub to adjust the view size.

◆ **Enter a view percentage.** Click the View percentage at the bottom of the Stage, enter a value, and then press Enter (Win) or Return (Mac).

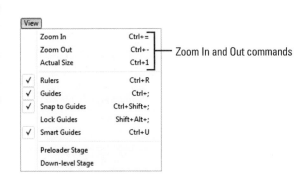

Zoom In and Out commands

View percentage; drag to adjust the view size

Using the Tools Panel

The Tools panel contains a set of tools—Selection, Transform, Rectangle, Rounded Rectangle, Ellipse, and Text—you can use to select, create, and transform shapes, such as rectangles, squares, circles, ovals, and text. For the shape tools, you can set the background and border colors. With either rectangle tool, you can create other shapes by changing the border radius. The difference between the two shape tools is that the Rounded Rectangle tool remembers border radius settings for next use while the Rectangle tool doesn't. The Ellipse tool is actually the Rounded Rectangle tool with settings to create ovals and circles. The shapes and text you create in Edge Animate are saved as media elements in the Elements panel. Before you create new elements, you can set and apply layout defaults for consistency and save time. After you create an element, you can use the Selection tool to select it, and then use the Transform tool to change its shape or the Clipping tool to crop it. When you position the pointer over a button on the Tools panel, a tooltip appears, displaying the button name and a shortcut key, which you can press (lowercase or uppercase) to quickly switch between tools.

Use the Tools Panel

◆ **Show or Hide the Tools Panel.**
Click the **Window** menu, and then click **Tools** to select (show) or deselect (hide) the check mark.

◆ **Use Tools on the Panel.** Use a tool on the Tools panel as follows:

  ◆ **Selection Tool.** Click the tool or press V, and then click individual elements or drag to select multiple elements.

  ◆ **Transform Tool.** Click the tool or press Q, select the element, and then drag to scale it.

  ◆ **Clipping Tool.** Click the tool or press C, select the element, and then drag to set a cropping area.

  ◆ **Rectangle Tool.** Click the tool or press M, and then drag to draw a rectangle.

  ◆ **Rounded Rectangle Tool.** Click the tool or press R, and then drag to draw a rounded rectangle.

  ◆ **Ellipse Tool.** Click the tool or press O, and then drag to draw an Ellipse or circle.

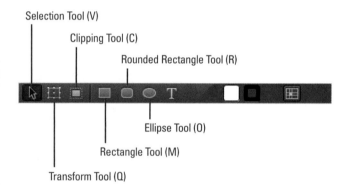

Selection Tool (V)

Clipping Tool (C)

Rounded Rectangle Tool (R)

Ellipse Tool (O)

Rectangle Tool (M)

Transform Tool (Q)

- ◆ **Text Tool.** Click the tool or press T, click or drag to draw a text box, and then type text.

- ◆ **Background Color and Border Color.** Click the color box, and then select a color to specify the one you want when you draw a shape.

◆ **Set Layout Defaults for New Elements.** Use the button to set default options as follows:

- ◆ **Relative point.** Click a square to specify the Relative point position (upper-left, upper-right, lower-left, or lower-right).

  The Relative point indicates the element position when the screen size changes.

- ◆ **L and T.** Set the units for the horizontal (L) and vertical (T) position.

- ◆ **W and H.** Set the units for the width (W) and height (H).

- ◆ **Use 'img' tag for images.** Select to use the <img> tag to embed images. Deselect to use the <div> tag.

- ◆ **'auto' for image width.** Select to use *auto* option for the embedded image, instead of a specific width size in pixels. Deselect to use the width in the Properties panel.

- ◆ **'auto' for image height.** Select to use *auto* option for the embedded image, instead of a specific height size in pixels. Deselect to use the height in the Properties panel.

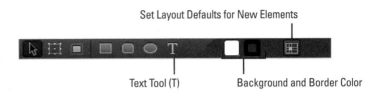

Set Layout Defaults for New Elements

Text Tool (T)   Background and Border Color

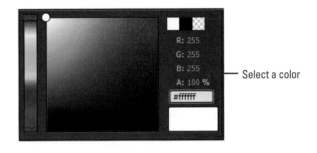

Select a color

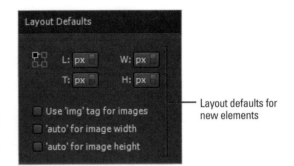

Layout defaults for new elements

Using the Properties Panel

The Properties panel displays the attributes of the current selection on the Stage or in the Timeline. After you select an element on the Stage or in the Elements panel, relevant commands and attributes for it appear in the Properties panel. You can set attributes—such as name, HTML tag, position, size, opacity, overflow, color, transform, corners, shadow, clipping (crop), playback, and accessibility—for shapes, graphics, and text. The attributes you set in the Properties panel are used to create CSS (Cascading Style Sheet) code for use in HTML. You can change attributes (values in gold) by clicking and entering a value or pointing to and dragging a scrub (cursor changes to double-arrow with pointing finger). You can even enter expressions as a value, such as 360*5 to rotate an element 5 times. A diamond next to an attribute represents a keyframe, which allows you to animate an element using the attribute. When you select two or more different types of elements, the Properties panel displays the common attributes for the elements; a dash appears where they are different.

Use the Properties Panel

◆ **Show or Hide the Properties Panel.** Click the **Window** menu, and then click **Properties** to select (show) or deselect (hide) the check mark.

◆ **Show or Hide Properties.** Click the **Expand** or **Collapse** arrow next to a heading.

◆ **Name an Element.** Select an element, select the ID name, type a name, and then press Enter (Win) or Return (Mac).

◆ **Select an Element HTML Tag.** Select an element, click the **Tag** button, and then select a tag.

◆ **Name a Class.** Select an element, click the **Class** button, enter a class, and then press Enter (Win) or Return (Mac).

◆ **Open Actions.** Select an element, and then click the **Open Actions** button. A script allows you to add functionality to the element. Click the **Close** button to exit.

◆ **Add a Keyframe Animation.** Select an element, position the Playhead, click the keyframe diamond to the left of the attribute name, and then adjust attributes.

Element ID name

Tag button

Class button

Open Actions button

Keyframe diamond

Use the Properties Panel to Change Attributes

1 Select an element on the Stage or in the Elements panel.

2 Do any of the following:

◆ **Change Values.** Point to a value in gold, click it, enter a value, and then press Enter (Win) or Return (Mac), or point to a value (cursor changes to double-arrow with pointing finger) and drag a scrub to adjust it.

◆ **Change Colors.** Click a Color box, and then select a color from the palette.

◆ White Color. Click the **White** box.

◆ Black Color. Click the **Black** box.

◆ Transparent. Click the **Transparent** box.

◆ Any Color. Drag the color spectrum slider, and then click and drag the white color circle.

◆ Specific RGB Color. Enter color values for **R**ed, **G**reen, and **B**lue.

◆ Specific Transparency. Enter a value (%) for **A**lpha. (0% is fully transparent, while 100% is completely solid).

◆ Specific Hex Color. Enter a six digit color value starting with a hash (#) in the Hex box, and then press Enter (Win) or Return (Mac).

Change values

Color box

Color circle   White Black

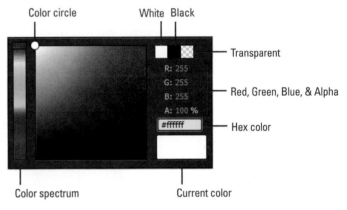

Transparent

Red, Green, Blue, & Alpha

Hex color

Color spectrum   Current color

For Your Information

Selecting a RGB Color

In the color palette, you can drag to select a color or enter specific color RGB or Hex values. RGB stands for Red, Green, and Blue. RGB is an additive color model in which red, green, and blue light is added together to create colors. It's designed to display images on electronic systems, such as televisions and computers. The Hex value, also known as a hex triplet, is a six digit, three-byte hexadecimal number with a hash (#) in front used in HTML, CSS, SVG, and other applications to represent colors in RGB in another way.

Using the Elements Panel

The Elements panel provides a convenient way to view and organize all media elements within an animation in a structured list. All elements are assigned a user-defined ID name and HTML tag and is represented with an associated element type icon. The Elements panel includes controls (Eye, Lock, and Actions icons) that allow you to quickly hide, show, lock, or unlock elements, and access element scripts. When you show or hide an element, an Eye icon (show) or grey dot (hide) appears in the Visibility column. When you lock or unlock an element, a padlock (lock) or grey dot (unlock) appears in the Lock column. To the left of the Visibility column is a light bar. The light bar gives you a visual indicator of an elements use. For example, when the light bar is grey, the element is not animated or when it's a color, the element is animated using keyframes. When you have a long list in the Elements panel, you can collapse or expand an element group to hide or show its contents. You can also move an element to change its stacking order position on the Stage. Elements appears in a layer stacking order with the ones at the bottom of the list appearing in the back and ones at the top appearing in front.

Use the Elements Panel

- **Show or Hide the Elements Panel.** Click the **Window** menu, and then click **Elements** to select (show) or deselect (hide) the check mark.

- **Collapse or Expand Element Groups.** Click the **Collapse** arrow (down) to collapse a group or click the **Expand** arrow (right) to expand a group.

- **Show or Hide Elements.** Click the **grey dot** (to show) or **Eye** icon (to hide) in the Visibility column to show or hide it.

- **Lock or Unlock Elements.** Click the **grey dot** (to lock) or **Lock** icon (to unlock) in the Lock column to unlock or lock it.

- **Open Element Actions.** Click the **Open Actions** button. A script allows you to add functionality to the element. To exit the Actions panel, click the **Close** button.

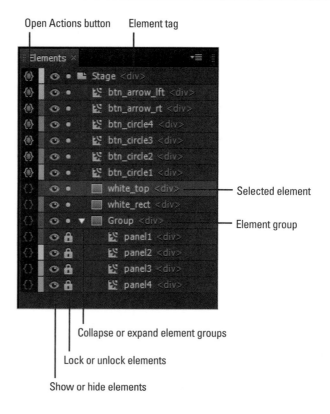

Open Actions button   Element tag

Selected element

Element group

Collapse or expand element groups

Lock or unlock elements

Show or hide elements

Work with Elements in the Elements Panel

◆ **Select an Element.** Click an element in the Elements panel or click an element on the Stage.

◆ **Rename an Element.** Double-click an element ID name, type a name, and then press Enter (Win) or Return (Mac).

◆ **Move Elements Stacking Position.** Drag an element name to a new position; a thick bold bar indicates the new location when you release the mouse.

Elements appear in a layer stacking order with the ones at the bottom of the list appearing in the back, and the ones at the top appears in front.

◆ **Group Elements in DIV.** Select the elements, click the **Modify** menu, and then click **Group Elements in DIV**.

TIMESAVER *Press Ctrl+G (Win) or ⌘+G (Mac) to group.*

A DIV is a container that allows you to work with multiple elements, such as moving. However, the elements are still looked at as individual ones.

◆ **Ungroup Elements.** Select the group of elements in a DIV, click the **Modify** menu, and then click **Ungroup Elements**.

TIMESAVER *Press Ctrl+Shift +G (Win) or ⌘+Shift+G (Mac) to ungroup.*

◆ **Modify Elements.** Right-click (Win) or Control-click (Mac) an element, and then select a command, such as Copy, Paste, Duplicate, and Delete, on the context menu.

◆ You can also use the Properties panel to change element attributes.

Selected element

Element commands

Using the Library Panel

The Library panel is where all of the assets, symbols, and web fonts in your animation in Edge Animate are stored. An **asset** is any artwork or element, such as images, buttons, and fonts, you have added into your composition. A **symbol** is a reusable asset that is turned into an instance, or copy, which you can modify and animate, on the Stage. A **web font** is a font that is optimized for use in web pages and resides on a web server instead of the user's local computer. You can click the Add button (+) to the right of Assets, Symbols, or Fonts to add items to the Library panel. You can use the Window menu to show or hide the Library panel as needed.

Use the Library Panel

◆ **Show or Hide the Library Panel.** Click the **Window** menu, and then click **Library** to select (show) or deselect (hide) the check mark.

◆ **Collapse or Expand Groups.** Click the **Collapse** arrow (down) to collapse a group or click the **Expand** arrow (right) to expand a group.

◆ **Add Assets.** Click the **Add** button (+) next to Assets, select the files, and then click **Open**.

◆ **Add Symbols.** Select an element on the Stage, click the **Add** button (+) next to Symbols, and then click **Convert selection to symbol**, enter a name, and then click **OK**, or click the **Add** button (+) next to Symbols, click **Import Symbols**, select the files, and then click **Open**.

◆ **Add Web Fonts.** Click the **Add** button (+) next to Fonts, type the web font name and fallback fonts, paste in embed code from web site for the web font, and then click **Add Font**.

Collapse or expand groups

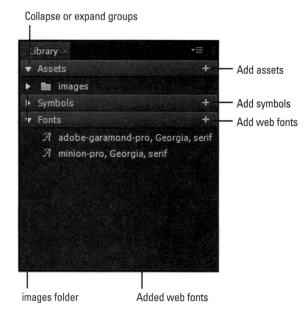

Add assets

Add symbols

Add web fonts

images folder   Added web fonts

Work with Elements in the Library Panel

◆ **Use Assets and Symbols.** Open the Library panel, click **Expand** arrow (down) next to Assets or Symbols, and then drag the asset you want at a location on the Stage.

As you drag on the Stage, X and Y location values in pixels appear along with the asset name as part of the cursor.

◆ **Modify a Symbol.** Right-click (Win) or Control-click (Mac) a symbol element, and then select a command, such as Edit, Delete, Rename, Duplicate, or Export, on the context menu.

◆ **Export a Symbol.** Right-click (Win) or Control-click (Mac) the symbol element, click **Export**, navigate to a destination folder, enter a name, and then click **Save**.

The program saves the exported symbol with the Edge Animate Symbol File (.ansym) file format.

◆ **Locate an Image Location.** Right-click (Win) or Control-click (Mac) the image, and then click **Reveal in Explorer**.

◆ **Delete a Web Font.** Right-click (Win) or Control-click (Mac) the web font, and then click **Delete**.

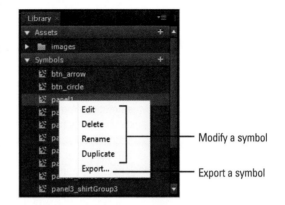

— Modify a symbol

— Export a symbol

— Locate an image location

— Delete a web font

Using the Timeline Panel

The Timeline panel, more commonly known as the Timeline, controls the content on the Stage. The Timeline consists of elements and layers. Elements along with their properties appear on the left side of the Timeline while layers (denoted as bars) along with their keyframes (denoted as diamonds) appear on the right. You use keyframes in layers to change element properties over time and space to create animations. You can arrange and adjust the layers in the Timeline to fine-tune the animation. You can work with elements in the Timeline just as you can in the Elements panel. The number of elements can grow quickly, especially when you open an existing HTML document. To make it easier to work with the elements and their properties in the Timeline, you can collapse or expand element property groups, show only animated elements, and search for specific elements. At the bottom of the Timeline, you can show a grid and change the grid size in seconds. You can also zoom in the time code from quarter-second increments to milliseconds for more timing control. Timeline commands are available on the Timeline panel and Timeline menu.

Use the Timeline Panel

◆ **Show or Hide the Timeline Panel.** Click the **Window** menu, and then click **Timeline** to select (show) or deselect (hide) the check mark.

◆ **Zoom In or Out the Timecode.** Drag the slider to the right to zoom in and to the left to zoom out.

> **TIMESAVER** *Press = (equal) to Zoom In. Press - (minus) to Zoom Out.*

◆ **Zoom Timeline to Fit.** Click the **Zoom Timeline to Fit** button to display the animation to fit in the Timeline view.

> **TIMESAVER** *Press \ (back slash) to Zoom to Fit.*

◆ **Show the Grid.** Click the **Show Grid** button to toggle on or off.

◆ **Change the Grid Size.** Click the **Grid Size** button, and then select a grid size.

Animated elements   Timeline grid   Timeline

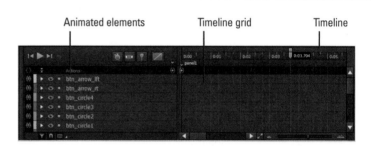

Grid Size button

Show Grid button

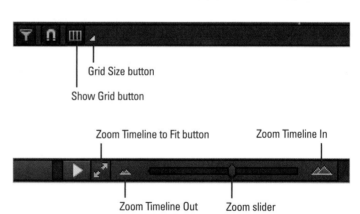

Zoom Timeline to Fit button   Zoom Timeline In

Zoom Timeline Out   Zoom slider

Display Elements in the Timeline Panel

◆ **Collapse or Expand Selected Property Group.** Click the **Collapse** arrow (down) to collapse a property group or click the **Expand** arrow (right) to expand a property group.

   TIMESAVER *Press Ctrl+. (period) (Win) or ⌘+. (period) (Mac) to Expand/Collapse Selected.*

◆ **Collapse or Expand All Property Groups.** Click the **Timeline** menu, and then click **Expand/Collapse All**.

   TIMESAVER *Press Ctrl+Shift+. (period) (Win) or ⌘+Shift +. (period) (Mac) to Expand/ Collapse All.*

◆ **Show or Hide Elements.** Click the **grey dot** (to show) or **Eye** icon (to hide) in the Visibility column to show or hide it.

◆ **Lock or Unlock Elements.** Click the **grey dot** (to lock) or **Lock** icon (to unlock) in the Lock column to unlock or lock it.

◆ **Filter Animated Elements.** Click the **Only Show Animated Elements** button to toggle on (highlighted) and off (non-highlighted). When turned on, only animated elements show in the Timeline, which helps reduce the Timeline clutter.

   When the light bar is grey, the element is not animated; when it's a color, the element is animated using keyframes.

◆ **Timeline Snapping.** Click the **Timeline Snapping** button to toggle on (highlighted) and off (non-highlighted). You can set **Snap To** options on the Timeline menu. When turned on, Timeline items snap to the **Grid**, **Playhead**, or **Keyframes**, **Labels**, **Triggers**.

Show and hide elements Expanded elements Element animations

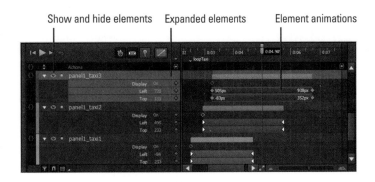

Lock and unlock elements

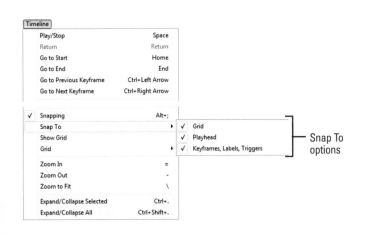

Timeline Snapping button

Only Show Animated Elements button

Snap To options

Working with Timeline Panel Controls

The order in which content appears in the Timeline determines the order in which it appears in the animation. The Timeline displays content in sequential order from 0:00 seconds to the end of the animation. The timecode in seconds appears below the Stage and next to the Playhead. The **Playhead** appears in the header with a red line going down the Timeline to indicate the current position in the animation. As you play an animation, the Playhead moves through the Timeline displaying the current content on the Stage. If you want to display specific content on the Stage or review the animation, you can move (drag) the Playhead, known as **scrubbing**, across the Timeline to a specific position or through a section to display it. A **keyframe** (denoted as a diamond) defines a point in time where an element property changes in an animation or uses actions to modify content. It sets the start and end points for an animation. In the Timeline, you can also toggle options on and off to create auto-keyframes, auto-transitions and one-step pin animations. Playhead and Iimeline commands are available on the Timeline panel and Timeline menu as well as with keyboard shortcuts.

Work with the Playhead in the Timeline Panel

- ◆ Move Playhead. Do any of the following:

  - ◆ **Move Playhead to Start.** Click the Rewind button (left of Play/Pause) or press Home.

  - ◆ **Move Playhead to End.** Click the Forward button (right of Play/Pause) or press End.

  - ◆ **Move Playhead to Last Play Position.** Click the Return button (right of Forward) or press Enter (Win) or Return (Mac).

  - ◆ **Move Playhead to Exact Time.** Click and enter a time value or point to the time value and drag.

  - ◆ **Move/Scrub Playhead.** Drag the Playhead.

  - ◆ **Move/Scrub Playhead without Snapping.** Ctrl (Win) or ⌘ (Mac)+drag the Playhead.

- ◆ Play Animation. Click the **Play/Pause** button or press Space to play or pause the animation.

Play/Pause button   Playhead   Playhead timecode

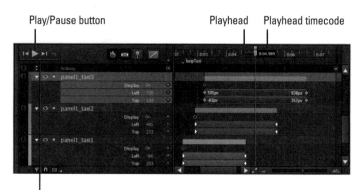

Rewind, Forward, and Return to Last Play Position

Work with Timeline Panel Controls

◆ **Create Auto-Keyframes.** Click the **Auto-Keyframe Mode** button or press K to toggle on (highlighted). When you move an element on the Stage, Edge Animate automatically inserts keyframes.

Using this option makes animation easy, however it also adds extras keyframes you may not want and need to delete later.

◆ **Add a Keyframe.** Position the Playhead, click the **Add Keyframe** diamond to the right of the attribute name on the Timeline or Properties panel, and then adjust attributes.

◆ **Create Auto-Transitions.** Click the **Auto-Transition Mode** button or press X to toggle on (highlighted). Creates a visible easing transition. When you click to toggle off (non-highlighted), the transition pops in instantly.

◆ **Toggle Pin.** Click the **Toggle Pin** button or press P to toggle on (highlighted). Create a from and to keyframe in a single edit.

◆ **Easing.** Click the **Easing** button to select an easing in or out of an animation.

◆ **Insert Label.** Position the Playhead where you want the label, click the **Insert Label** button, type a label, and then press Enter (Win) or Return (Mac).

TIMESAVER *Press Ctrl+L (Win) or ⌘+L (Mac) to insert a label.*

◆ **Open Element Actions.** Click the **Open Actions** button. A script allows you to add functionality to the element. To exit the Actions panel, click the **Close** button.

Auto-Keyframe Mode button

Auto-Transition Mode button

Toggle Pin button

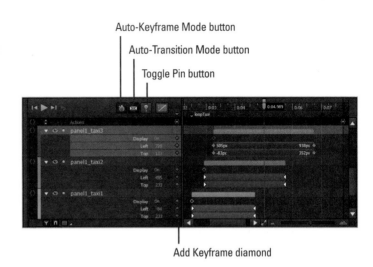

Add Keyframe diamond

Easing button

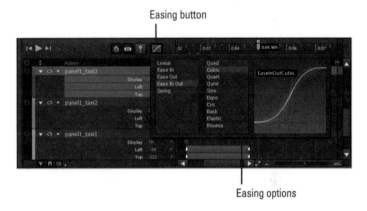

Easing options

Insert Label button   Label on the Timeline

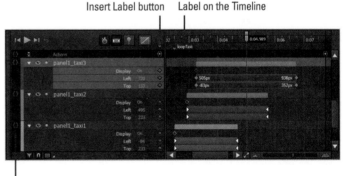

Open Actions button

Using the Code Panel

With the Code panel you can view and work with all the code in your composition. The Code panel allows you to view, create, and edit your own code or built-in code snippets (predefined segments of JavaScript code). An action enables you to invoke a script to perform a function. The script is invoked when a certain "event" or "trigger" occurs. You can attach a script to an element that responds when a specific event occurs or attach a script to a place in the Timeline. For example, you can attach the Mouseover event script to a button that runs whenever the user hovers over the button, or you can attach the Stop script to the Timeline that stops playing when the Playhead reaches it. You can use the Window menu to show or hide the Code panel as needed. The Code panel displays in an separate window as an undocked panel for ease of use; however, you can docked if you use it on a regular basis.

Use the Code Panel

◆ **Open the Code Panel.** Click the **Window** menu, and then click **Code** to select (show) the check mark.

The panel opens in a separate window as an undocked panel.

TIMESAVER *Press Ctrl+E (Win) or ⌘+E (Mac).*

◆ **Close the Code Panel.** Click the **Window** menu, and then click **Code** to deselect (hide) the check mark, or click the **Close** button on the panel.

◆ **Change Code Font Size.** In the Code panel, click the **Options** button, point to **Font Size**, and then click **Small**, **Medium**, or **Large** to select (show) the check mark.

◆ **Show Code Line Numbers.** Click the **Options** button, and then click **Show Line Numbers** to select (show) the check mark.

◆ **Include Code Snippet Comments.** Click the **Options** button, and then click **Include Snippet Comments** to select (show) the check mark.

Selected action

Options button

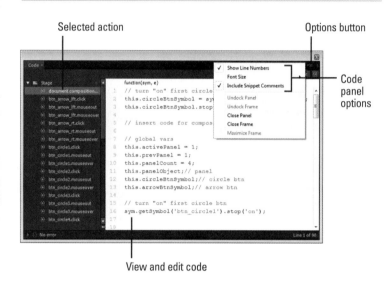

Code panel options

View and edit code

Work with Code in the Code Panel

◆ **View and Edit Code.** Select the element with the code you want to work with, and then modify it as you would in any word processing program.

◆ **Add Code.** Click the **Add Code** button (+) to the right of the element, click **Event**, **Elements**, or **Timeline**, and then select an action or trigger.

◆ **Show or Hide Code Snippets.** Click the **Toggle Display of Code Snippets** button to show or hide it.

◆ **Insert a Code Snippets.** Click to place the insertion point where you want to insert the snippet, click the **Toggle Display of Code Snippets** button to show it, and then click a snippet button.

After you insert a code snippet, you can edit it. Code in red is placeholder text that you can modify to suit your own needs.

◆ **View and Edit the Entire Actions JavaScript File.** Click the **Full Code** button to display it; the circle icon next to it turns color. To exit the view, click the **Full Code** button again; the circle icon turns gray.

Add Code button   Toggle Display of Code Snippets button

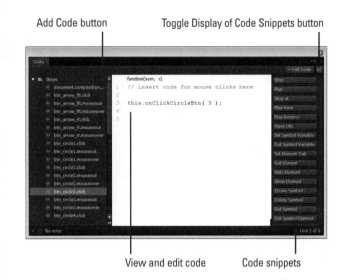

View and edit code   Code snippets

Full Code button

View and edit the entire actions JavaScript file

Working with Panels

Panels are windows that allow you to view, organize, and change elements and related options in a document. In Edge Animate, you work with several panel windows at one time. If the default layout of the panels doesn't work with your style, you can open, close, or rearrange panels within the Edge Animate window to save space or meet your individual needs. You can use the Windows menu to open and close a panel. A panel appears with a tab title, Close button, Options menu, and header bars. The Close button allows you to close a panel or close a document. The Options menu provides you with panel and frame specific commands, including undock, close, and maximize/restore a panel or frame. You can also drag a panel edge to resize it. The header bars (two rows of dotted lines on the left and right side of a panel) allow you to move a panel to a different position within the Edge Animate window.

Open and Close Panels

◆ **Open a Panel.** Click the **Window** menu, and then click a panel to select (show) the check mark.

◆ **Close a Panel.** Click the **Window** menu, and then click a panel to deselect (hide) the check mark.

> **TIMESAVER** *Click the Close button on the panel tab to close it.*

◆ You can also click the **Options** button on the panel, and then click **Close Panel**.

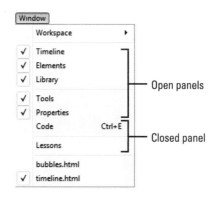

Work with Panels

- **Resize a Panel.** Point to the edge (left, right, top, or bottom) of a panel (cursor changes to double bars), and then drag to resize.

- **Maximize/Restore a Panel.** Click the **Options** button on the panel, and then click **Maximize Frame** or **Restore Frame Size**.

- **Move a Panel.** Point to a panel tab or header icon, and then drag it to another panel. As you drag the panel, the destination panel tints blue and sections off. Point to the section (above, below, left, right, or tab in the center) where you want to move the panel, and then release the mouse button.

See Also

See "Docking and Undocking Panels" on page 48 for more information on moving a panel.

Header icon/panel tab   Options button

Resize a panel

Left   Above

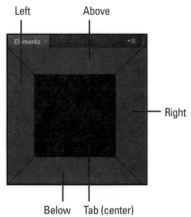

Right

Below   Tab (center)

Docking and Undocking Panels

You can dock and undock—or temporarily attach and detach—panels or panel groups, or frame. You can display panels using the Window menu, and then drag them around the program window to dock or undock them to other panels. When you drag a panel using its panel tab or panel header icon over a dockable area, the destination panel tints to blue and displays frame zones (above, below, left, right, or tab in the center) or tints to green for a program window edge, where you can specify the final destination of the panel. When you release the mouse button, the panel snaps to the dockable area and stays there until you move it. If you attempt to dock a panel over an undockable area, no frame zones appear. If you want to put a panel in a separate window, you need to undock it from the program window.

Dock a Panel

1 Position the pointer on the panel tab or panel header icon (two rows of dots on the left and right side of the header bar).

2 Drag the window away from the panel to a destination panel or the edge of the program window.

As you drag to a destination panel, the panel sections off into frame zones and highlights zones to indicate the destination. As you drag to a program window edge, a bar highlights the edge as the destination.

3 Point to the frame zone where you want to dock the panel.

- **Above.** Places the panel above the destination panel.

- **Below.** Places the panel below the destination panel.

- **Left.** Places the panel to the left of the destination panel.

- **Right.** Places the panel to the right of the destination panel.

- **Center (Tab).** Places the panel as a tab in the destination panel.

- **Program Edge.** Places the panel vertically or horizontally along the edge.

4 Release the mouse button.

Left   Above

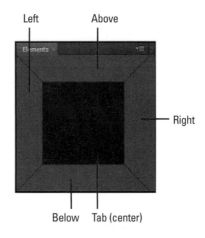

Right

Below   Tab (center)

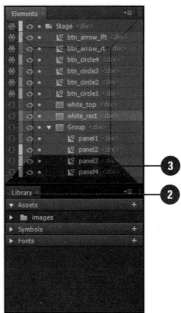

Undock a Panel

1. Click the tab in the panel to select and display it, if necessary.

2. Click the **Options** button on the right side of the panel header bar, and then click **Undock Panel**.

3. Drag the undocked panel window to an empty area of the program window.

4. To close the window, click the **Close** button.

See Also

See "Working with Panels" on page 46 for more information on opening, closing, and resizing panels.

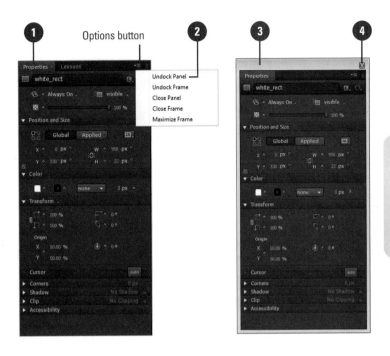

Options button

Undock a Frame

1. Click the tab in the panel with more than one tab to select and display it.

2. Click the **Options** button on the right side of the panel header bar, and then click **Undock Frame**.

   All the tabs in the panel frame are undocked into a separate window.

3. Drag the undocked panel window to an empty area of the program window.

4. To close the window, click the **Close** button.

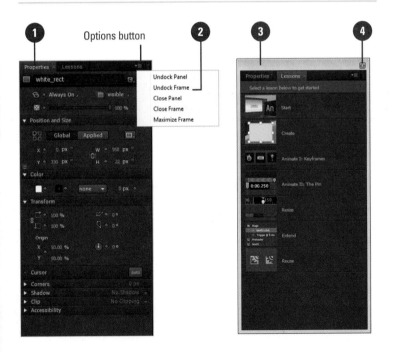

Options button

Creating and Use Workspaces

As you work with Edge Animate, you'll open, close, and move around panels to meet your individual needs. You can create custom workspaces, or use the default workspace provided by Edge Animate. After you customize the Edge Animate workspace, you can save the location of panels as a workspace, or custom panel set or reset the current workspace back to its original state. You can switch the display to a workspace by using the Workspace submenu on the Window menu. If you no longer use a custom workspace, you can remove it at any time. Before you can delete a workspace, you need to display a workspace that is not the one you want to remove. Edge Animate doesn't include the current workspace in the list of available workspaces you can remove.

Create a Workspace

1. Open and position the panels you want to include in a panel set.

2. Click the **Window** menu, point to **Workspace**, and then click **New Workspace**.

   The New Workspace dialog box opens.

3. Type a name in the Name box.

4. Click **OK**.

   The workspace is now saved and available on the Workspace submenu.

Did You Know?

You can reset a workspace back to its original state. Click the Window menu, point to Workspace, and then select a workspace. Change the layout of the workspace. To reset it back, click the Window menu, point to Workspace, click Reset "Workspace Name," and then click Yes to confirm the change.

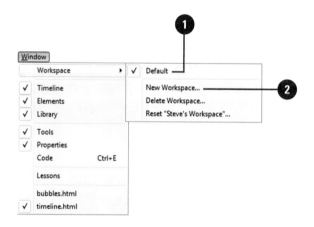

Switch to a Workspace

1. Click the **Window** menu, point to **Workspace**, and then select a panel option:

   ◆ **Default.** Displays the default panel layout created by Adobe for Edge Animate.

   ◆ **Custom panel name.** Displays a custom panel layout that you created.

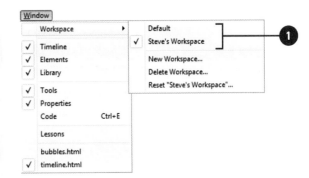

Delete a Workspace

1. Click the **Window** menu, point to **Workspace**, and then select a workspace you don't want to delete.

2. Click the **Window** menu, point to **Workspace**, and then click **Delete Workspace**.

3. Click the **Name** list arrow, and then select the panel set you want to delete.

4. Click **OK**.

   The workspace is now deleted.

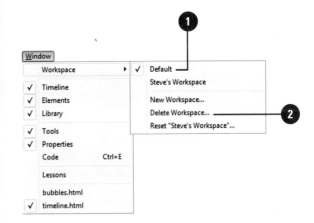

Defining Keyboard Shortcuts

A wise man once wrote "time is money," and Edge Animate is a program that can consume a lot of time. That's why the Edge Animate program uses keyboard shortcuts. **Keyboard Shortcuts**, as their name implies, let you perform tasks in a shorter period of time. For example, if you want to open a new composition in Edge Animate, you can click the File menu, and then click New, or you can abandon the mouse and press Ctrl+N (Win) or ⌘+N (Mac) to use shortcut keys. Using shortcut keys reduces the use of the mouse and speeds up operations. In fact, a recent study in the American Medical Journal suggested that the use of shortcut keys significantly cuts down on repetitive stress, and reduces instances of carpal tunnel syndrome. Edge Animate raises the bar by not only giving you a lot of possible shortcut keys, but also actually allowing you to define your own shortcuts, even multiple ones for the same command.

Create a Keyboard Shortcut

1. Click the **Edit** menu, and then click **Keyboard Shortcuts**.

   TIMESAVER *Press Alt+K (Win) or Option+K (Mac).*

2. Click an arrow (left column) to expand the menu that contains the command for which you want to create a shortcut.

3. Select an item from the Commands list, and then click under Shortcut for the item.

4. Use the keyboard to create the new shortcut. For example, press Ctrl+N (Win) or ⌘+N (Mac).

   If the shortcut is already used, an alert appears in the dialog box.

5. If a conflict appears, click **Undo** to reverse it or click **Go To Conflict** to change it.

6. Click **Add**.

7. Click **OK**.

Change a Keyboard Shortcut

1. Click the **Edit** menu, and then click **Keyboard Shortcuts**.

2. To search for a command, enter it in the Search box, and then press Enter (Win) or Return (Mac).

3. Click an arrow (left column) as needed to expand the menu that contains the command for which you want to create a shortcut.

4. Select an item from the Commands list, and then click the item you want to change under Shortcut.

5. Use the keyboard to change the shortcut. For example, press Ctrl+N (Win) or ⌘+N (Mac).

   If the shortcut is already used, an alert appears in the dialog box.

6. If a conflict appears, click **Undo** to remove it or click **Go To Conflict** to change it.

7. Click **Add**.

8. To add another one for the selected command, click to the right of the shortcut, use the keyboard to create the shortcut, and then click **Add**.

9. To remove a shortcut, select it, and then click **Remove All**.

10. Click **OK**.

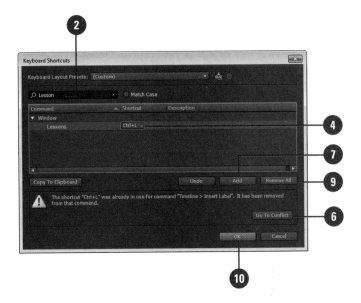

Changing the Language

If you prefer to use Edge Animate in another language, you can use the Change Language command on the Help menu to switch to another one. You can change the language to German, English, Spanish, French, Italian, or Japanese. When you switch to a different Language, the change takes effect when you exit and restart the Edge Animate program.

Change the Language

1. Click the **Help** menu, and then click **Change Language**.

   TIMESAVER *Press Alt+K (Win) or Option+K (Mac).*

2. Click the **Locale** list arrow, and then select a language.

3. Click **OK**.

4. Exit Edge Animate.

   ◆ Click the **Edge Animate** menu, and then click **Quit Edge Animate** (Mac).

   ◆ Click the **Close** button, or click the **File** menu, and then click **Exit** (Win).

5. If necessary, click **Yes** (Win) or **Save** (Mac) to save any changes you made to your open compositions before the program quits.

6. Start Edge Animate.

Undoing and Redoing Changes

You may realize you've made a mistake shortly after completing a task or command. The Undo command lets you "take back" one or more previous tasks, including shapes you created, edits you made, or commands you selected. For example, if you were to make several property changes, and then decide you don't like the adjustment, you could undo the changes instead of trying to re-create the previous look. A few moments later, if you decide the changes you just undid were not so bad after all, you could use the Redo command to restore them back. Edge Animate remembers your tasks in order. The Undo command takes you back one task/command at a time, so you can keep using the Undo command to take you back multiple tasks/commands. The Redo command works the same way in reverse.

Undo and Redo Commands

① Perform tasks and commands in Edge Animate.

② To perform an undo, click the **Edit** menu, and then click **Undo** *command name*.

TIMESAVER *Press Ctrl+Z (Win) or ⌘+Z (Mac).*

③ To perform a redo, click the **Edit** menu, and then click **Redo**.

TIMESAVER *Press Ctrl+Shift+Z (Win) or ⌘+Shift+Z (Mac).*

TROUBLE? *The Redo command is only available after you use the Undo command.*

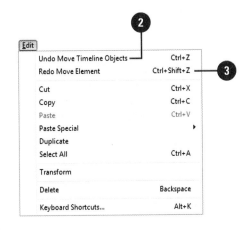

Taking In-App Lessons

3

Introduction

From the Welcome screen or the Lessons panel, you can use In-App Lessons to help you get started with the project in Edge Animate. The In-App Lessons provide seven step-by step topics with the aid of the Lessons panel to walk you through the process of creating animations with Edge Animate. The lessons include *Quick Start* to help you get going, *Create* to teach you how to work with shapes, text and images, *Animate I: Keyframes* and *II: The Pin* to show you how to use keyframes and pins, *Resize* to learn how to respond to size changes, *Extend* to learn how to loop and handle user interaction, and *Reuse* to show you how to create reusable elements with symbols.

If you want further help and instructional materials, you can use links in the Welcome screen to access a list of key features and product release notes, and helpful resources from online content, including Help and Tutorials, videos on Adobe TV, community forums, and sample projects. In addition, you can access Facebook and Twitter to get more information about Edge Animate.

What You'll Do

Start a Lesson

Use the Lessons Panel

Take the Quick Start Lesson

Take the Create Lesson

Take the Animate with Keyframes Lesson

Take the Animate with the Pin Lesson

Take the Resize Lesson

Take the Extend Lesson

Take the Reuse Lesson

Starting a Lesson

Within Edge Animate you can take In-App Lessons to help you get started with the project. Edge Animate provides seven In App step-by step lessons with the aid of the Lessons panel. The lessons include *Quick Start* to help you get going, *Create* to teach you how to work with shapes, text and images, *Animate I: Keyframes* and *II: The Pin* to show you how to use keyframes and pins, *Resize* to learn how to respond to size changes, *Extend* to learn how to loop and handle user interaction, and *Reuse* to show you how to create reusable objects with symbols. You can start an In App Lesson from the Welcome screen or the Lessons panel. After you start a lesson, the Lessons panel walks you through topic as you perform the steps in the Edge Animate window.

Start a Lesson from the Welcome Screen

1. Start Adobe Edge Animate, or close all open documents (click the **File** menu, and then click **Close All**).

2. Click **Getting Started**, if necessary.

3. Point to a lesson tile to view a brief description.

4. Click a lesson tile to start it.

   The Welcome screen closes, Edge Animate creates a new Untitled project, and the Lessons panel opens with the selected lesson.

5. Read and perform the lesson steps in the Edge Animate window as indicated in the Lessons panel.

6. At the bottom of the Lessons panel, click the **Next Step** link.

7. Follow the additional steps or click links to start other lessons.

   After you complete the lesson, you can save or close the Untitled project.

8. To close the Lessons panel, click the **Window** menu, and then click **Lessons** or click the **Close** button on the panel.

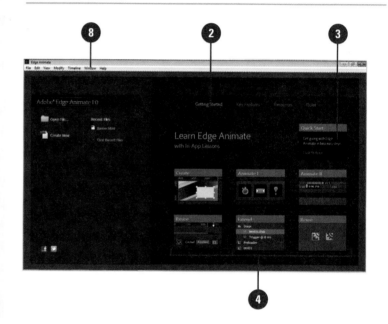

Start a Lesson from the Lessons Panel

① Click the **Window** menu, and then click **Lessons** to select (show) the check mark.

The Lessons panel opens, displaying a list of In-App Lessons.

② Click a lesson tile to start it.

Edge Animate creates a new Untitled project, and the Lessons panel displays the start of the selected lesson.

③ Read and perform the lesson steps in the Edge Animate window as indicated in the Lessons panel.

④ At the bottom of the Lessons panel, click the **Next Step** link.

⑤ Follow the additional steps or click links to start other lessons.

After you complete the lesson, you can save or close the Untitled project.

⑥ To close the Lessons panel, click the **Window** menu, and then click **Lessons** or click the **Close** button on the panel.

Lessons panel

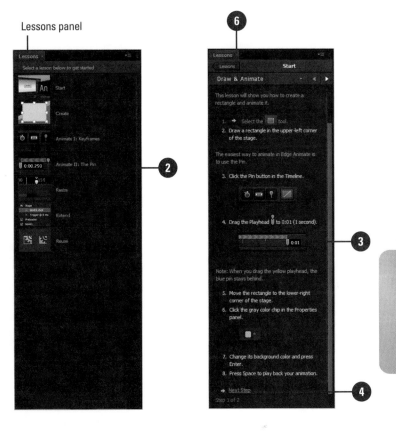

Using the Lessons Panel

After you start a lesson, you use the Lessons panel to walk you through the step by step instructions to complete the topic. If the Lessons panel takes up too much room in the Edge Animate window, you can dock it to another panel—the Properties panel is a good place to put it—or undock it as a separate window. As you work through a lesson, you can use the navigation at the top of the Lessons panel to get around. You can use the Lessons button to display all the lessons or the navigation buttons to switch between panels in the Lessons panel.

Use the Lessons Panel

1. Click the **Window** menu, and then click **Lessons** to select (show) the check mark.

   The Lessons panel opens, displaying a list of In-App Lessons.

2. Click a lesson tile to start it.

   Edge Animate creates a new Untitled project, and the Lessons panel displays the start of the selected lesson.

3. Follow the lesson steps in the Edge Animate window, and then click the **Next Step** link at the bottom of the panel.

4. To go back and forth between the Step panels, click the **Previous** or **Next** button or click the **Pane Name** list arrow, and then click a pane name.

5. To display the list of lessons, click the **Lessons** button.

6. To close the Lessons panel, click the **Window** menu, and then click **Lessons** or click the **Close** button on the panel.

Navigation options

Taking the Quick Start Lesson

With the Quick Start lesson, you can quickly create your first animation in Edge Animate. It's quick and easy, but it gives you simple way to see how an animation works. You'll create a rectangle on the Stage and then use the Pin button and the Playhead in the Timeline to make the shape move across the screen. After you create the animation, you'll play it back on the Stage and in the Timeline to see how it works.

Take the Quick Start Lesson

1. From the Welcome screen under Getting Started or the Lessons panel, click the **Quick Start** lesson tile to start it.

   The Welcome screen closes, Edge Animate creates a new Untitled project, and the Lessons panel displays the start of the lesson.

2. Select the **Rectangle Tool** on the Tools panel.

3. Draw a rectangle in the upper-left corner of the Stage.

4. Click the **Pin** button in the Timeline.

5. Drag the **Playhead** to 0:01 (1 second).

6. Move the rectangle to the lower-right corner of the Stage.

7. Click the gray color chip (diamond) in the Properties panel.

8. Click the **Background Color** box on the Tools panel, and then select a color from the palette.

9. Click the **Play** button or press Space to play back the animation.

10. At the bottom of the Lessons panel, click the **Next Step** link.

    The lesson is complete.

11. Click the **File** menu, click **Save**, navigate to a folder, create a folder, enter a name for the composition, and then click **Save**.

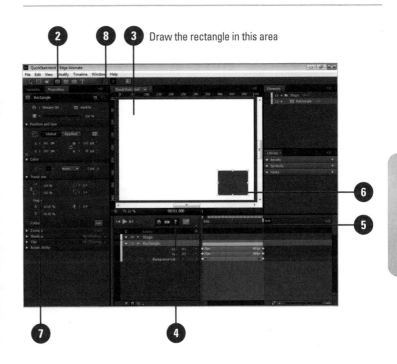

Draw the rectangle in this area

Taking the Create Lesson

With the Create lesson, you'll learn how to quickly draw and work with assets in Edge Animate. An asset is any artwork or element, such as shapes, images, buttons, and fonts, you have created or imported into your composition. In this lesson, you start from a sample file, and then use it to work create and work with elements. You'll create a rounded rectangle, add text, add graphics from the Library panel, and organize elements in the Elements panel.

Take the Create Lesson

1. From the Welcome screen under Getting Started or the Lessons panel, click the **Create** lesson tile to start it.

    The Welcome screen closes, Edge Animate creates a new Untitled project, and the Lessons panel displays the start of the lesson.

2. Click the **Click to open the sample** link.

    The content_creation.html file opens, displaying a blank Stage.

3. Click the **Next Step** link to create content (Step 2 of 5).

4. Select the **Rounded Rectangle Tool** on the Tools panel.

5. Draw a rounded rectangle in the center of the Stage.

6. In the Properties panel, click on the **link** between W and H, and then set the size of **W** to 220 and **H** to 130.

7. Click the **Next Step** link to add text (Step 3 of 5).

8. Click the **Text Tool** on the Tools panel.

9. Click in the center of the rectangle and type **Hello World**.

10. Click the **Close** button in the Text editor.

Continue Next Page

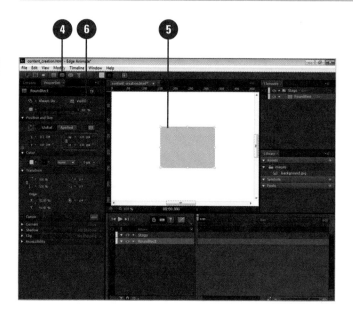

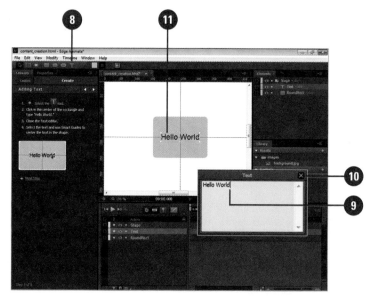

11. Select the text, and then drag to center the text in the shape.

As you drag towards the center, Smart Guides (horizontal and vertical) appear to indicate the center.

12. Click the **Next Step** link to import graphics (Step 4 of 5).

13. Drag the **background.jpg** icon from the Library pane onto the Stage and place it at 0,0 (the upper-left corner of the Stage). As you drag, the position appears on the Stage.

The background image covers all the other elements on the Stage.

14. In the Elements panel, drag the **background.jpg <div>** element below the **RoundRect <div>** element. As you drag a black bar appears indicating the new location.

The background image moves to the back of the Stage.

15. Click the **Next Step** link to organize elements (Step 5 of 5).

16. In the Elements panel, drag the **Text <div>** element onto the **RoundRect <div>** element. As you drag on top, the destination element changes to gray.

The Text element is now associated with the Rounded Rectangle element.

The lesson is complete.

17. Click the **File** menu, click **Save As**, navigate to a folder, create a folder, enter a name for the composition, and then click **Save**.

18. To open a finished version of the lesson, click the **Click to open the finished sample** link.

Drag image to (0,0)   Drag element here

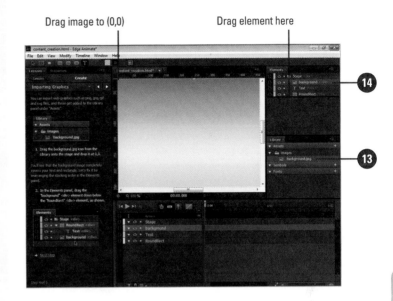

Completed lesson

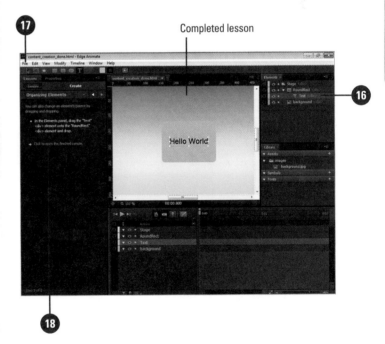

Taking the Animate with Keyframes Lesson

With the Animate I: Keyframes lesson, you can create an animation by setting keyframes at specific times on the Timeline and changing property values between them. The property changes from one keyframe to another over time on the Timeline creates animation. As an indicator, when a keyframe is hollow, it means that it has different value than the previous keyframe. Using keyframes is a little more time consuming, however, you have more control over the results. To help make it easier, you can use Auto Keyframe Mode, which automatically creates keyframes when a property is modified, and Auto Transition Mode, which automatically creates a transition as needed.

Take the Animate with Keyframes Lesson

1 From the Welcome screen under Getting Started or the Lessons panel, click the **Animate I: Keyframes** lesson tile to start it.

The Welcome screen closes, Edge Animate creates a new Untitled project, and the Lessons panel displays the start of the lesson.

2 Click the **Click to open the sample** link.

The keyframe_animation.html file opens, displaying a blank Stage.

3 Click the **Next Step** link to create keyframes (Step 2 of 7).

4 Move the **Playhead** to 0:01.

5 Select the **E** element on the Stage.

6 In the Properties panel, click the **Y keyframe** (diamond) to add a keyframe on the Timeline.

7 Move the **Playhead** to 0:00.

8 In the Properties panel, click the **Y keyframe** again.

9 Change the **Y** value to -90.

10 Click the **Play** button or press Space to play back the animation.

The E letter jumps to its position.

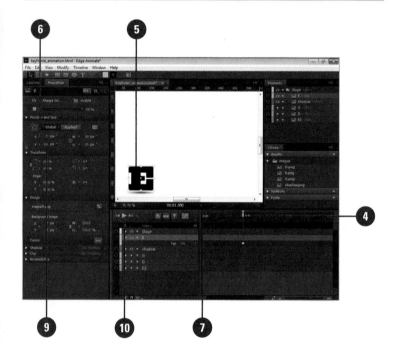

① Click the **Next Step** link to add a transition (Step 3 of 7).

When two keyframes have different values, you can add a transition between the two values.

② Right-click (Win) or Control-click (Mac) either of the keyframes, and then click **Create Transition**.

A transition appears connecting the keyframes in the Timeline.

③ Click the **Play** button or press Space to play back the animation.

The E letter smoothly transitions to its position.

④ Click the **Next Step** link to specify easing for the transition (Step 4 of 7).

⑤ Click the transition in the Timeline to select it.

⑥ Click the **Easing** button in the Timeline, select **Ease Out**, select **Bounce**, and then press Enter (Win) or Return (Mac).

⑦ Click the **Play** button or press Space to play back the animation.

The E letter falls and lands with a bounce to its position.

⑧ Click the **Next Step** link to animate the shadow element (Step 5 of 7).

⑨ Click the **Auto Keyframe Mode** button in the Timeline to select it.

This automatically creates keyframes when a property is modified.

⑳ Click the **Auto Transition Mode** button in the Timeline to select it.

This automatically adds a transition when a property is modified.

Continue Next Page

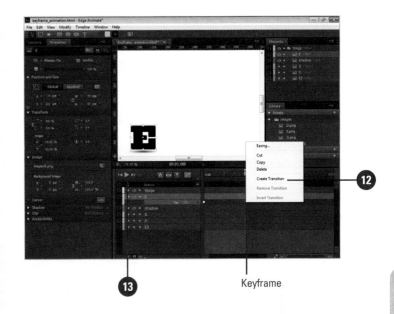

Keyframe

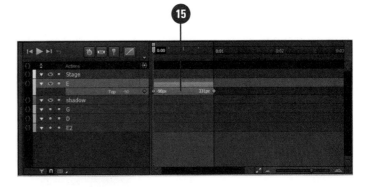

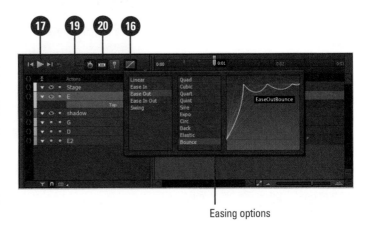

Easing options

Continue from Previous Page

21 Select the **shadow** element on the Stage.

22 Move the **Playhead** to 0:01.

23 In the Properties panel under Transform, click the **Scale X** and **Scale Y** keyframe.

24 Move the **Playhead** to 0:00.

25 In the Properties panel under Transform, set the **Scale X** value to 0. Since the X and Y are linked, both values change.

This creates an automatic animation and transition using the current one (Bounce).

26 Click the **Play** button or press Space to play back the animation.

The shadow animates along with the E element.

27 Click the **Next Step** link to reuse keyframes (Step 6 of 7).

28 Select the **E** element on the Stage.

29 Click the **Time Snapping** button in the Timeline to deselect it.

30 Move the **Playhead** to where the E first hits bottom, around 0.364.

31 In the Properties panel, click the **Rotation** keyframe.

32 Move the **Playhead** to where the E reaches the top of the bounce, around 0.544.

33 In the Properties panel, set the **Rotate** value to -10.

34 Move the **Playhead** to where the E hits bottom again, around 0.729.

35 Select the first rotation keyframe, making sure that only the one keyframe is selected.

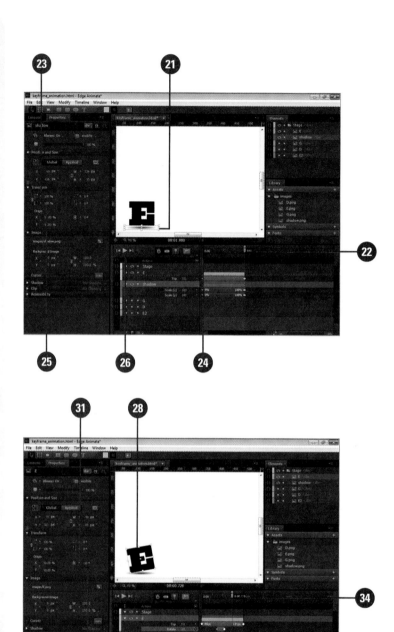

36 Press Ctrl+C (Win) or ⌘+C (Mac) to copy the keyframe, and then press Ctrl+V (Win) or ⌘+V (Mac) to paste it.

37 Click the **Next Step** link to reuse transitions (Step 7 of 7).

38 Click the **Time Snapping** button in the Timeline to select it.

39 In the Elements panel, click the **gray dot** under Visibility for G, D, and E2 to display them on the Stage.

40 In the Timeline, select the bar on top of the transitions for the E animation to select all transitions.

41 Press Ctrl+C (Win) or ⌘+C (Mac) to copy it.

42 Select the **G** element on the Stage, move the **Playhead** to 0:01, and then press press Ctrl+V (Win) or ⌘+V (Mac) to paste it.

43 Select the **D** element on the Stage, and then press press Ctrl+V (Win) or ⌘+V (Mac) to paste it.

44 Select the **E2** element on the Stage, and then press press Ctrl+V (Win) or ⌘+V (Mac) to paste it.

45 Click the **Play** button or press Space to play back the animation.

Each letter bounces in, one after the other.

The lesson is complete.

46 Click the **File** menu, click **Save As**, navigate to a folder, create a folder, enter a name for the composition, and then click **Save**.

47 To open a finished version of the lesson, click the **Click to open the finished sample** link.

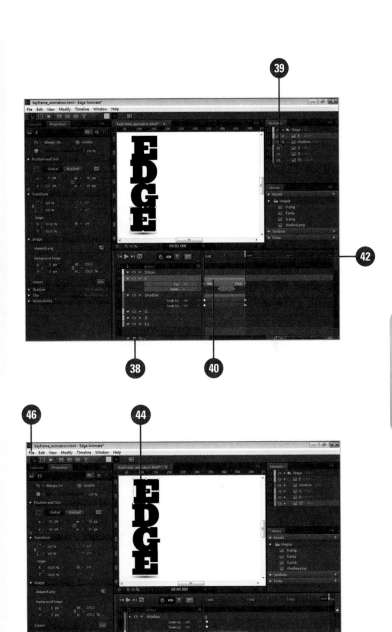

Pasted animation for G, D, and E2

Taking the Animate with the Pin Lesson

With the Animate II: The Pin lesson, you can quickly create an animation by using the Pin to help you create keyframes. You'll learn how to work with the Playhead and the Pin to create an animation region. You'll use the completed file from the Create lesson (*Hello World*) and then add an entrance and exit animation to it.

Take the Animate with the Pin Lesson

1. From the Welcome screen under Getting Started or the Lessons panel, click the **Animate II: The Pin** lesson tile to start it.

   The Welcome screen closes, Edge Animate creates a new Untitled project, and the Lessons panel displays the start of the lesson.

2. Click the **Click to open the sample** link.

   The animation_start.html file opens, displaying *Hello World*.

3. Click the **Next Step** link to add easing (Step 2 of 5).

4. Click the **Easing** button in the Timeline, select **Ease Out**, select **Quad**, and then press Enter (Win) or Return (Mac).

5. Click the **Next Step** link to add an entrance animation (Step 3 of 5).

6. Move the **Playhead** to 0:00.250 (0.25 seconds).

7. Double-click the **Playhead** to display a blue pin on top.

8. Drag the **Pin** (blue) to 0:00.750 (0.75 seconds). This displays a blue region for the animation.

9. In the Elements panel, select the **RoundRec <div>** element.

10. Shift-drag the shape element off the Stage to the left.

11. In the Properties pane, set the **Rotate** value to 720, and then click the Stage.

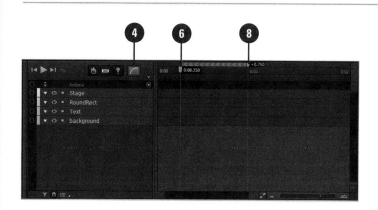

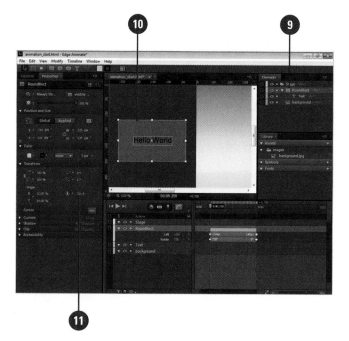

12 Click the **Next Step** link to add an entrance animation (Step 4 of 5).

13 Drag the left Rotate keyframe right to 0:00.500 (0.5 seconds).

14 Press Enter (Win) or Return (Mac) to activate the blue region.

15 Drag the blue region right to 0:00.750 (0.75 seconds).

16 Select the *Hello World* text element on the Stage.

17 In the Properties panel, set the **Scale X** or **Y** value to 0, and set the **Opacity** value to 0.

18 Click the **Next Step** link to add an exit animation (Step 5 of 5).

19 Click the **Easing** button in the Timeline, select **Ease In**, select **Quad**, and then press Enter (Win) or Return (Mac).

20 Drag the **Pin** (blue) to 0:01.75 (1.75 seconds).

21 Drag the **Playhead** (gold) to 0:02.250 (2.25 seconds).

22 Select the *Hello World* text element on the Stage.

23 In the Properties panel, set the **Opacity** value to 0.

24 Drag the Yellow region to 0:00.500 (0.5 seconds) so the pin is at 0:02.

25 Select the **RoundRect** element on the Stage, and then Shift-drag it off the Stage to the right.

26 Click the **Go to Start** button, and then click the **Play** button or press Space to play back the animation.

The lesson is complete.

27 Click the **File** menu, click **Save**, navigate to a folder, create a folder, enter a name for the composition, and then click **Save**.

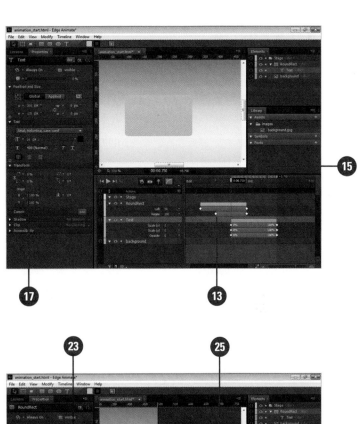

Taking the Resize Lesson

With the Resize lesson, you can create an animation that is responsive to the size of the screen. For example, when you resize your browser window, the composition resizes too. You can make the Stage and individual elements responsive to the screen size by changing their units from pixels (fixed) to percentage (adjustable). In addition, you can change the relative change position to any corner of an element. Instead of testing changes to your composition in your browser, you can quickly check them on the Stage in Edge Animate.

Take the Resize Lesson

1. From the Welcome screen under Getting Started or the Lessons panel, click the **Resize** lesson tile to start it.

   The Welcome screen closes, Edge Animate creates a new Untitled project, and the Lessons panel displays the start of the lesson.

2. Click the **Click to open the sample** link.

   The resize_start.html file opens, displaying an animation.

3. Click the **File** menu, and then click **Preview In Browser** or press Ctrl+Enter (Win) or ⌘+Return (Mac).

4. Resize the browser window to see how it responds.

   The animation doesn't respond to changes in the windows size.

5. Click the **Close** button to exit your browser.

6. Click the **Next Step** link to % resize the Stage (Step 2 of 8).

7. In the Elements panel, select the **Stage <div>** element.

8. In the Properties panel, point to the units for **W**, and then change from pixels (px) to percentage (%).

9. Click the **File** menu, and then click **Preview In Browser** or press Ctrl+Enter (Win) or ⌘+Return (Mac).

10 Resize the browser window to see how it responds, and then click the **Close** button to exit.

The Stage fills the width of the browser with its light blue background to the right of the animation.

11 Click the **Next Step** link to % resize on the Stage (Step 3 of 8).

12 Move the Stage adjustment handle on the top ruler back and forth to preview, and then return it to its original position at 800 px.

13 Click the **Next Step** link to % resize object's location on the Stage (Step 4 of 8).

14 In the Elements panel, select the **Text1 <div>** element.

15 Hold down Shift, and then select the **Text2 <div>** element.

16 In the Properties panel, point to the units for **X**, and then change from pixels (px) to percentage (%).

17 Move the Stage adjustment handle on the top ruler back and forth to preview, and then return it to its original position at 800 px.

The text boxes adjust as the Stage is resized.

18 Click the **Next Step** link to resize objects of the parents (Step 5 of 8).

19 In the Elements panel, select the **red_ribbon <div>** element.

20 In the Properties panel, point to the units for **W**, and then change from pixels (px) to percentage (%).

Continue Next Page

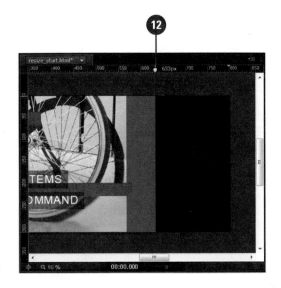

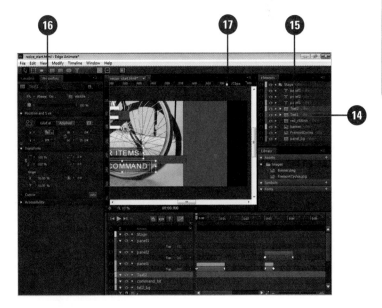

Continue from Previous Page

21 Move the Stage adjustment handle on the top ruler back and forth to preview, and then return it to its original position at 800 px.

22 Click the **Next Step** link to resize the relative position of objects their parents (Step 6 of 8).

By default, objects are positions relative to the upper-left corner of their parent. You can change the relative position to any corner using the Coordinate Space Picker in the Properties panel.

23 In the Elements panel, select the **panel_bg <div>** element.

24 In the Properties panel, select the **Bottom Right** square in the Coordinate Space Picker.

25 Point to the units for **W**, and then change from pixels (px) to percentage (%).

26 In the Elements panel, select the **panel1 <div>** element.

27 Hold down Shift, and then select the **panel3 <div>** element.

This selects panel1, panel2, and panel3.

28 In the Properties panel, select the **Bottom Right** square in the Coordinate Space Picker.

29 Point to the units for **W**, and then change from pixels (px) to percentage (%).

30 Move the Stage adjustment handle on the top ruler back and forth to preview, and then return it to its original position at 800 px.

This keeps the blue panel and the animated text relative to the right side of the Stage.

31 Click the **Next Step** link to apply layout presets to objects (Step 7 of 8).

32 In the Elements panel, select the **FremontCycles <div>** element.

33 In the Properties panel, click the **Layout Presets** button, click the **Center Background Image** preset, and then click **Apply**.

34 Move the Stage adjustment handle on the top ruler back and forth to preview, and then return it to its original position at 800 px.

This makes the element resize on both X and Y axis while keeping the image centered.

35 Click the **Next Step** link to set resize constraints of objects their parents (Step 8 of 8).

36 In the Elements panel, select the **Stage <div>** element.

37 In the Properties panel, set the **Min W** value to 650 px.

38 Click **Max W**, and then deselect **None**.

39 Set the **Max W** value to 1280 px.

40 Click the **File** menu, and then click **Preview In Browser** or press Ctrl+Enter (Win) or ⌘+Return (Mac).

41 Resize the browser window to see how it responds, and then click the **Close** button to exit.

This keeps the size range of the composition between 650 px and 1280 px.

The lesson is complete.

42 Click the **File** menu, click **Save**, navigate to a folder, create a folder, enter a name for the composition, and then click **Save**.

Taking the Extend Lesson

With the Extend lesson, you can code to your composition to extend the functionality of your animation. With the code you can add interactivity to animation. For example, you can add code to start an animation when you click a button. When you click the button, it triggers an event to take place. With Edge Animate, you don't have to be a programmer to add interactivity. It comes with Code snippets, segments of code, that you can quickly insert to perform a task.

Take the Extend Lesson

1. From the Welcome screen under Getting Started or the Lessons panel, click the **Extend** lesson tile to start it.

   The Welcome screen closes, Edge Animate creates a new Untitled project, and the Lessons panel displays the start of the lesson.

2. Click the **Click to open the sample** link.

   The interactivity_start.html file opens, displaying an animation.

3. Click the **File** menu, and then click **Preview In Browser** or press Ctrl+Enter (Win) or ⌘+Return (Mac).

   The animation plays in your browser.

4. Click the **Close** button to exit your browser.

5. Click the **Next Step** link to add a trigger (Step 2 of 7).

6. Move the **Playhead** to 0:00 in the Timeline.

7. Click the **Timeline** menu, and then click **Insert Trigger** or press Ctrl+T (Win) or ⌘+T (Mac).

8. In the Snippets list, click the **Stop** button.

9. Click the **Close** button to exit.

10. Click the **Next Step** link to add an action (Step 3 of 7).

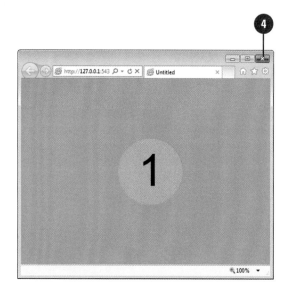

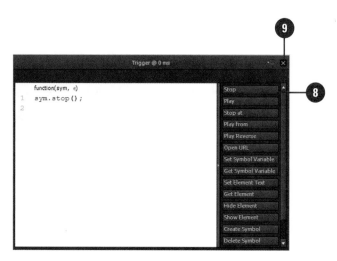

11. In the Elements panel, click the **Open Actions** button for the play <div> element.

12. Select **click** from the menu.

13. In the Snippets list, click the **Play** button.

14. Click the **Close** button to exit.

15. Click the **Next Step** link to add a label on the Timeline (Step 4 of 7).

16. Move the **Playhead** to 0:00.500 (0.5 seconds).

17. Click the **Timeline** menu, and then click **Insert Label** or press Ctrl+L (Win) or ⌘+L (Mac).

18. Type **Loop** for the label, and then press Enter (Win) or Return (Mac).

19. Click the **Next Step** link to add a timeline action (Step 5 of 7).

20. In the Timeline, click the **Timeline Actions** button to the left of the Actions row.

21. Select **complete** from the menu.

22. In the Snippets list, click the **Play** button.

23. Replace 1000 with **loop**.

24. Click the **Close** button to exit.

25. Click the **File** menu, and then click **Preview In Browser** or press Ctrl+Enter (Win) or ⌘+Return (Mac).

26. Click the **Play** button to start the animation in your browser, and then click the **Close** button to exit.

27. Click the **Next Step** link to open the Code window (Step 6 of 7).

Continue Next Page

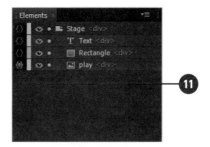

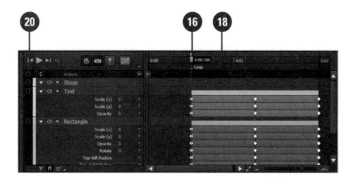

Continue from Previous Page

28 Click the **Window** menu, and then click **Code**.

The Code panel opens in a separate window.

29 Click the **Next Step** link to create a loop counter (Step 7 of 7).

30 In the tree, select **play.click**.

31 Click to place the insertion point below the code: sym.play();

32 Click the **Code Snippets** button to display the Snippets panel.

33 Click **Set Symbol Variable** from the Snippets list.

34 Modify the code to the following: sym.setVariable("count",1);

This stores a value that you'll use to count the number of loops.

35 In the tree, select **Timeline.complete**.

36 Click to place the insertion point before the code: sym.play(loop);

37 Click **Get Symbol Variable** from the Snippets list.

38 Modify the code to the following: var count =sym.getVariable ("count");

39 Click to place the insertion point on the line after the code: var count =sym.getVariable ("count");

40 Click **Set Symbol Variable** from the Snippets list.

41 Modify the code to the following: sym.setVariable ("count", count + 1);

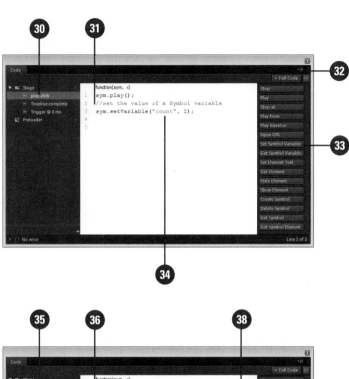

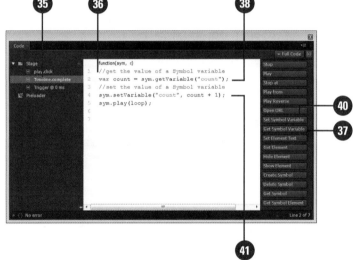

42 Move the **Playhead** to 0:00.500 in the Timeline.

43 Click the **Timeline** menu, and then click **Insert Trigger** or press Ctrl+T (Win) or ⌘+T (Mac).

44 In the Snippets list, click the **Get Symbol Variable** button.

45 Modify the code to the following: var count = sym.getVariable ("count");

This displays the count.

46 Click to place the insertion point on the line after the code: sym.getVariable ("count");

47 Click **Set Element Text** from the Snippets list.

Set Element Text uses jQuery code to modify the text of an element.

48 Modify the code to the following: sym.$("Text").html("" + count);

49 Click the **Close** button to exit.

50 Click the **File** menu, and then click **Preview In Browser** or press Ctrl+Enter (Win) or ⌘+Return (Mac).

51 Click the **Play** button to start the animation in your browser.

The animation continue to count until you close your browser.

52 Click the **Close** button to exit.

The lesson is complete.

53 Click the **File** menu, click **Save**, navigate to a folder, create a folder, enter a name for the composition, and then click **Save**.

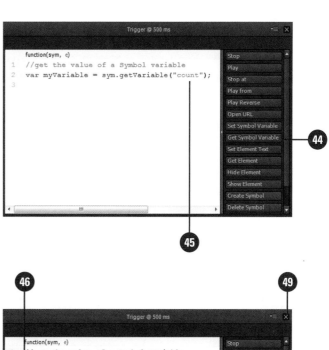

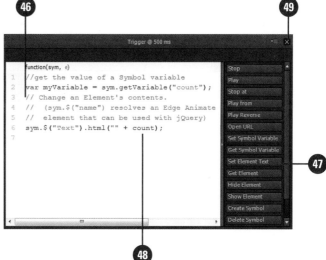

Taking the Reuse Lesson

With the Reuse lesson, you can create symbols of an element so that you can reuse it multiple times in you composition. When you import an asset as a symbol or convert an existing element to a symbol, it's known as a definition. When you use the symbol definition in your animation, it becomes an instance, which you can uniquely modify. You can add multiple instances of the same symbol and animate them differently. By using the same symbol definition, you're only using the asset once, which reduces time it takes to load it.

Take the Reuse Lesson

①　From the Welcome screen under Getting Started or the Lessons panel, click the **Reuse** lesson tile to start it.

The Welcome screen closes, Edge Animate creates a new Untitled project, and the Lessons panel displays the start of the lesson.

②　Click the **Click to open the sample** link.

The interactivity_start.html file opens, displaying an animation.

③　Click the **File** menu, and then click **Preview In Browser** or press Ctrl+Enter (Win) or ⌘+Return (Mac).

The animation plays in your browser.

④　Click the **Close** button to exit your browser.

⑤　Click the **Next Step** link to convert an object to a symbol (Step 2 of 5).

⑥　Move the **Playhead** to 0:01 (1 second).

⑦　In the Elements panel, select the **SpinRect <div>** element.

⑧　Click the **Modify** menu, and then click **Convert to Symbol**.

⑨　Type **Spin**, and then click **OK**.

This creates a symbol, which you can reuse. These are known as instances.

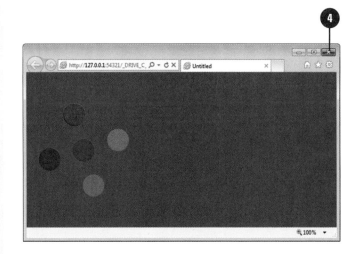

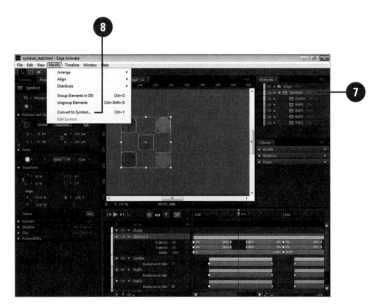

10 Click the **Next Step** link to create instances of a symbol (Step 3 of 5).

11 In the Library panel, drag the **Spin** icon from Symbols to the right of the first instance.

12 Alt-drag the second instance on the Stage to create another copy to the right of it.

13 Click the **Next Step** link to convert an object to a symbol (Step 4 of 5).

14 Double-click one of the instances on the Stage.

The symbol opens to in-place symbol editing mode.

15 In the Properties panel, deselect the **Autoplay** check box, so the symbol doesn't play automatically.

16 In the Timeline, click the **Timeline Actions** button to the left of the Actions row.

17 Select **complete** from the menu.

18 To loop, click the **Play from** button in the Snippets list.

19 Change the time of 1000 to 0. The time is in milliseconds.

20 Click the **Close** button to exit.

21 In the Elements panel, click the **Open Actions** button for the Center <div> element.

22 Select **click** from the menu.

23 Add the code from the illustration.

24 Click the **Close** button to exit.

25 Click **Back** button or **Stage** on the Edit bar to exit symbol editing mode.

Continue Next Page

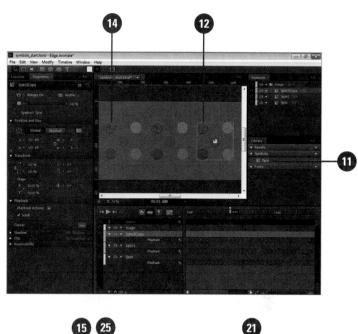

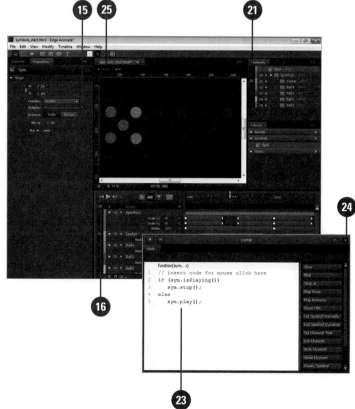

Continue from Previous Page

26 Move the **Playhead** to 0:00 (0 seconds).

27 In the Timeline, click the **Add** button (+) in the Playback row for the Spin element.

28 Click **Play** from the menu.

29 Move the Playhead to 0:00.750 (0.75 seconds).

30 Click the **Add** button (+) in the Playback row for the Spin2 element, and then click **Play**.

31 Move the Playhead to 0:01.500 (1.5 seconds).

32 Click the **Add** button (+) in the Playback row for the Spin3 element, and then click **Play**.

33 Click the **File** menu, and then click **Preview In Browser** or press Ctrl+Enter (Win) or ⌘+Return (Mac).

34 Click the **Close** button to exit.

The lesson is complete.

35 Click the **File** menu, click **Save**, navigate to a folder, create a folder, enter a name for the composition, and then click **Save**.

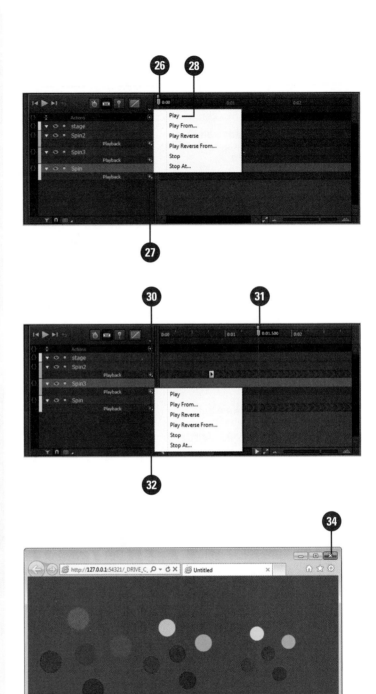

Working with Shapes and Graphics

Introduction

Edge Animate offers several tools for creating and editing shapes. When you draw in Edge Animate, you create vector art. **Vectors** are mathematical descriptions of lines and points that, when connected, form shapes. Vector-defined art is not limited by resolution like bitmaps are, so they can be scaled to any size without a loss in quality or increase in file size.

Included in Edge Animate are the main vector drawing tools—Rectangle, Rounded Rectangle and Ellipse—you need to create squares, rectangles, ovals, and circles. Vector shapes are fully editable after they are created so you can continue to adjust their properties. When you select a shape or graphic image on the Stage, the Properties panel displays the attributes of that element that are modifiable, such as name, position, size, border, shadow, opacity (transparency), and color.

In addition to the vector drawing tools that allow you to create animations in Edge Animate, you can also import graphic images in other formats. Edge Animate provides support for PNG, JPG/JPEG, and GIF files—bitmapped graphics—as well as SVG files—vector graphics. Edge Animate drawing tools create and edit vector shapes, not pixels, so preparation is necessary for bitmap graphics in a paint application outside of Edge Animate, such as Adobe Photoshop or Fireworks. As for vector graphics, you can prepare them in Adobe Illustrator. An important thing to remember is that any bitmap used in your project can add considerable size to your Edge Animate animation, so it's important to optimize and compress graphics as much as possible before importing them into Edge Animate.

What You'll Do

Understand Vector and Bitmap Graphics

Gather and Use Graphics

Examine Import Graphic Formats

Import Graphics

Draw Shapes

Use Smart Guides with Elements

Select Elements

Name Element IDs or Classes

Change Element Tags

Change Element Display

Change Element Overflow and Opacity

Change Element Position and Size

Change Element Adjustability

Change Shape Borders and Corners

Change Shape Background Color

Add Shadows to Elements

Change Cursors Over Elements

Modify Image Elements

Transform Element Origin

Rotate, Skew, and Scale Elements

Change Element Clipping

Add Accessibility to Elements

Understanding Vector and Bitmap Graphics

Vector graphics—including SVG—are comprised of anchor points connected to each other by lines and curves called **vectors**. These anchor points and vectors describe the contour and surface of the artwork with some included information about color, opacity, and line width. Because they are general descriptions of the coordinates of a shape, they are resolution-independent; that is they can be resized without any loss to the quality of the artwork. Resolution represents the amount of information contained within a linear inch represented by a grid. The vector artwork is rendered or drawn on the screen at view time. Edge Animate's native format is vector-based because it produces smaller file sizes.

Bitmap graphic

Bitmapped, also known as raster, graphics—PNG, GIF, and JPG/JPEG files to name a few—are made up of small, colored squares called **pixels** that form a grid. Each pixel is given a specific color and a grid of these pixels forms a mosaic, which is your image. Because of this, bitmaps are dependent on resolution (the number of pixels in the grid). The size and quality of a bitmap depends on the number of pixels per inch. Images saved for onscreen display have a resolution of 72 pixels per inch because that's what most monitors can handle, whereas images saved for print can require 300 pixels per inch or more. Resizing up or down forces pixels to be created or removed to accommodate the new grid size, which can result in a loss of image quality. Bitmaps must be rendered each time they change positions on the Stage, which can slow down playback; and bitmaps must store one bitmap image in each frame of an animation, which increases file size.

Vector graphic

Both vectors and bitmaps have their strengths and weaknesses. Vector shapes are simple and graphic in nature. They are a good choice for creating high-contrast, geometric art or art with limited color shifts. Vectors take up less space than bitmaps. However, if you need to implement artwork with a richer surface texture, color depth, and shading, like those qualities found in a photograph, a bitmap better suits this purpose. The strength of Edge Animate as a content developer is that you can combine the

Gathering and Using Graphics

As you gather and import your files, you also need to know about some federal regulations regarding the use of graphics and accessibility issues for the public with disabilities.

Understanding Copyright Rules

U.S. copyright rules are in place to protect the creator of an image—whether it's a photograph, illustration, drawing, painting or other type—from other people trying to profit from its use. Copyright rules cover ownership, the term the copyright applies, and how to register a copyright. A copyright is created when the image is first created, and the person who created the image or the person/organization that commissioned it in a contract places a copyright mark (©) on the image. For example, "Copyright © 2013 by Perspection, Inc." However, it is very difficult to provide ownership unless the copyright is registered through the U.S. Copyright Office. To copyright an image, go to the electronic Copyright Office (eCO) section of the web site at *www.copyright.gov.*

For images that are sold but not commissioned, the person who created the image retains the copyright. A copyright expires 70 years after the death of the person who created the image, unless the image was commissioned. Public domain images are pictures for which the owner's copyright has expired. Images created by the U.S. government are also considered public domain.

If you want to use an image, you need to get permission from the author or copyright holder. The U.S. Copyright Act provides for fines per use of a copyrighted image. If you take a photograph with people in it, you may need to get their permission to use it. If you are using their image for editorial purposes, you don't need it. However, if you are using it to advertise, you do need it.

Understanding Section 508 Rules

You also need to be aware of accessibility issues. Section 508 refers to Section 508 of the Rehabilitation Act of 1973, as amended by the Workforce Investment Act of 1998. The law requires Federal agencies to purchase electronic and information technology that is accessible to employees and to the public with disabilities.

In response to Section 508, the World Wide Web Consortium (W3C) created Web Content Accessibility Guidelines (WCAG) that provide recommendations for making Web content more accessible. Following these guidelines will make Web content accessible to a wider range of people with disabilities, including blindness and low vision, deafness and hearing lost, speech disabilities, and combinations of these. You can view the latest guidelines at *www.w3.org.*

Examining Import Graphic Formats

In addition to the vector drawing tools that allow you to create shapes in Edge Animate, you can also import graphics in the following web friendly formats: PNG, GIF, JPG/JPEG, and SVG. A web friendly format is designed to help the image display well on the screen, load as quickly as possible, and be compatible with all major browsers on any operating system. PNG, GIF, and JPG/JPEG are bitmap graphic formats, while SVG is a vector graphic format.

PNG (Portable Network Graphic) is a bitmapped file format designed for use in 8-bit (like a GIF) or 24-bit (like a JPG/JPEG) images. It can store text with the image making it possible for search engines to gather information and offer subject searching. In addition, the PNG format adjusts the gamma of an image so that it appears the same on a Macintosh or Windows monitor. PNG is also the native file format in Adobe Fireworks. You can import Adobe Fireworks PNG files into Edge Animate as bitmap images. When you import a PNG file as a bitmap image, the file, including any vector data, is flattened, or rasterized, and converted to a bitmap.

GIF (Graphics Interchange Format) is a bitmapped file format designed for use with images that contain distinct colors, such as clip art, line drawings, or small text. The GIF format supports 8-bit color, and creates a graphic with a maximum of 256 colors (the fewer the colors, the smaller the file size). GIF images support transparency, where one or more colors can be set to transparent (100% opacity) to let the color on the underlying web page to show through.

JPG/JPEG (Joint Photographic Experts Group) is a bitmapped file format designed for use with images that contain a log of continuous tones, like photographs. The JPG/JPEG supports 24-bit color and creates a graphic with up to 16 million colors. JPG/JPEG images do not support transparency, and fill transparent areas of the image with a user-defined matte color.

SVG (Scalable Vector Graphics) is an XML-based file format designed for describing two-dimensional vector graphics. SVG graphics and their associated behaviors are defined in XML (Extensible Markup Language) text files. SVG can contain three types of objects: vector graphics, bitmap graphics (including PNG and JPG/JPEG), and text. You can save vector graphics in the SVG format in applications like Adobe Illustrator.

Compressing Graphics

The web can be slow to navigate and your visitors typically don't have much patience. When you compress a graphic, you're essentially removing information from the image to reduce its file size and speed up the loading time. The unfortunate result of that reduction is loss of image quality. Web friendly graphics are not always the best quality; however, reducing the file size is a necessary evil to keep visitors from clicking off your site and moving to another.

Some formats, such as PNG and GIF, use **lossless compression**, which allows the exact original data to be reconstructed from the compressed data when you open it. Other formats, such as JPG/JPEG use **lossy compression**, which allows for some original data to be lost and not be reconstructed, possibly affecting image quality. Therefore, it's best when editing a JPG/JPEG image to save a copy without compression to retain the original data. The degree of compression can be adjusted, allowing for a tradeoff between size and image quality. You can specify this tradeoff in applications like Adobe Photoshop.

Importing Graphics

You can import graphics of several file types—including PNG, GIF, JPG/JPEG, and SVG—directly into Edge Animate to use in your animation. PNG, GIF, and JPG/JPEG are bitmap graphics while SVG is a vector graphic. Since vectors are based on mathematical descriptions of lines and points, file size and quality issues are typically not a problem. That's not the case with bitmaps. If file size is an issue, it's best to import your bitmaps in at the size you want. For example, if your bitmap image is going to be 160 pixels by 160 pixels, it's best to import it at this size and not resize it up or down in Edge Animate; you will end up with higher-quality images and smaller files. Unlike vectors, resizing or scaling bitmaps reduces the quality of the image. If you need to scale a bitmap in Edge Animate, it's a good idea to import the image at a slightly larger size, so when you scale it down, loss of quality is minimized. When you import a graphic, a copy is stored in a folder called images and linked to Edge Animate related-documents and added to the Library panel under Assets. In addition, the original filename of the graphic is used as the element ID, so you don't have to rename it.

Import a Graphic

1 Click the **File** menu, and then click **Import**.

TIMESAVER *Press Ctrl+I (Win) or ⌘+I (Mac).*

2 Click the **Show** popup (Mac) or **Files Of Types** list arrow (Win), and then click **All Formats** or select the format of the file you want to import:

◆ **PNG.** Bitmap file format.

◆ **GIF.** Bitmap file format.

◆ **JPG/JPEG.** Bitmap file format.

◆ **SVG.** Vector file format.

3 Navigate to the drive or folder where the file is located.

4 Select the file you want to import.

◆ To import multiple files, hold down the ⌘ (Mac) or Ctrl (Win) key and click additional files to select them.

5 Click **Open**.

Edge Animate uses the original filename as the element ID.

Adding Graphics

In addition to importing graphics into a composition by using the Import command, you can also add graphics directly from your computer file system, either Windows Explorer (Win) or Finder (Mac), or the Library panel in Edge Animate to the Stage by using drag and drop. You can add graphics with the file types—including PNG, GIF, JPG/JPEG, and SVG—directly into Edge Animate to use in your animation. PNG, GIF, and JPG/JPEG are bitmap graphics while SVG is a vector graphic. When you add a graphic directly from your file system to the Stage in Edge Animate, a copy is stored in a folder called images and linked to Edge Animate related-documents and added to the Library panel under Assets. In addition, the original filename of the graphic is used as the element ID, so you don't have to rename it.

Add a Graphic from the File System

1. Switch to your file system, either Windows Explorer (Win) or Finder (Mac).

2. Navigate to the location with the graphic file you want to add to your animation.

3. Adjust the folder window location so you can view the Stage in Edge Animate, and then select the graphic files you want to add.

4. Drag the graphic you want from the folder window in your file system to a location on the Stage.

   As you drag the asset on the Stage, X and Y location values in pixels appear along with the asset name as part of the cursor.

   When you release the mouse button, the asset is added to the composition, copied to the Images folder, and added to the Library panel under Assets.

See Also

See "Importing Graphics" on page 85 for information on file size and quality issues.

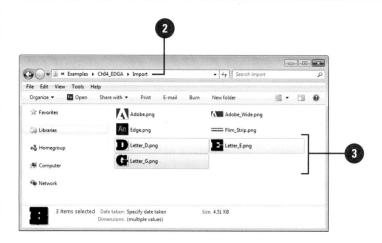

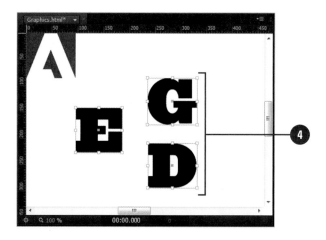

Add a Graphic Asset from the Library Panel

1. Open the Library panel.

    ◆ Click the **Window** menu, and then click **Library**.

2. Click the **Add** button (+) on the Assets heading bar on the Library panel.

3. Navigate to the drive or folder where the file is located.

4. Select the file you want to import.

5. Click **Open**.

    The graphic appears in the Library panel in the Images folder under Assets. The graphic is copied into the Images folder within your composition.

6. Click the **Expand** arrow (down) next to Assets to expand the group, and then click the **Expand** arrow next to the Images folder.

7. Drag the graphic you want to a location on the Stage.

    As you drag the asset on the Stage, X and Y location values in pixels appear along with the asset name as part of the cursor.

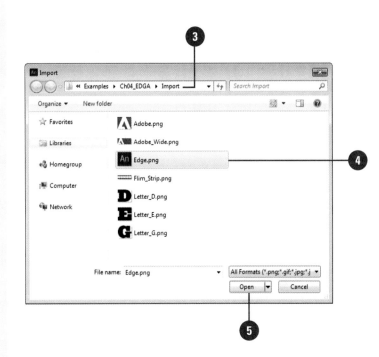

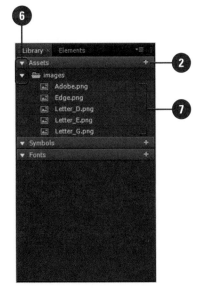

Did You Know?

You can locate the file path, name, and extension of a graphic. Select the graphic you want to view file information. In the Properties panel under Image, you can view the file path (based on the location of your Edge Animate composition folder as the root) along with the filename and extension.

Drawing Shapes

The Edge Animate Tools panel includes several tools—Rectangle, Rounded Rectangle, and Ellipse—for quickly creating vector shapes, such as rectangles, squares, circles, and ovals. They are easy to use; you just click and drag on the Stage to create the shapes. The Rectangle Tool creates rectangles with square corners, while the Rounded Rectangle Tool creates rectangles. The Ellipse Tool creates circles and ovals with rounded corners. The Rounded Rectangle Tool remembers corner radius settings for next use while the Rectangle Tool doesn't. With any drawing tool, you can create other shapes by changing the corner radius attribute in the Properties panel, all four at once or one at a time. Shapes are composed of attributes—such as location, size, opacity, fill color, border color, border thickness, border style, corner radius, rotate, skew, scale, and shadow—that you can change in the Properties panel, in the Tools panel (background and border color), or on the Stage (in some cases) to create other looks and shapes.

Draw Shapes

1. Select a drawing tool (**Rectangle**, **Rounded Rectangle**, or **Ellipse**) on the Tools panel.

   TIMESAVER *Press M to select the Rectangle Tool, press R to select the Rounded Rectangle Tool, or press O to select the Ellipse Tool.*

2. Click a color box for **Background Color** or **Border Color** on the Tools panel, and then select a color.

3. Position the pointer on the Stage where you want to start drawing the shape with the selected tool.

   The pointer becomes a crosshair that you can drag on the Stage.

4. To constrain the width and height to the same size (like a square or circle), press and hold the Shift key.

5. Drag to draw the shape.

   IMPORTANT *If Smart Guides are enabled on the Modify menu, alignment guides appear when working with multiple shapes.*

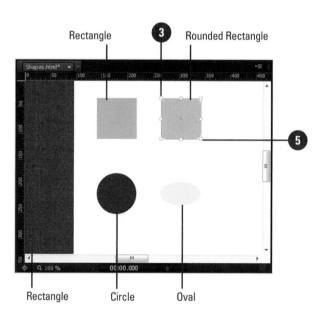

Rectangle   Rounded Rectangle

Rectangle   Circle   Oval

Create Other Shapes with Properties

1. Select a drawing tool (**Rectangle**, **Rounded Rectangle**, or **Ellipse**) on the Tools panel.

2. Click a color box for **Background Color** or **Border Color** on the Tools panel, and then select a color.

3. Position the pointer on the Stage, and then drag to draw a shape close to the size you want.

    IMPORTANT *If Smart Guides are enabled on the Modify menu, alignment guides appear when working with multiple shapes.*

4. Do any of the following:

    ◆ **Properties Panel.** Click the tab with the number of values, either **1**, **4**, or **8**, you want to change, enter a radius value in pixels or percentages, and then press Enter (Win) or Return (Mac), or drag (scrub) a radius value to the one you want.

    ◆ **Stage.** Select the **Transform Tool** on the Tools panel, position the pointer over a black diamond handle (cursor changes to a white arrow), and then drag to adjust the corner to the size you want.

    As you drag, all the corners adjust to the same size.

    ◆ **Adjust Individual Corners.** Hold down the Ctrl key, and then drag a black diamond handle.

    As you drag, only the individual corner adjusts.

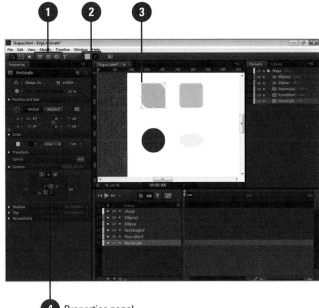

4 Properties panel

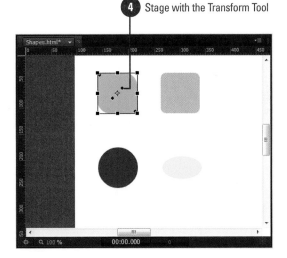

4 Stage with the Transform Tool

Using Smart Guides with Elements

Smart Guides are dimension markers and alignment guides that allow you to create shapes and text or resize elements to the same size as other elements on the Stage. They appear automatically as you draw a shape or text box, resize any element, or move elements and then disappear when not needed. They allow you to visually create same size elements or align one element to another with a minimum of effort. As you create or resize an element, dimension markers (double arrow guides) appear along the element's width or height when it matches another element on the Stage. As you drag, it also displays horizontal and vertical guides when the edge or middle of the element aligns with another element on the Stage or to the center of the Stage. Smart Guides are automatically turned on by default. You can turn Smart Guides on and off by selecting the Smart Guides command on the Modify menu.

Turn Smart Guides On and Off

1. To turn Smart Guides on (enabled), click the **View** menu, and then click **Smart Guides**.

   A check mark appears next to the menu command.

   TIMESAVER *Press Ctrl+U (Win) or ⌘+U (Mac) to toggle Smart Guides on and off.*

2. To turn Smart Guides off (disabled), click the **View** menu, and then click **Smart Guides**.

   The check mark next to the menu command disappears.

See Also

See "Aligning and Distributing Elements" on page 162 for more information on aligning elements using Smart Guides.

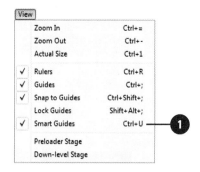

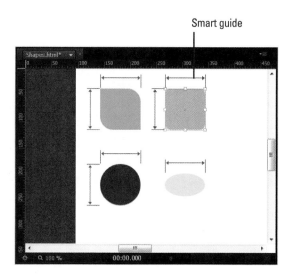

Smart guide

Draw Shapes with Smart Guides

1. Select a drawing tool (**Rectangle**, **Rounded Rectangle**, or **Ellipse**) on the Tools panel.

2. Position the pointer on the Stage where you want to start drawing the shape with the selected tool.

   The pointer becomes a crosshair that you can drag on the Stage.

3. Drag to draw the shape.

   As you draw the shape, Smart Guides appear to help you size it with the same width or height as other elements on the Stage, or align it to the edge or middle of other elements on the Stage or to the center of the Stage.

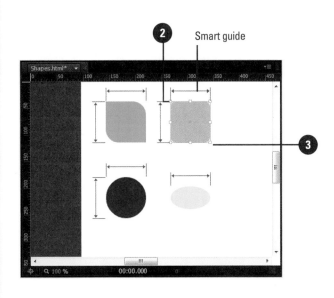

Smart guide

Resize Elements with Smart Guides

1. Click the **Selection Tool** on the Tools panel.

2. Select the element you want to resize.

3. Position the pointer over a resize handle (cursor changes to a black two-headed arrow), and then drag to the size you want.

   As you resize the element, Smart Guides appear to help you size it with the same width or height as other elements on the Stage, or align it to the edge or middle of other elements on the Stage or to the center of the Stage.

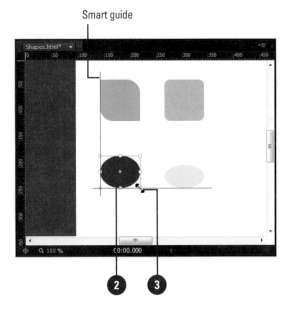

Smart guide

Selecting Elements

There are several ways to select elements in Edge Animate. You can select a shape using the Selection Tool on the Stage or in the Timeline or Elements panel. You can use the Selection Tool to select one or more shapes by clicking individual elements or dragging over them. When you select one or more elements, a bounding box appears around each one with resize handles (white squares) on the border edge, and a transform origin point (blue square) in the middle. The **resize handles** change the size of the bounding box. The **transform origin** changes the transformation position, the orientation where elements are transformed (rotate, skew, or scale). The Properties panel displays the attributes for what is selected—including location, size, opacity, fill color, border color, border thickness, border style, corner radius, rotate, skew, scale, and shadow. When you select multiple elements, the Properties panel displays a dash (-) where attributes are different; for operations, such as resizing, it takes effect on the group, rather than the last selected element.

Select Elements with the Selection Tool

1. Click the **Selection Tool** on the Tools panel.

   The pointer becomes an arrow.

   TIMESAVER *Press V to select the Selection Tool.*

2. Position the arrow on any part of the bounding box (cursor changes to a black four-headed arrow) for a shape on the Stage.

3. Click within the bounding box of the shape.

4. To select multiple shapes, press and hold the Shift key, and then click on any part of the shapes you want to select.

   ◆ You can also drag a selection rectangle over elements bounding box to select them.

   TIMESAVER *Press Ctrl+A (Win) or ⌘+A (Mac) to select all.*

   The elements are selected on the Stage and in the Timeline and Elements panel.

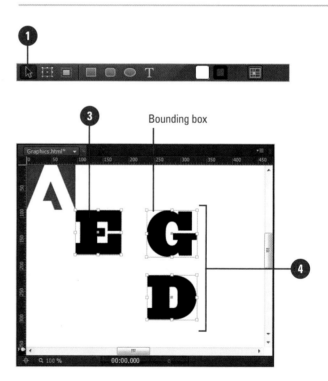

Bounding box

Select Elements with the Timeline and Elements Panel

1. Click the **Selection Tool** on the Tools panel.

   The pointer becomes an arrow.

   TIMESAVER *Press V to select the Selection Tool.*

2. In the Timeline or Elements panel, click the element name you want to select.

3. To select multiple elements, do any of the following:

   ◆ **Contiguous (Sequential Order).** Press and hold the Shift key, and then click the last element name you want in the list. All elements between the first and last one are selected.

   ◆ **Non-Contiguous (Not in Sequential Order).** Press and hold the Ctrl (Win) or ⌘ (Mac) key, and then click the element name you want in the list. The elements you select are added to the selection.

   The elements are selected on the Stage and in the Timeline and Elements panel.

   IMPORTANT *Depending on the Only Show Animated Elements button setting, not all elements appear in the Timeline.*

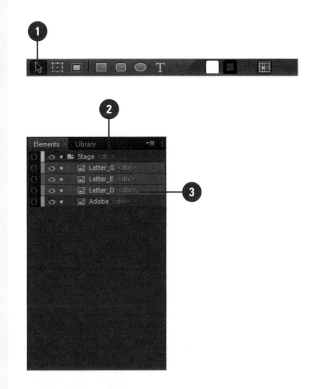

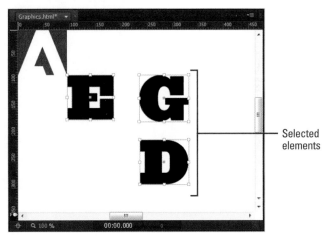

Selected elements

Naming Element IDs or Classes

When you create a shape, add text, or import a graphic, Edge Animate automatically provides a unique ID name based on the element type. For example, the first drawn rectangle is named Rectangle1. The second one is named Rectangle2, etc. For an imported graphic, the element is named with the original filename as the ID. For example, the imported file named Banner.jpg is named Banner. Naming an element allows you to reference it in an Action using JavaScript code to perform a function, such as changing element properties, based on an event, such as clicking an element. You can also use the ID to apply a CSS style. However, you can only apply it to the specific element, because element IDs must be unique. If you want to apply the same CSS style to multiple elements, you can specify a class. You can change an element ID or specify a class name in the Properties panel. If you try to rename an element ID with an existing name, Edge Animate disregards the change to avoid errors.

Name an Element ID or Class

1. Click the **Selection Tool** on the Tools panel.

2. Select the element you want to name.

3. In the Properties panel, select the current name in the ID box.

   ◆ **ID.** Select the current name in the ID box.

   ◆ **Class.** Click the **Class** button.

4. Type the ID or class name you want for the element, and then press Enter (Win) or Return (Mac).

   ◆ If you enter an existing element name, Edge Animate disregards the change, even though the text changes.

4 ID name   **3** Class button

See Also

See "Getting to Know HTML" on page 248 and "Getting to Know CSS" on page 252 for more information on using classes.

Changing Element Tags

When you create a shape, add text, or import a graphic, Edge Animate automatically assigns the element an HTML division (DIV) tag and creates CSS code based on the attributes set in the Properties panel. A **tag** is HTML's basic way to identify items. A DIV tag is an HTML element that defines generic containers or sections within the content of a web page. The DIV tag is a general way to define an element in HTML; it's not based on the content of the element. Defining an element with a content specific HTML tag provides information and predefined attributes to help your web browser more accurately display the web page content. Some content specific tags, such as the heading tags h1 thru h6, are used by search engines to index the structure and content of your web pages. When you view HTML code, tags always appear with **angle brackets** (< >), such as <div>. So, it's a good idea to define HTML elements using appropriate HTML tags whenever possible.

Change Element Tags

1. Click the **Selection Tool** on the Tools panel.

2. Select the element you want to change.

3. In the Properties panel, click the **Tag** list arrow, and then select an element specific tag; tags vary depending on the selected element.

   ◆ Graphic.

     ◆ **img.** Defines an image.

   ◆ Text.

     ◆ **address.** Defines contact information for the author of a document/article.

     ◆ **article.** Defines self-contained content, like a news article or blog post; new tag in HTML5.

     ◆ **blockquote.** Defines a section that is quoted from another source.

     ◆ **p.** Defines a paragraph.

     ◆ **h1 - h6.** Defines HTML headings.

     ◆ **pre.** Defines preformatted text.

     ◆ **code.** Defines a piece of computer code.

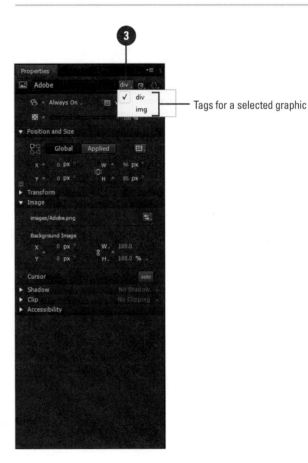

Tags for a selected graphic

Changing Element Display

With the Display property, you can control if or when an element appears on the Stage. This is useful for hiding and showing elements during an animation. The Display property can be set to Always On, On, and Off in the Properties panel. By default, all elements are set to Always On. When you set an element to On at a specified point in the animation, the element is set to Off (none) until the specified point and then set to On (visible). When an element is set to Off, it's displayed in a crosshatch pattern to make it easier to see when it's active.

Change Element Display

1. Click the **Selection Tool** on the Tools panel.

2. Select the element you want to change.

3. In the Properties panel, click the **Element Display** list arrow, and then select an option:

   ◆ **Always On.** Sets the element to always display (default).

   ◆ **On.** Sets the element to display at a specified point; the element is set to Off (none) until the specified point.

   ◆ **Off.** Sets the element to not display.

4. To reset the Display property to Always On after setting it to On or Off, click the **Element Display** list arrow, click **Always On**, and then click **Continue**.

Changing Element Overflow

If an element is located off the Stage, you can specify how you want to display the area off the Stage in the overflow area. There are four values for the overflow property: visible (default), hidden, scroll, and auto. The visible option displays content that extends beyond the Stage; the content off the Stage won't move any other content. The hidden option hides content—makes it inaccessible—that extends beyond the Stage. The scroll option hides the content off the Stage and displays horizontal and vertical scrollbars, even if you don't need them. The auto option is similar to the scroll option, however, it only displays the scrollbars you need. You can set the Overflow option in the Properties panel.

Change Element Overflow

1. Click the **Selection Tool** on the Tools panel.

2. Select the element you want to change.

3. In the Properties panel, click the **Overflow** list arrow, and then select an option:

   ◆ **Visible.** Shows the element in the overflow area (default).

   ◆ **Hidden.** Hides the element in the overflow area, which is not accessible.

   ◆ **Scroll.** Hides the element in the overflow area and always shows horizontal and vertical scroll bars.

   ◆ **Auto.** Hides the element in the overflow area and shows scroll bars as needed (horizontal, vertical, or both).

Changing Element Opacity

With the Opacity property, you can change the transparency level by percentage for an element. This is useful for creating a fade animation effect for an element. The Opacity property can take a value from 0% to 100%, where a lower value makes the element more transparent. When you change the opacity for a shape element, the background fill color and border color adjust to the same set percentage. For a text element, the color for individual characters adjust to the same set percentage. For an imported graphic, the entire image adjusts to the set percentage.

Change Element Opacity

1 Click the **Selection Tool** on the Tools panel.

2 Select the element you want to change.

3 In the Properties panel, drag the **Opacity** slider to the transparency percentage you want, or click the **Opacity** value, enter a value in a percentage, and then press Enter (Win) or Return (Mac).

0% is completely transparent, while 100% is a full display.

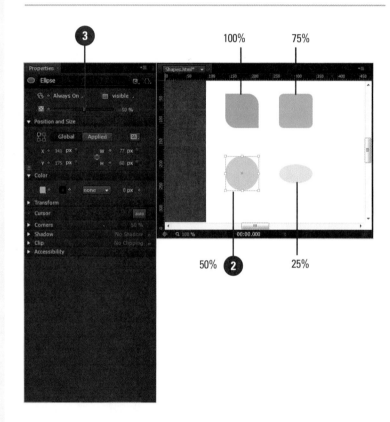

Changing Element Position

An element's position on the Stage is based on X and Y coordinates in pixels, denoted as px (pixel) or % (percentage). X is the horizontal axis position and Y is the vertical axis position. Together, the X and Y coordinates locate any specific pixel location on the Stage. The 0, 0 coordinates for the X and Y location is the upper-left corner of the Stage. A positive X value moves the X location to the right along the horizontal axis (even off the Stage) and a positive value moves the Y location down the vertical axis (even off the Stage). A negative X value moves the X location off the Stage to the left and a negative Y value moves the Y location off the Stage above it. The element location on the Stage is determined by the upper-left corner of an element. You can drag an element to another location on the Stage or set specific Position X and Y coordinates in the Properties panel.

Change Element Position

1. Click the **Selection Tool** on the Tools panel.

2. Select the element you want to change.

3. In the Properties panel under Position and Size, do any of the following:

   ◆ **Stage.** Position the pointer over the element (cursor changes to a black four-headed arrow), and then drag to the location you want.

   ◆ **Properties Panel.** Click the **Position X** or **Y** value, enter a value, and then press Enter (Win) or Return (Mac), or drag (scrub) the **Position X** or **Y** value to the one you want.

X and Y position

Stage

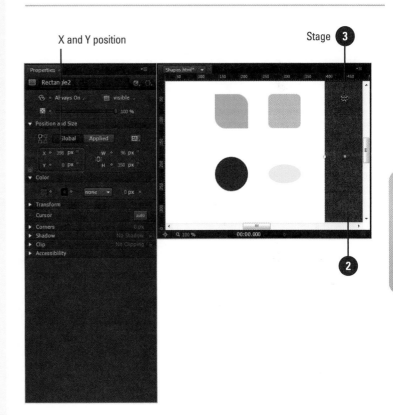

Changing Element Size

When you select an element in Edge Animate, a bounding box appears around each one with resize handles (white squares) on the border edge and a transform origin point (blue square) in the middle. You can change the size of an element on the Stage by dragging a resize handle or set specific W (width) and H (height) settings in the Properties panel. When you drag a middle resize handle, the size change is constrained to the left and right, or top and bottom. When you drag a corner resize handle, the size change is not constrained, unless you hold down the Shift key. As you drag to resize an element on the Stage with Smart Guides turned on (Modify menu), guides automatically appear to help you size and align the element with other elements already on the Stage. The size of an element is denoted in pixels or percentage, as shown in the Properties panel.

Change Element Size

1 Click the **Selection Tool** on the Tools panel.

2 Select the element you want to change.

3 Do any of the following:

◆ **Stage.** Position the pointer over a resize handle (cursor changes to a black two-headed arrow), and then drag to the size you want.

 ◆ **Variable.** Drag a corner resize handle.

 ◆ **Constrain Left and Right or Top and Bottom.** Drag a middle resize handle.

 ◆ **Constrain Width and Height Proportionally.** Hold down the Shift key, and then drag a corner resize handle.

◆ **Properties Panel.** Click the **Size W** or **H** value, enter a value in pixels or percentages, and then press Enter (Win) or Return (Mac), or drag (scrub) the **Size W** or **H** value to the one you want.

 ◆ **Constrain/Unconstrain.** Click the **Link/Unlink** icon to toggle on and off.

W and H position

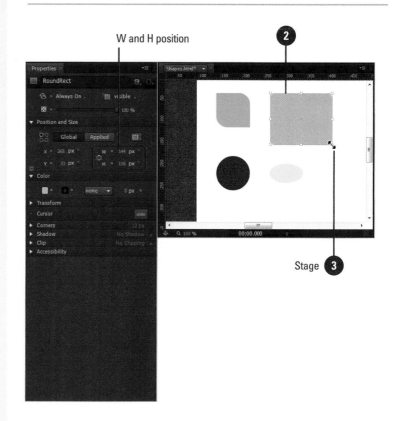

Stage

Changing Element Adjustability

In Edge Animate, you can create an animation that is responsive to the size of the screen. For example, when you resize your browser window, the composition resizes too. You can make the Stage and individual elements responsive by changing their units from pixels (fixed) to percentage (adjustable). In addition, you can change the relative change position to any corner of an element, either relative to the Stage (Global) or to its parent (Applied). By default, elements are positions relative to the upper-left corner of their parent. You can change the relative position to any corner in the Properties panel. Instead of changing individual values for an element, you can apply a layout preset. The presets include Scale Position (X and Y), Scale Size (W and H), Scale Background Image, Center Background Image, Clip Background Image, and Static Background Image. Instead of testing changes to your composition in your browser, you can quickly check them on the Stage by using a ruler adjustment handle (pin) in Edge Animate.

Change Element Adjustability

1. Click the **Selection Tool** on the Tools panel.

2. Select the element you want to change.

3. To use preset options, click the **Layout Preset** button, select a preset and view its settings, and then click **Apply**.

4. To set individual adjustable options, point to units for the position (**X** and **Y**) and size (**W** and **H**), and then drag the slider from px (pixels) to % (percentage).

5. To set the relative position (upper-left, upper-right, lower-left or lower-right) of the element on the screen, click the corner square in the Coordinate Space Picker, and then click **Global** or **Applied**.

   Global calculates the position relative to the Stage, while Applied calculates it relative to its parent.

6. To preview the results on the Stage, move the Stage adjustment handle (pin) on a ruler back and forth, and then return it to its original position marker.

Apply Layout Preset

Adjustment handle (pin)

Changing Shape Corners

After you create or select a shape element, either a rectangle or rounded rectangle, you can adjust the corners to create different degrees of roundedness, which is known as the **corner radius**. You can change the corner radius of a shape element on the Stage by setting specific corner values in the Properties panel. You can make changes in pixels or percentages by the number of settings—either 1, 4, or 8—in the Properties panel. When you select the number 1 tab, the same corner radius is set for all four corners. When you select the number 4 tab, you can set individual values for each of the four corners. When you select the number 8 tab, you can set individual values for each side of the four corners.

Change Shape Corners in the Properties Panel

1. Click the **Selection Tool** on the Tools panel.

2. Select the shape element you want to change.

3. In the Properties panel under Corners, click the tab with the number of values, either **1**, **4**, or **8**, you want to change.

   For tab 1, one value appears (one for all corners). For tab 4, four values appear (one for each corner). For tab 8, eight values appear (two for each corner).

4. Click a **Border Radius** value, enter a value in pixels or percentages, and then press Enter (Win) or Return (Mac), or drag (scrub) a **Border Radius** value to the one you want.

5. To reset a rounded corner to a square corner, click a **Border Radius** button (corner changes from rounded to square).

   To reset a square corner to a rounded corner with a zero value, click a **Corner Radius** (corner changes from square to rounded).

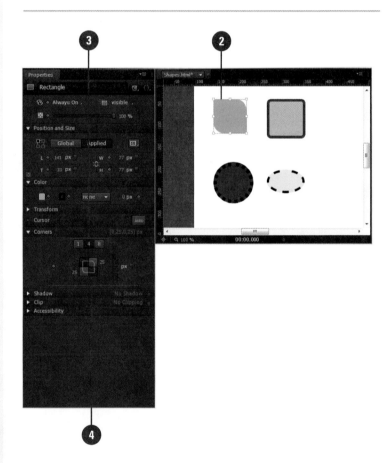

Change Element Corners with the Transform Tool

① Click the **Transform Tool** on the Tools panel.

② Select the shape or image element you want to change.

③ If you want to change the origin point, drag the transform origin (white circle and crosshairs) in the element on the Stage, or specify **Transform Origin X** or **Y** values by percentage in the Properties panel.

④ Position the pointer over a black diamond handle (cursor changes to a white arrow), and then drag to adjust the corner to the size you want.

As you drag, all the corners adjust to the same size.

◆ **Adjust Individual Corners.** Hold down the Ctrl key, and then drag a black diamond handle.

As you drag, only the individual corner adjusts.

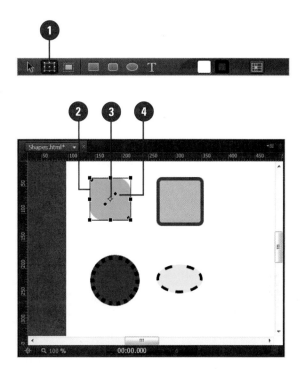

Origin point for an image

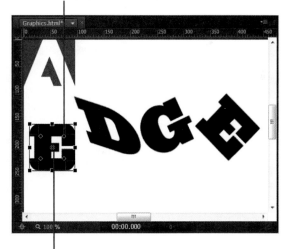

Black diamond handle for an image

Changing Shape Borders

When you draw a shape element, Edge Animate applies a background fill color, border color, border thickness in pixels, and border style. By default, when you draw a shape in a new composition, the background color is set to grey (RGB 192 each or #c0c0c0 in Hex), the border color is set to black, the border thickness is set to zero, and the border style is set to none. With the thickness set to zero and the style set to none, a border doesn't appear in the shape. However, you can change the border properties at any time. You can specify a border color, border thickness in pixels, and border style—none, solid, or dashed—in the Properties panel. For added convenience, you can also specify a border color in the Tools panel.

Change Shape Border Size and Style

1. Click the **Selection Tool** on the Tools panel.

2. Select the shape element you want to change.

3. In the Properties panel under Color, click the **Border Thickness** value, enter a value in pixels, and then press Enter (Win) or Return (Mac), or drag (scrub) the **Border Thickness** value to the one you want.

   ◆ **Zero.** Shows no border. The Border Thickness value is 0.

4. Click the **Border Style** list arrow, and then select an option:

   ◆ **None.** Shows no border. The Border Thickness value is ignored.

   ◆ **Solid.** Shows a solid border with the specified border thickness and color.

   ◆ **Dashed.** Shows a dashed border with the specified border thickness and color.

   ◆ **Dotted.** Shows a dotted border with the specified border thickness and color.

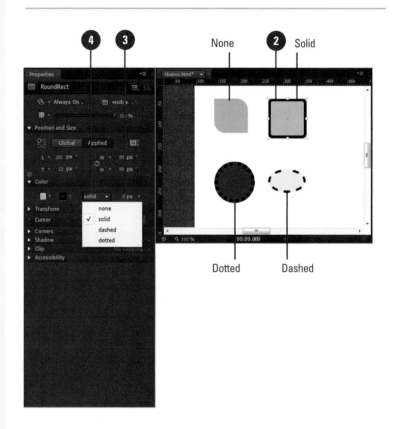

Change Shape Border Color

1 Click the **Selection Tool** on the Tools panel.

2 Select the shape element you want to change.

3 In the Tools panel or Properties panel under Color, click the **Border** color box, and then select a color:

◆ White Color. Click the **White** box.

◆ Black Color. Click the **Black** box.

◆ Transparent. Click the **Transparent** box.

◆ Any Color. Drag the color spectrum slider, and then click and drag the white color circle.

◆ Specific RGB Color. Enter color values for **R**ed, **G**reen, and **B**lue.

◆ Specific Transparency. Enter a value (%) for **A**lpha. (0% is fully transparent, while 100% is completely solid).

◆ Specific Hex Color. Enter a six digit color value starting with a hash (#) in the Hex box, and then press Enter (Win) or Return (Mac).

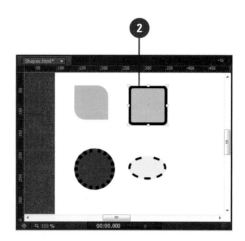

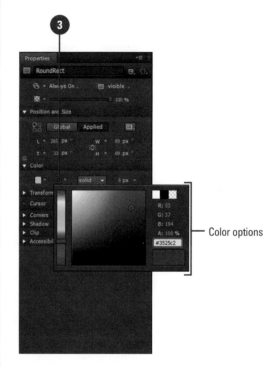

Color options

Changing Shape Background Color

When you draw a shape element, Edge Animate applies a background fill color along with other border properties. You can select a background color in the Properties or Tools panel by clicking the Background Color box and using the color palette. You can choose virtually any color you want from the color spectrum, as well as no color at all (transparent). In the color palette, you can drag to select a color or enter a specific color RGB using individual Red, Green, and Blue values or a single Hex value. The Hex value, also known as a hex triplet, is a six digit, three-byte hexadecimal number with a hash (#) in front used in HTML, CSS, SVG, and other programs to represent colors in RGB.

Change Shape Background Color

1. Click the **Selection Tool** on the Tools panel.

2. Select the shape element you want to change.

3. In the Tools panel or Properties panel under Color, click the **Background** color box, and then select a color:

   ◆ **White Color.** Click the **White** box.

   ◆ **Black Color.** Click the **Black** box.

   ◆ **Transparent.** Click the **Transparent** box.

   ◆ **Any Color.** Drag the color spectrum slider, and then click and drag the white color circle.

   ◆ **Specific RGB Color.** Enter color values for **R**ed, **G**reen, and **B**lue.

   ◆ **Specific Transparency.** Enter a value (%) for **A**lpha. (0% is fully transparent, while 100% is completely solid).

   ◆ **Specific Hex Color.** Enter a six digit color value starting with a hash (#) in the Hex box, and then press Enter (Win) or Return (Mac).

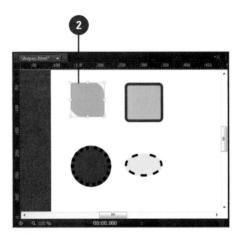

Adding Shadows to Elements

You can format any element in Edge Animate with a shadow. You can add drop shadow on the outside edge or an inset shadow on the edge of the element. After you add a shadow, you can specify the shadow X and Y position, color, blur, or feathering, and spread, or depth, of the shadow. This give you control of the overall design of the shadow. You can enable or disable the use of a shadow by dragging the slider on the Shadow header bar in the Properties panel. When you turn it on (enable) and off (disable), the shadow settings for the element remain in tact, so you don't have to reset them.

Add Shadows to Elements in the Properties Panel

1. Click the **Selection Tool** on the Tools panel.

2. Select the element you want to change.

3. In the Properties panel under Shadow, drag the **slider** on the header bar to turn it on.

4. Click the **Drop Shadow** or **Inset Shadow** button.

5. Click the **X** or **Y** value, enter a value, and then press Enter (Win) or Return (Mac), or drag (scrub) the **X** or **Y** value to the one you want.

6. Click the **Color** box, and then select a color for the shadow.

7. Click the **Blur** or **Spread** value, enter a value, and then press Enter (Win) or Return (Mac), or drag (scrub) the **Blur** or **Spread** value to the one you want.

   - **Blur.** The Blur value specifies the amount of shadow edge feathering.

   - **Spread.** The Spread value specifies the depth of the shadow.

8. To turn the Shadow property off, drag the **slider** on the header bar to turn it off.

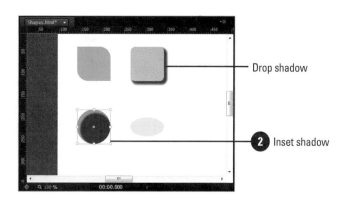

Drop shadow

Inset shadow

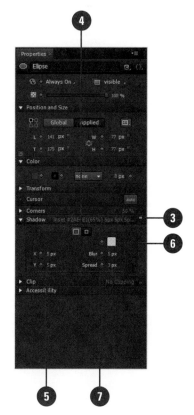

Changing Cursors Over Elements

When you move your cursor over an element on a web page, it can change to provide an indicator of its use. For example, when you hover over a link, it changes to a pointing finger. The cursor is set to auto by default, which lets the browser set the cursor. This is typically the best option, unless you have a unique design with specific requirements. If you want to change it, you can select a cursor for any element in the Properties panel. With the Cursor button, you can select from 24 different cursors, including resizing, drawing, and busy.

Change the Cursor Over Elements in the Properties Panel

① Click the **Selection Tool** on the Tools panel.

② Select the element you want to change.

③ In the Properties panel under Cursor, click the **Cursor** button.

④ Click a cursor icon on the pane.

   ◆ **Auto.** The browser sets the cursor (default).

   ◆ **Cursor.** When you point to an element in your browser, the selected cursor displays.

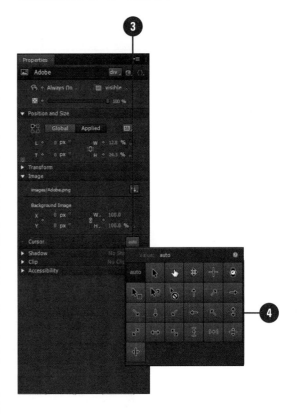

Modifying Image Elements

The Image settings in the Properties panel allow you to adjust a graphic's position in its bounding box using X and Y coordinates in pixels or percentages. X is the horizontal axis position and Y is the vertical axis position. The 0, 0 coordinates for the X and Y location is the normal default position in the bounding box. The graphic is positioned relative to its normal position. You can use positive or negative values to adjust the position. For example, X = 20 and Y = -20, moves the graphic position 20 pixels to the right (X) and -20 pixels up (Y). X moves the position left and right, while Y moves the position up and down. In addition to the image position in the bounding box, you can also change the width and height size of the image itself. You can specify the X and Y position and W and H values for an image in the Properties panel.

Change Image Elements in the Properties Panel

1. Click the **Selection Tool** on the Tools panel.

2. Select the graphic image element you want to change.

3. In the Properties panel under Image, click the **Background X** or **Y** value, enter a value in pixels or percentages, and then press Enter (Win) or Return (Mac), or drag (scrub) the **Background X** or **Y** value to the one you want.

4. To change the size of the image, click the **Background W** or **H** value, enter a value in pixels or percentages, and then press Enter (Win) or Return (Mac), or drag (scrub) the **Background W** or **H** value to the one you want.

   ◆ **Constrain/Unconstrain.** Click the **Link/Unlink** icon to toggle on and off.

5. To change the image element source, click the **Change Image Source** button, and then select the image asset you want from the Library Assets panel.

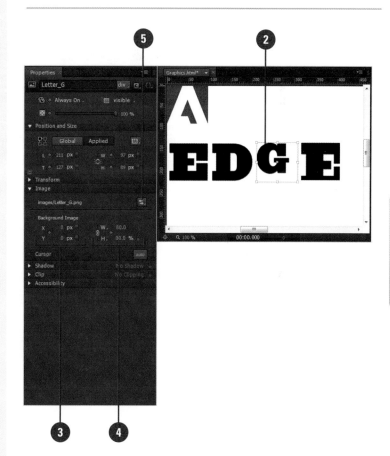

Transforming Element Origin

The transform origin point determines the center orientation position when you transform an element by changing the Rotate, Skew, or Scale properties. When you select one or more elements—either a shape, text, or imported graphic—a transform origin appears in the center of the element (X = 50% and Y = 50%) by default. You can change the transform origin of an element on the Stage by dragging the transform origin point with the Transform Tool or set specific Transform Origin X and Y settings in percentages in the Properties panel. You can set the transform origin inside or outside the boundary box of an element.

Change the Origin Point in the Properties Panel

① Click the **Selection Tool** on the Tools panel.

② Select the element you want to change.

③ In the Properties panel, click the **Transform Origin X** or **Y** value, enter a value in percentages, and then press Enter (Win) or Return (Mac), or drag (scrub) the **Transform Origin X** or **Y** value to the one you want.

◆ **50% - 50%.** Sets the origin point to the center.

◆ **25% - 25%.** Moves the origin point to the left for X and up for Y of center.

◆ **75% - 75%.** Moves the origin point to the right for X and down for Y of center.

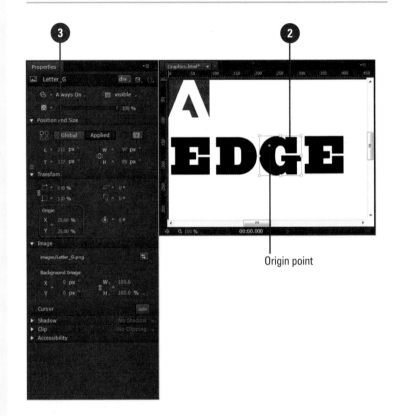

Origin point

Change the Origin Point with the Transform Tool

1. Click the **Transform Tool** on the Tools panel.

2. Select the element you want to change.

3. Position the pointer over the origin point (cursor changes to a white pointer), and then drag to another position.

    ◆ **Constrain Vertical or Horizontal.** Hold down the Shift key, and then drag the origin point.

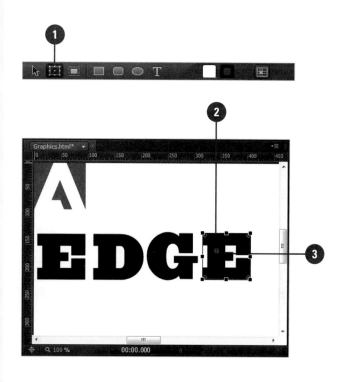

Rotating Elements

The Rotate value in the Properties panel or the Transform Tool on the Tools panel allows you to rotate an element to the right (positive) or left (negative). This is useful for creating a rotating animation effect for an element, such as a rolling ball or spinning star. You can specify a Rotate value in degrees for an element in the Properties panel or drag outside a selected corner (cursor changes to an arrow with a circle) on the Stage with the Transform Tool. An element rotates around the transform origin point, which is set to the center of an element (X = 50% and Y = 50%) by default, so if you want to adjust it, you should do it beforehand. If you want to rotate an element multiple times, you can enter an expression in the Rotate property value. For example, you can enter 360*5 to rotate an element five times (or 1800 degrees) to the right.

Rotate Elements in the Properties Panel

1. Click the **Selection Tool** on the Tools panel.

2. Select the element you want to change.

3. If you want to adjust the rotation point, specify **Transform Origin X** or **Y** values by percentage in the Properties panel under Transform.

4. In the Properties panel under Transform, drag the **Rotate (z)** slider to the degree you want, or enter or scrub (drag) a **Rotate (z)** value in degrees, either positive (right) or negative (left).

   ◆ **Expression.** In the Rotate (z) box, you can enter an expression to rotate multiple times. For example, enter 360*5 to rotate an element five times.

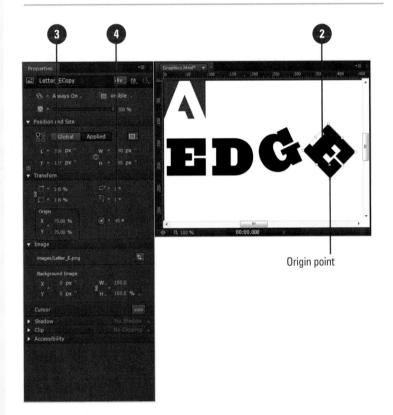

Origin point

Rotate Elements with the Transform Tool

1 Click the **Transform Tool** on the Tools panel.

2 Select the element you want to change.

3 If you want to adjust the rotation point, drag the Transform origin point in the element on the Stage.

4 Position the pointer outside a corner point (cursor changes to an arrow with a circle), and then drag to rotate the element.

The element rotates around the origin point.

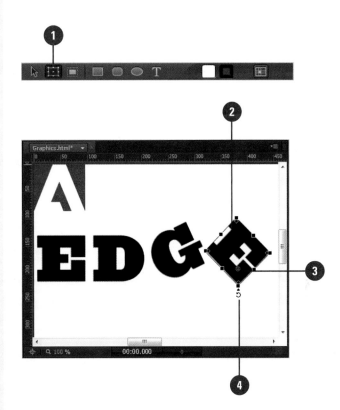

Skewing Elements

The Skew value in the Properties panel or the Transform Tool on the Tools panel allows you to adjust the horizontal or vertical plane of an element around the X and Y-axis. This is useful for creating a stretching animation effect for an element, such as creating a diamond from a square. For example, if you set X = 30 and Y = 20, the element skews 30 degrees around the X-axis and 20 degrees around the Y-axis. You can specify the Skew X and Y values in degrees for an element in the Properties panel or drag outside a selected horizontal or vertical edge (not a corner) (cursor changes to a double arrow in opposite directions) on the Stage with the Transform Tool. An element turns (skews) along the transform origin point, which is set to the center of an element (X = 50% and Y = 50%) by default, so if you want to adjust it, you should do it beforehand.

Skew Elements in the Properties Panel

1. Click the **Selection Tool** on the Tools panel.

2. Select the element you want to change.

3. If you want to adjust the skew point, specify **Transform Origin X** or **Y** values by percentage in the Properties panel under Transform.

4. In the Properties panel under Transform, click the **Skew X** or **Y** value, enter a value in degrees, and then press Enter (Win) or Return (Mac), or drag (scrub) the **Skew X** or **Y** value to the one you want.

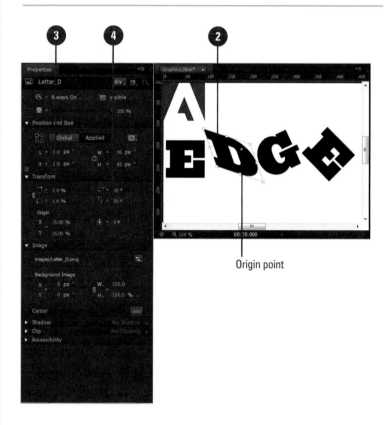

Origin point

Skew Elements with the Transform Tool

① Click the **Transform Tool** on the Tools panel.

② Select the element you want to change.

③ If you want to adjust the skew point, drag the Transform origin point in the element on the Stage.

④ Position the pointer outside a corner point (cursor changes to a double arrow in opposite directions), and then drag to rotate the element.

The element skew along the vertical or horizontal edge from the origin point.

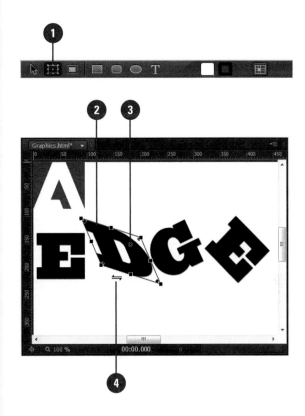

Scaling Elements

The Scale value in the Properties panel or the Transform Tool on the Tools panel allows you to increase or decrease the scale size of an element by a specified percentage. This is useful for creating a growing or shrinking animation effect for an element. You can specify the Scale X and Y values for an element on the Stage by dragging a black handle (cursor changes to a double arrow) with the Transform tool or set specific Scale X and Y settings in percentages in the Properties panel. A percentage greater than 100% increases the scale of an element, while a percentage less than 100% decreases the scale of an element. An element scales around the transform origin, which is set to the center of an element (X = 50% and Y = 50%) by default, so if you want to adjust the Transform Origin X and Y values on the Stage or in the Properties panel, you should do it beforehand.

Scale Elements in the Properties Panel

1. Click the **Selection Tool** on the Tools panel.

2. Select the element you want to change.

3. If you want to adjust the scale point, specify **Transform Origin X** or **Y** values in percentages in the Properties panel under Transform.

4. In the Properties panel under Transform, click the **Scale X** or **Y** value, enter a value in percentages, and then press Enter (Win) or Return (Mac), or drag (scrub) the **Scale X** or **Y** value to the one you want.

   ◆ **Proportional/Not Proportional.** Click the **Link/Unlink** icon (left of the Scale X and Y values) to toggle on and off.

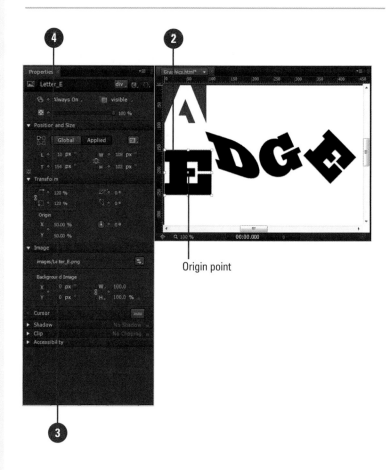

Origin point

Scale Elements with the Transform Tool

1 Click the **Transform** tool on the Tools panel.

2 Select the element you want to change.

3 If you want to adjust the scale point, specify **Transform Origin X** or **Y** values by percentage in the Properties panel under Transform.

4 Position the pointer over a black square handle (cursor changes to a double arrow), and then drag to the scale size you want.

◆ **Proportional.** Hold down the Shift key, and then drag a black handle.

◆ **Horizontal or Vertical.** Drag a middle black handle on a horizontal or vertical edge.

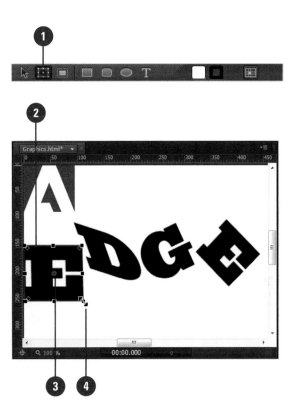

Changing Element Clipping

A clipping area describes the portion of an element's bounding box that is visible. The Clip property is like a mask or cropping. It allows you to mask the content of an element in a bounding box. To clip an element, you can use the Clipping Tool on the Tools panel to resize the clipping area or the Properties panel to specify exact values—left, top, right, and bottom—in pixels relative to the element. The Clip left value indicates the length from the left edge of the bounding box to the left side of the clip area. The Clip top value does the same but from the top. Here is where things get different. The bottom value indicates the length from the top edge of the bounding box to the bottom side of the clip area. The Clip right value does the same but from the left edge to the right side. For example, a new element's Clip values are Left = 0 px, Top = 0 px, Right = Left (0 px)+Width, and Bottom = Top (0 px)+Height. When you clip an element, a clip icon appears to the right of the name in the Element panel as an indicator of the element change.

Change Element Clipping in the Properties Panel

1. Click the **Selection Tool** on the Tools panel.

2. Select the element you want to change.

3. In the Properties panel under Clip, drag the **slider** on the header bar to turn it on (enabled).

4. Click a **Clip** (Left, Right, Top, or Bottom) value, enter a value in pixels, and then press Enter (Win) or Return (Mac), or drag (scrub) a **Clip** value to the one you want.

5. To turn the Clip property off and remove the clipping area, drag the **slider** on the header bar to turn it off (disabled).

   ◆ You can also right-click (Win) or control-click (Mac) the clipped element, and then click **Remove Clip**.

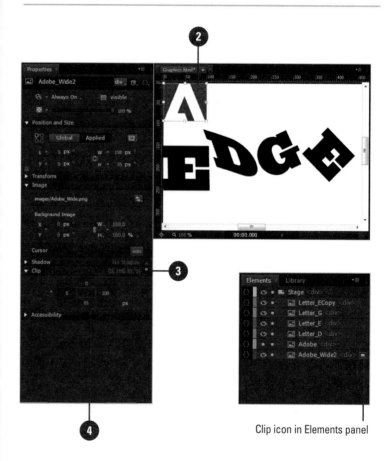

Clip icon in Elements panel

Change Element Clipping with the Clipping Tool

1. Click the **Clipping Tool** on the Tools panel.

2. Select the element you want to change.

   When you select an element, the bounding box appears in green instead of blue. A blue bounding box appears around element when it's selected with the Selection Tool.

3. To change the size of the clipping area, drag the resize handle on the green bounding box to change the clipping area.

   As you drag the resize handle, a black bounding box might appear for the element. The black bounding box is the size of the element. You can drag the resize handle for the black bounding box to resize the element itself.

4. To move the element within the clipping area, point the content grabber (a circle within a circle, the cursor changes to a hand), and then drag it.

5. To remove clipping from an element, right-click (Win) or control-click (Mac) the clipped element, and then click **Remove Clip**.

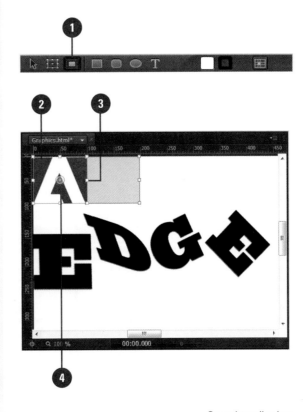

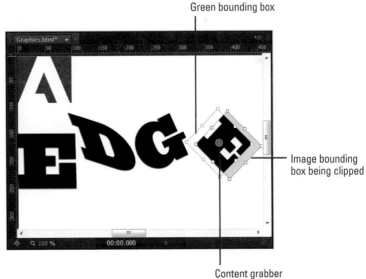

Green bounding box

Image bounding box being clipped

Content grabber

Adding Accessibility to Elements

Accessibility makes it easier for people with disabilities to use and interact with your animation. In the Properties panel under Accessibility, you can specify an accessibility title for an element and specify a numbered position in the tabbing order on the web page. The title is used by readers to help the visually impaired identify an element on the screen. The tabbing order provides a sequence to change the current focus on the screen. When you press Enter (Win) or Return (Mac), the current focus is executed, such as a button. The tab index attribute begins with the smallest value and ends with the largest value. The value can be between 0 and 32767.

Add Accessibility to Elements in the Properties Panel

1. Click the **Selection Tool** on the Tools panel.

2. Select the element you want to change.

3. In the Properties panel under Accessibility, enter a title for the selected element.

4. Click the **Tab Index** value, enter a value, and then press Enter (Win) or Return (Mac), or drag (scrub) the **Tab Index** value to the one you want.

5. To remove the Tab Index value, click the **Close** button.

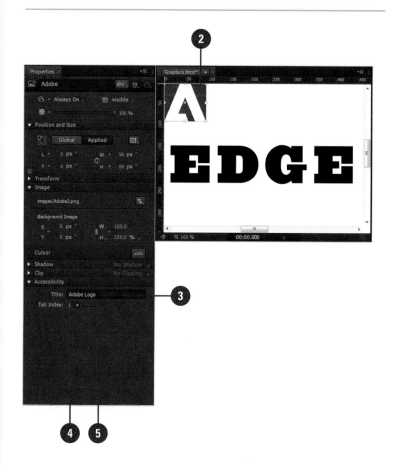

Working with Text

Introduction

In addition to the shape tools, the Tools panel includes a text tool for creating text elements in your animations. The Text Tool creates a text box container for holding text. Just like shapes and graphics, text elements are composed of attributes that you can change in the Properties panel. Edge Animate uses CSS (Cascading Style Sheet) text properties— such as font family, size, color, weight, italic, underline, alignment, and line spacing—to format the text. In addition to the text properties, you can also use the Transform and Clipping Tools on the Tools panel or attributes in the Properties panel, just like shapes and graphics, to scale, rotate, skew, clip (crop), and shadow a text box for use in an animation or to create a special effect.

   In addition to the standard list of fonts that comes with Edge Animate, you can also add web fonts to your compositions. A web font is a font that is optimized for use in web pages and resides on a web server instead of the user's local computer. Web fonts are available from font providers, such as Adobe, Google, Typekit, Fontsquirrel.com, and Fonts.com. Adobe provides a free online service called Edge Web Fonts with hundreds of web fonts for you to use in your projects. Edge Web Fonts are powered by Typekit, a premium web font service from Adobe that provides access to a library of commercial web fonts.

   With Edge Animate, you can assign standard HTML tags to text. This is useful to help you format text consistently. When you create a text box, Edge Animate automatically assigns an HTML division <div> tag, however, you can change it to other text specific tags, such as paragraph <p> and headings <h1>...<h6>.

What You'll Do

Create Text Boxes

Add Text

Edit Text

Dictate Text

Insert Special Characters

Examine Text Properties

Change Text Properties

Get Web Fonts

Add Web Fonts

Resize Text Boxes

Clip Text

Transform Text

Add Shadows to Text

Change Text Tags

Add Links to Text

Creating Text Boxes

Along with the shape tools, the Tools panel includes a text tool for creating text elements in your animations. The Text Tool creates a text box container for holding text. When you click and drag on the Stage to create a text box, Edge Animate opens a separate Text window, where you enter and edit text for the text box. Text elements are composed of attributes—such as font family, size, color, weight, italic, underline, alignment, and line spacing—that you can change in the Properties panel. The size of the text box is determined by W (width) and H (height) and not by the text within it, so you might need to adjust it on the Stage or in the Properties panel.

Create a Text Box

1 Click the **Text Tool** on the Tools panel.

TIMESAVER *Press T to select the Text Tool.*

2 Position the pointer on the Stage where you want to start drawing the text box.

The pointer becomes a crosshair that you can drag on the Stage.

3 Drag to create a text box.

IMPORTANT *If Smart Guides are enabled on the Modify menu, alignment guides appear when working with multiple elements.*

When you release the mouse, a separate Text window appears for entering text.

4 In the Text window, enter the text you want. As you type, text wraps within the window.

◆ You can press Enter (Win) or Return (Mac) in the window to start text on the next line.

◆ You can modify the text in the window like you're in an editor.

5 When you're done, click the **Close** button or click off the window.

6 If the text displays below the bottom edge of the bounding box, you can drag a bottom resize handle to modify the size.

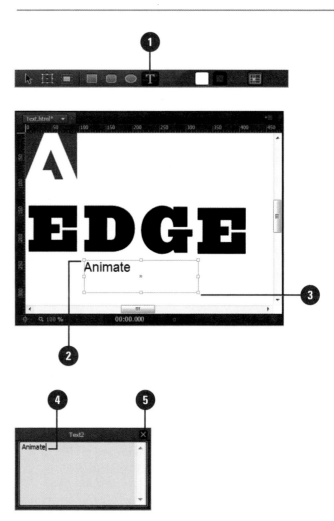

Adding Text

In addition to creating a text box and entering text, you can also add text to a text box by copying text from another file, such as a word processing document, and pasting text from the Clipboard in the open Text window. If you have an existing web page with text already in it that was created from another HTML editor or web development tool, such as Adobe Dreamweaver, you can open the HTML document in Edge Animate and use the existing text boxes on the page in an animation. When you open the HTML document, you lose any text formatting, however, any links within the text are preserved. Edge Animate displays all the text you enter whether it fits within the size of the text box or not. If the text doesn't fit, the text extends out past the bottom. You can drag a resize handle on the text box on the Stage or change the W (width) and H (height) attributes in the Properties panel.

Paste Text into a Text Box

1. Open the program and file with the text you want, copy the text, and then exit it.

2. Start or switch to Edge Animate, and then open the composition where you want to add text.

3. Click the **Text Tool** on the Tools panel.

4. Drag to create a new text box or click an existing text box.

   A separate Text window appears for entering or pasting text.

   TIMESAVER *With the Selection Tool, you can double-click a text box to edit its contents.*

5. Click to place the insertion point in the Text window where you want to paste the text.

6. Press Ctrl+V (Win) or ⌘+V (Mac) to paste the text from the Clipboard into the Text window.

7. When you're done, click the **Close** button or click off the window.

8. If the text displays below the bottom edge of the bounding box, you can drag a bottom resize handle to modify the size.

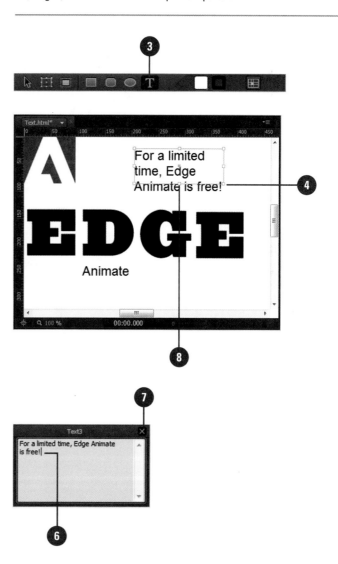

Editing Text

Before you can edit text, you need to open the Text window for an existing text box. You can do this by clicking the text box with the Text Tool or double-clicking the text box with the Selection Tool. In the Text window, you can delete, replace, move (cut), or copy text within different text boxes or between compositions or other documents even if they're from different programs. In either case, the steps are the same. Text you cut or copy is temporarily stored in the Clipboard.

Edit Text

1. Click the **Text Tool** on the Tools panel.

2. Click an existing text box.

   A separate Text window appears for entering or pasting text.

   TIMESAVER *With the Selection Tool, you can double-click a text box to edit its contents.*

3. Click to place the insertion point or drag to select text in the Text window.

4. Perform one of the following editing commands:

   ◆ To delete text, press the Backspace key or the Delete key.

   ◆ To replace selected text, type your text.

   ◆ To cut selected text, press Ctrl+X (Win) or ⌘+X (Mac).

   ◆ To copy selected text, press Ctrl+C (Win) or ⌘+C (Mac).

5. When you're done, click the **Close** button or click off the window.

6. If the text displays below the bottom edge of the bounding box, you can drag a bottom resize handle to modify the size.

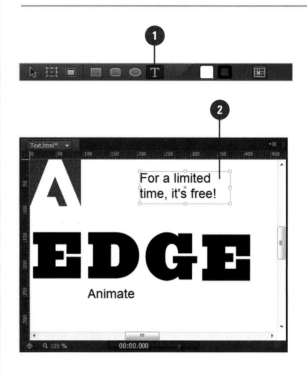

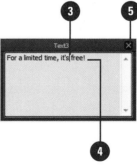

Dictating Text

If you're using Edge Animate with OS X Mountain Lion (v10.8) or later, you can use the Start Dictation command to dictate the text into the Text window. Before you get started, make sure a microphone is available on or connected to your computer, and then enable the dictation option in Dictation & Speech preferences. You can start the dictation in a place that accepts text by selecting the Start Dictation command from the Edit menu or specifying a keyboard shortcut for easy access when you need it. After you start, a Dictation box appears at the insertion point. At this point, dictate your text, and then click Done to convert it to type. Dictation understands basic commands, such as new line or punctuation (period, comma, etc.) in the current language. If you don't want it converted or it's taking too long, click Cancel.

Start and Use Dictation

1. In Edge Animate (Mac), click the **Text Tool** on the Tools panel.

2. Create a new text box or click an existing text box to open the Text window.

3. Click to place the insertion point or drag to select text in the Text window.

4. Start the dictation using any of the following:

   ◆ Click the **Edit** menu, and then click **Start Dictation.**

   ◆ Use the shortcut specified in Dictation preferences.

   If prompted, click **OK**, and then click **Enable Dictation**.

   TROUBLE? *Dictation is only available with OS X Mountain Lion (v10.8) or later.*

5. Dictate the text you want converted into type on the screen.

6. Click **Done** in the Dictation box.

   ◆ To stop the conversion, click **Cancel** in the Dictation box.

   The text is converted to type.

7. When you're done, click the **Close** button or click off the window.

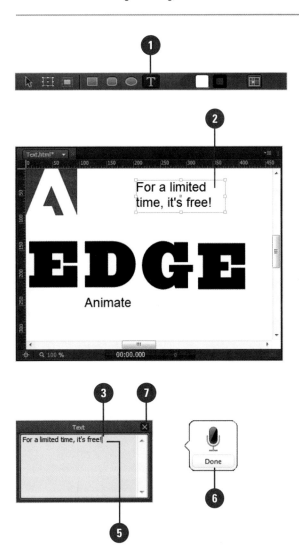

Inserting Special Characters

If you're using Edge Animate with Mac OS X, you can insert special characters such as ©, ™, or ® that don't appear on your keyboard into the Text window using an accessory called Character. Character is available in Mac applications and displays all the characters that are available for each of the fonts on your computer. You can insert special characters in a variety of symbol fonts, including arrows, punctuations, currency symbols, pictographs, bullets/stars, math symbols, letter like symbols, emoji (emoticons), and latin. Each one of the fonts also includes style variations.

Insert a Special Character

1. In Edge Animate (Mac), click the **Text Tool** on the Tools panel.

2. Create a new text box or click an existing text box to open the Text window.

3. Click in the text to place the insertion point where you want to insert a special character.

4. Click the **Edit** menu, and then click **Special Characters**.

   TIMESAVER *Press Option+⌘+T to open the Character program.*

5. Select a category, click **Recently Used**, or click **Favorites** to select from your favorites, and then click a subcategory, if available.

6. Click the special character you want to insert.

7. Click a font variation, if desired.

8. To add the character to a favorites list, click **Add To Favorites**.

9. To insert a special character into a document, double-click the character.

10. Click the **Close** button to exit the Character program.

11. When you're done, click the **Close** button or click off the window.

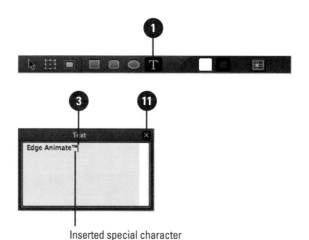

Inserted special character

Examining Text Properties

When you create a text box, Edge Animate uses CSS (Cascading Style Sheet) text properties to format the text. You change the CSS text properties in the Properties panel.

◆ **Font Family.** Specifies the font typeface in the order of availability. The default is Arial, Helvetica, sans-serif.

If a user your animation doesn't have the selected font, their web browser will substitute it with another one. The Font Family list displays the order of substitution. In the case of the default, it tries Arial, then Helvetica, and then any sans-serif font.

There are three main categories of fonts: serif, sans-serif, and monospace. **Serif** fonts use extra bars and strokes at the ends of letters. **Sans-serif** fonts don't use the extra bars and strokes. Sans-serif is taken from the French and means without serifs. **Monospace** fonts use the same space horizontally for each character.

◆ **Font Size.** Specifies the font size in pixels (px), percentage (%), or ems (em). The font size is a relative measure instead of a fixed point size because you can change the font display in a web browser. Pixels use the resolution of the screen; percentage uses browser preferences; and em uses browser preferences and the font size of its parent element (for nested elements). For most browsers, 16px = 1em. The default is 24 pixels.

When you change the units for the Font Size, it changes the units for other text attributes, such as letter spacing, word spacing, line height, and line indent.

◆ **Font Color.** Specifies the color of the text. The default is black (#000000).

◆ **Font Weight.** Specifies how bold the text displays. The weight is assigned from 100 (lightest) to 900 (boldest). The default is 400 (Normal).

◆ **Font Style.** Specifies whether the font is italic or normal. The default is italic style off (normal).

◆ **Font Decoration.** Specifies whether the font is underline or normal. The default is underline style off (normal).

◆ **Text Align.** Specifies whether the text is align left, center, or right. The default is left align.

◆ **Letter Spacing.** Specifies the spacing between letters in pixels (px) or ems (em). The default is zero pixels (normal font spacing).

◆ **Word Spacing.** Specifies the spacing between words in pixels (px) or ems (em). The default is zero pixels (normal font spacing).

◆ **Line Height.** Specifies the line height between words in pixels (px) or percentage (%). The default is 29 pixels.

◆ **Line Indent.** Specifies whether to indent the first line of text in pixels (px) or percentage (%). The default is zero pixels (no indent).

Changing Text Properties

After you create a text box with the Text Tool on the Tools panel, you can change the text properties to format the text in the Properties panel. When you select a text box, the Text panel appears in the Properties panel with text-specific attributes. Edge Animate uses CSS (Cascading Style Sheet) text properties to format the text. The text properties are similar to the ones in many word processing programs, however the terminology and the use of fonts and sizes are a little different. For example, italic is denoted as text-style and underline is denoted as text-decoration. The Font Family includes a list of alternate fonts in case one or more fonts is not available on the web, and the font size is specified in relative sizes using pixels (px), percentage (%), or ems (em) instead of a fixed point size in case the web browser window size changes.

Change Text Properties

1 Select the text box with the text you want to change.

2 In the Properties panel under Text, view and change any of the following:

◆ **Font Family.** Select a font typeface. The font family list includes alternate fonts. The default is Arial, Helvetica, sans-serif.

◆ **Font Size.** Specify the font size in pixels (px), percentage (%), or ems (em). The units are a relative size instead of a fixed one. The default is 24 pixels. For most browsers, 16px = 1em.

IMPORTANT *When you change the units, it also changes the units for other text attributes.*

◆ **Font Color.** Select a font color on the color palette. The default is black (#000000).

◆ **Font Weight.** Select a boldness attribute from 100 (lightest) to 900 (boldest). The default is 400 (Normal).

◆ **Font Style.** Click the button to turn on (enable) or off (disable) the italic style. The default is italic style off (normal).

- ◆ **Font Decoration.** Click the button to turn on (enable) or off (disable) the underline style. The default is underline style off (normal).

- ◆ **Text Align.** Click the Left, Center, or Right Align button to align the text. The default is left align.

3 Click the **Expand** double-arrow button at the bottom of the Text pane.

This displays additional options. The button toggles to expand and collapse the extended pane.

4 In the Properties panel under Text in the extended pane, view and change any of the following:

- ◆ **Letter Spacing.** Specify the spacing between letters in pixels (px) or ems (em). The default is zero pixels (normal font spacing).

- ◆ **Word Spacing.** Specify the spacing between words in pixels (px) or ems (em). The default is zero pixels (normal font spacing).

- ◆ **Line Height.** Specify the line height between words in pixels (px) or percentage (%). The default is 29 pixels.

- ◆ **Line Indent.** Specify indent spacing for the first line of text in pixels (px) or percentage (%). The default is zero pixels (normal font spacing).

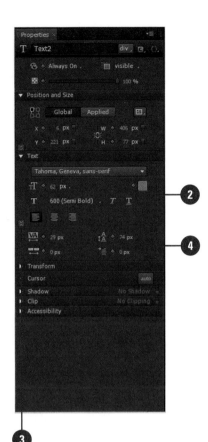

Getting Web Fonts

In addition to the standard list of fonts that comes with Edge Animate, you can also add web fonts to your compositions. A web font is a font that is optimized for use in web pages and resides on a web server instead of the user's local computer. Web fonts are available from font providers, such as Adobe, Google, Typekit, Fontsquirrel.com, and Fonts.com. Adobe provides a free online service called Edge Web Fonts with hundreds of web fonts for you to use in your projects. Edge Web Fonts are powered by Typekit, a premium web font service from Adobe that provides access to a library of commercial web fonts. Edge Web Fonts and other providers use a web site to provide embed code for you to copy and paste into your HTML. The embed code tells a browser where to find the web fonts. If a browser is not connected to the web, the web fonts won't be available for use. If you use a lot of web fonts, you can slow down your web pages, so only use the font styles that you actually need on your web pages.

Get Edge Web Fonts

1 In your web browser, go to *html.adobe.com/edge*.

2 Click the **Edge Web Fonts** icon.

3 Scroll to the Preview Edge Web Fonts area of the page.

4 Click the **Font** list arrow, and then select the font you want.

The web site displays the embed code you need to paste into the head of your HTML, and then font-family name you need in your CSS.

5 Select the embed code for the selected web font.

6 Right-click (Win) or Control-click (Mac), and then click **Copy**.

The embed code is copied to the Clipboard.

Now, you're ready to add the web font to your Edge Animate project; see the next topic for details.

7 When you're done, close your web browser.

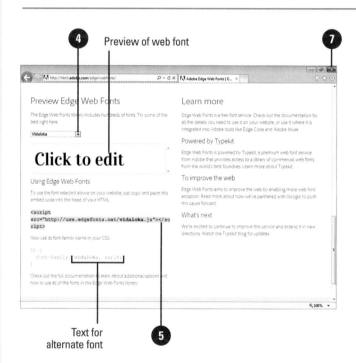

Preview of web font

Text for alternate font

Get Google Web Fonts

1. In your web browser, go to *www.google.com/webfonts*.

2. Locate the fonts you want to use.

3. Click **Add to Collection** for each one you want to use.

4. Click **Review** to preview the fonts.

5. Click **Use**, and then select the check boxes with the fonts you want to use.

6. Click the **Standard** tab.

7. Select the embed code for the selected web font.

8. Right-click (Win) or Control-click (Mac), and then click **Copy**.

   The embed code is copied to the Clipboard.

   Now, you're ready to add the web font to your Edge Animate project; see the next topic for details.

9. When you're done, close your web browser.

Preview of web font

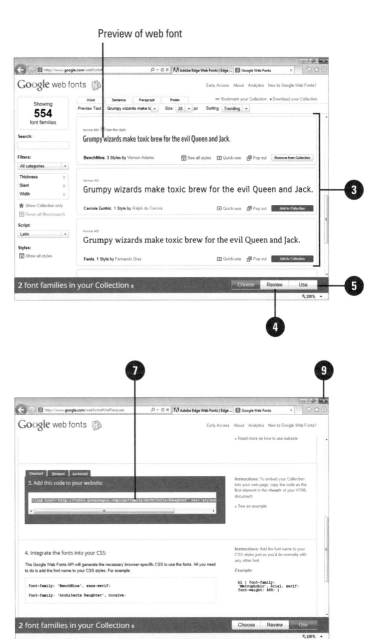

Adding Web Fonts

Before you can use a web font, you need to copy its embed code from a web font provider, such as Adobe, Google, Typekit, Fonts.com, and Fontsquirrel.com. Many of them provide web fonts for free. After you copy a web font's embed code, you paste it in the Add Web Fonts dialog box where you can use it from the Font list in Edge Animate. The embed code tells a browser where to find the web fonts. If a browser is not connected to the web, the web fonts won't be available for use. To fix the problem, you provide a substitute font for use when the specified web font is not available. The web fonts are only available for the compositions in which you add them.

Add Edge Web Fonts

1 Open the composition that you want to add web fonts.

2 In the Library panel, click the **Add Web Fonts** button (+).

3 Paste the embed code in the Embed Code text box.

4 Type the name of the font along with the fonts (separated by commas) that should be used if the web font is not available.

5 Click **Add Font**.

You can select the font from the Font list from use in your project.

If the font doesn't take effect, continue with the following steps.

6 Start an HTML editor, such as Adobe Edge Code.

Adobe Edge Code is a program you can download and install from the Edge Tools & Services web site.

7 Open the HTML document for the composition.

8 Paste the embed code (copied from the web font site; see the previous page for details) within the Head code, anywhere between <head> and </head>.

9 Save and close the HTML file and exit the HTML editor program.

Font Family list   Web font applied to text box

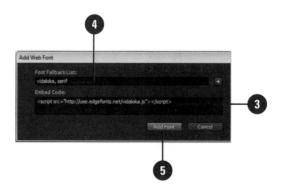

Add Google or Other Web Fonts

1 Open the composition that you want to add web fonts.

2 In the Library panel, click the **Add Web Fonts** button (+).

3 Paste the embed code in the Embed Code text box.

4 Type the name of the font along with the fonts (separated by commas) that should be used if the web font is not available.

5 Click **Add Font**.

You can select the font from the Font list from use in your project.

Did You Know?

You can delete a web font. To delete a web font, right-click (Win) or control-click (Mac) the web font in the Fonts section of the Library panel, and then click Delete.

Font Family list   Web font applied to text box

Resizing Text Boxes

As you enter and edit text, you may see a situation where the text within a text box displays below the bottom edge of the bounding box. The size of the text box is determined by W (width) and H (height) attributes and not by the text within it, so you might need to adjust it on the Stage or in the Properties panel. You can resize it on the Stage by dragging a resize handle with the Selection Tool on the Tools panel or by setting specific W (width) and H (height) values in the Properties panel. When you change the W value, the text within the text box wraps to the adjusted right edge. As it wraps, all the text within the text box reflows to display on the Stage.

Resize a Text Box

1. Click the **Selection Tool** on the Tools panel.

2. Select the text box you want to change.

3. Position the pointer over a black square handle (cursor changes to a double arrow) on the right side, and then drag to the size you want.

   ◆ **Proportional.** Hold down the Shift key, and then drag a black handle.

   ◆ **Horizontal or Vertical.** Drag a middle black handle on a horizontal or vertical edge.

4. To set specific size values in the Properties panel, click the **Size W** or **H** value, enter a value in pixels or percentages, and then press Enter (Win) or Return (Mac), or drag (scrub) the **Size W** or **H** value to the one you want.

   ◆ **Constrain/Unconstrain.** Click the **Link/Unlink** icon to toggle on and off.

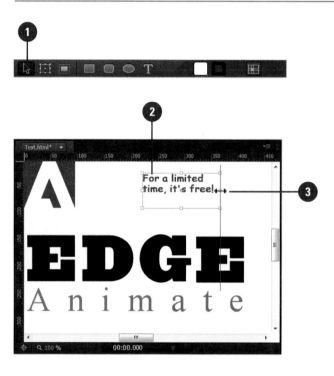

Clipping Text

A clipping area describes the portion of an element's bounding box that is visible. The Clip property is like a mask or cropping. It allows you to mask the content of an element in a bounding box. This is useful for animating a text box from a clipped position to full display. To clip an element, you can use the Clipping Tool on the Tools panel to resize the clipping area or the Properties panel to specify exact values—left, top, right, and bottom—in pixels relative to the element. When you clip an element, a clip icon appears to the right of the name in the Element panel as an indicator of the element change.

Change Text Box Clipping with the Clipping Tool

1 Click the **Clipping Tool** on the Tools panel.

2 Select the text box you want to change.

When you select an element, the bounding box appears in green instead of blue.

3 To change the size of the clipping area, drag the resize handle on the green bounding box to change the clipping area.

As you drag the resize handle, a black bounding box might appear for the text box. The black bounding box is the size of the text box. You can drag the resize handle for the black bounding box to resize the text box itself.

4 To remove clipping from an element, right-click (Win) or control-click (Mac) the clipped element, and then click **Remove Clip**.

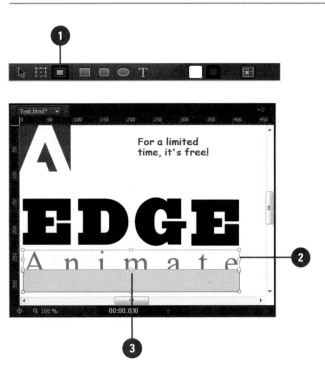

See Also

See "Changing Element Clipping" on page 118 for more information on changing element clipping in the Properties panel.

Transforming Text

With the Transform Tool on the Tools panel or attributes in the Transform area of the Properties panel, you can scale, rotate, and skew a text box for use in an animation or to create a special effect. If you want to set an exact value to scale, rotate, or skew a text box, you change values in the Properties panel. However, if you want to scale, rotate, or skew a text box on the Stage, you can drag handles using the Transform Tool. When you select a text box with the Transform Tool, you can position the pointer over or near a black handle to Transform it. Before you transform a text box, you need to specify the origin point, or the new center position where the scale, rotate, or skew takes place.

Transform a Text Box in the Properties Panel

1. Click the **Selection Tool** on the Tools panel.

2. Select the text box you want to change.

3. If you want to adjust the origin point, specify **Transform Origin X** or **Y** values by percentage in the Properties panel under Transform.

4. In the Properties panel under Transform, change any of the following:

   ◆ Scale. Click the **Scale X** or **Y** value, enter a value in percentages, and then press Enter (Win) or Return (Mac), or drag (scrub) the **Scale X** or **Y** value to the one you want.

   ◆ Skew. Click the **Skew X** or **Y** value, enter a value in degrees, and then press Enter (Win) or Return (Mac), or drag (scrub) the **Skew X** or **Y** value to the one you want.

   ◆ Rotate. Drag the **Rotate (z)** slider to the degree you want, or enter or scrub (drag) a **Rotate (z)** value in degrees, either positive (right) or negative (left).

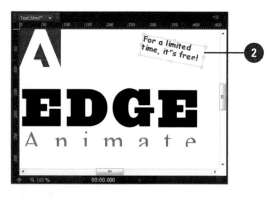

Transform a Text Box with the Transform Tool

1. Click the **Transform Tool** on the Tools panel.

2. Select the text box you want to change.

3. If you want to adjust the origin point, drag the Transform origin point in the text box on the Stage.

4. On the Stage, use any of the following:

   ◆ Scale. Position the pointer over a black square handle (cursor changes to a double arrow), and then drag to the scale size you want.

      ◆ Proportional. Hold down the Shift key, and then drag a black handle.

      ◆ Horizontal or Vertical. Drag a middle black handle on a horizontal or vertical edge.

   ◆ Skew. Position the pointer outside a corner point (cursor changes to a double arrow in opposite directions), and then drag to skew the element.

   ◆ Rotate. Position the pointer outside a corner point (cursor changes to an arrow with a circle), and then drag to rotate the element.

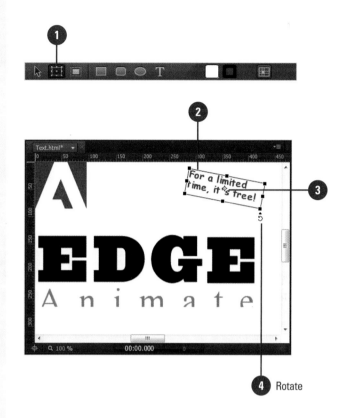

4 Rotate

Adding Shadows to Text

You can add a shadow to text within a text box in Edge Animate. After you add a shadow, you can specify the X and Y position, color and blur in the Properties panel. The blur value specifies the amount of shadow edge feathering you want. You can add or remove a shadow to a text box by dragging the slider to on (enable) or off (disable) on the Shadow header bar in the Properties panel. When you turn it on and off, the shadow settings for the text box remain in tact, so you don't have to reset them.

Add Shadows to a Text Box in the Properties Panel

1. Click the **Selection Tool** on the Tools panel.

2. Select the text box you want to change.

3. In the Properties panel under Shadow, drag the **slider** on the header bar to turn it on.

4. Click the **X** or **Y** value, enter a value, and then press Enter (Win) or Return (Mac), or drag (scrub) the **X** or **Y** value to the one you want.

5. Click the **Color** box, and then select a color for the shadow.

6. Click the **Blur** value, enter a value, and then press Enter (Win) or Return (Mac), or drag (scrub) the **Blur** value to the one you want.

7. To turn the Shadow property off, drag the **slider** on the header bar to turn it off.

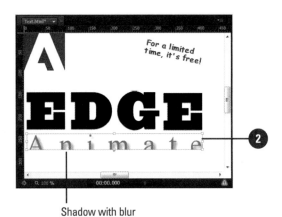

Shadow with blur

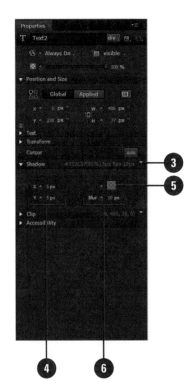

Changing Text Tags

With Edge Animate, you can assign standard HTML tags to text. This is useful to help you format text consistently. When you create a text box, Edge Animate automatically assigns an HTML division (DIV) tag and creates CSS code based on the attributes set in the Properties panel. A DIV tag is an HTML element that defines generic containers or sections within the content of a web page. Defining an element with a content specific HTML tag provides information and predefined attributes to help your web browser more accurately display the content of the web page. Some content specific tags, such as the heading tags, are used by search engines to index the structure and content of your web pages. So, it's a good idea to define HTML elements using appropriate HTML tags whenever possible.

Change Text Tags

1. Click the **Selection Tool** on the Tools panel.

2. Select the text box you want to change.

3. In the Properties panel, click the **Tag** list arrow, and then select an element specific tag.

   ◆ **div.** Defines a general way to define an element in HTML; it's not based on its content.

   ◆ **address.** Defines contact information for the author of a document/article.

   ◆ **article.** Defines self-contained content, like a news article or blog post; new tag in HTML5. It specifies content that might be from another source.

   ◆ **blockquote.** Defines a section that is quoted from another source.

   ◆ **p.** Defines a paragraph.

   ◆ **h1 - h6.** Defines HTML headings.

   ◆ **pre.** Defines preformatted text. It retains defined white space, which usually gets ignored by HTML.

   ◆ **code.** Defines a piece of computer code, which typically uses a monospaced font.

Tags for a selected text box

Adding Links to Text

With Edge Animate, you can add links to your compositions in two ways. One way is to add an action script using a code snippet to open a URL. Another way is to open an existing HTML document with code to add a link using the <a> and </a> tags. For example, <a href="http://www.perspection.com"> ww.perspection.com</a>. After you have a text box with a link, you can animate it just like another element in a composition. At this time, Edge Animate doesn't allow you to edit HTML code. However, you can use Adobe Edge Code or another HTML editor to do the job. You can even have both programs and HTML files open at the same time and go back and forth between them making changes.

Add Links to Text

1. Create a text box with the text you want to use as the link.

2. In the Properties panel, click the **Cursor** button, and then click the Pointer cursor.

3. In the Elements panel, click the **Open Actions** button next to the Text box element.

4. In the Snippets panel, click the **Open URL** button.

   The code to open a link appears in the window. The default link is set to *www.adobe.com*, which you can select and change.

5. Click the **Close** button.

6. Click the **File** menu, and then click **Preview In Browser**.

   Your default web browser opens displaying the composition.

7. Point to the text to display the pointer, and then click to open the web page.

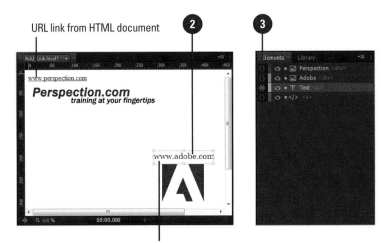

URL link from HTML document

Open URL script in Edge Animate

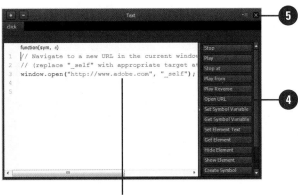

URL link in script

See Also

See "Using the Open URL Snippet" on page 210 for more information on creating a URL using a snippet or HTML code.

Add HTML Links to Text with an HTML Editor

1. Start Adobe Edge Code or another HTML editor.

2. Click the **File** menu, and then click **Open**.

3. Navigate to and select the HTML file that you want to add a link.

4. Click **Open**.

5. Within the <body> and </body> tags of the HTML code, add the following code:

   <a href="http://www.perspection.com">ww.perspection.com</a>

6. Click the **File** menu, and then click **Save**.

7. Click the **Close** button to exit the HTML editor.

8. Start or switch back to Edge Animate.

   If the HTML file is already open in Edge Animate, click **Yes** to update and reload it.

9. If the HTML file is not already open, click the **File** menu, click **Open**, select the HTML file, and then click **Open**.

10. Click the **File** menu, and then click **Preview In Browser**.

    Your default web browser opens displaying the composition.

11. Point to the text to display the pointer, and then click to open the web page.

See Also

See "Downloading Edge Animate and Tools" on page 282 for more information on downloading Adobe Edge Code.

Edge Code

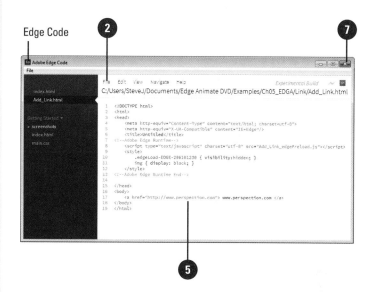

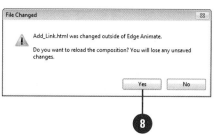

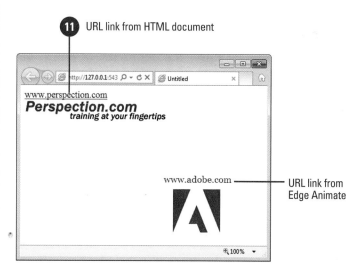

URL link from HTML document

URL link from Edge Animate

Working with Symbols and Elements

6

Introduction

A symbol is a special asset that allows you to group together elements with its own Timeline, which is independent from the main Timeline for your composition. A symbol is a reusable asset that is turned into an instance, which you can modify and animate, on the Stage and in the Timeline. You can use the instance of a symbol many times as unique elements on the Stage, which you can animate and use separately. Each instance stands on its own, yet can still be changed for all instances in the symbol.

A symbol allows you to reuse elements without having to increase the amount of disk space the asset takes up on your system. When you copy and paste an element, such as an image, it increases the disk space usage for each copy. However, if you need a slightly different element or want to use an element in another composition, then copy and paste or duplicate is the way to go.

After you get all your content on the Stage, you can use rulers and guides to place the elements where you want for use in your composition. In the Elements panel, you can work with individual elements. You can stack and group elements one in front of the other to properly display them on the Stage, show or hide elements to make them easier to work with on the Stage, lock or unlock elements, such as a background, to keep them in place or allow them to move, or rename an element for better identification.

What You'll Do

Create Symbols

Import Symbols

Export Symbols

Create an Instance from a Symbol

Modify an Instance from a Symbol

Edit Symbols

Nest Symbols

Copy or Duplicate Elements

Delete Elements

Display Rulers and Guides

Use Guides with Elements

Align and Distribute Elements

Stack Elements

Hide and Show Elements

Group Elements

Reparent Elements

Lock and Unlock Elements

Rename Elements

Creating Symbols

A symbol is a special asset that allows you to group together elements with its own Timeline, which is independent from the main Timeline for your composition. A symbol allows you to reuse elements without having to increase the amount of disk space the asset takes up on your system. When you copy and paste an element, such as an image, it increases the disk space usage for each copy. When you create a symbol, it's known as a definition. When you use the symbol definition in your composition, it becomes an instance, which you can uniquely modify. You can add multiple instances of the same symbol and animate them differently. Each instance stands on its own. By using the same symbol definition, you're only using the asset once, which reduces the time it takes to load it. When you create a symbol, you can specify whether to have it automatically play when the symbol starts.

Convert an Element to a Symbol

1. Click the **Selection Tool** on the Tools panel.

2. Select the existing element you want to convert into a symbol.

3. Click the **Modify** menu, and then click **Convert to Symbol**.

   TIMESAVER *Press Ctrl+Y (Win) or* ⌘+Y *(Mac) to convert to symbol.*

   ◆ You can also click the **Add** button (+) next to Symbols in the Library panel, and then click **Convert selection to symbol**.

4. Enter a name for the symbol.

5. To have the symbol automatically play when you display the symbol in the timeline, select the **Autoplay timeline** check box.

6. Click **OK**.

   The symbol appears under Symbols in the Library panel, and the element in the Elements panel is changed and renamed with a number at the end to be an instance.

   The converted element on the Stage is now an instance of the symbol.

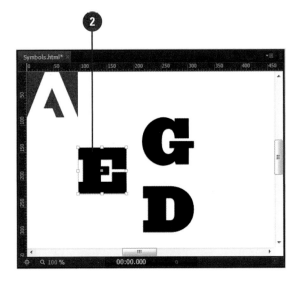

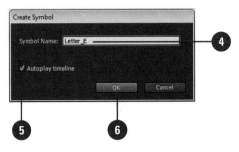

Importing Symbols

In addition to creating a symbol directly in an Edge Animate composition, you can also create symbols by importing them from another composition. An imported symbol uses the Edge Animate Symbol File (*.ansym) format, which you export from Edge Animate. The imported symbol is actually a compressed file that looks very similar to the contents of a composition. When you import a symbol, it's placed in the Library panel under Symbols. You can access the Import Symbols command from the Add button (+) next to Symbols in the Library panel.

Import Symbols

1 In the Library panel, click the **Add** button (+) next to Symbols, and then click **Import Symbols**.

The default file format is set to Edge Animate Symbol File (*.ansym; *.eglib).

2 Navigate to the drive or folder where the file is located.

3 Select the file you want to import.

◆ To import multiple files, hold down the ⌘ (Mac) or Ctrl (Win) key and click additional files to select them.

4 Click **Open**.

The symbol appears under Symbols in the Library panel.

Did You Know?

You can delete a symbol. In the Library panel under Symbols, right-click or control-click the symbol element, click Delete, and then click Yes, if prompted delete any instances.

You can rename a symbol. In the Library panel under Symbols, right-click or control-click the symbol element, click Rename, type a name, and then press Enter (Win) or Return (Mac).

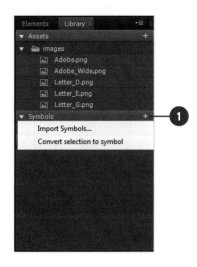

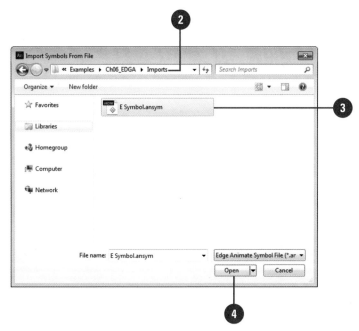

Exporting Symbols

As you create and animate symbols for use in one animation, you may have use for it in another animation. In Edge Animate, you can export a symbol from a composition as an Edge Animate Symbol File (*.ansym), and then import into another composition. The exported symbol is actually a compressed file that looks very similar to the contents of a composition. The single exported file makes it easy to import into other Edge Animate compositions.

Export a Symbol

1 In the Library panel, right-click (Win) or control-click (Mac) the symbol element, and then click **Export**.

◆ You can also right-click or control-click a symbol on the Stage or Elements panel, and then click **Export Symbol** *name*.

The default file format is set to Edge Animate Symbol File (*.ansym).

2 Type the new file name.

3 Navigate to the drive and folder location where you want to export the symbol file.

◆ To create a new folder, click the **New Folder** button, type a folder name, and then press Enter (Win) or click **Create** (Mac).

4 Click **Save**.

The program saves the exported symbol with the Edge Animate Symbol File (.ansym) file format.

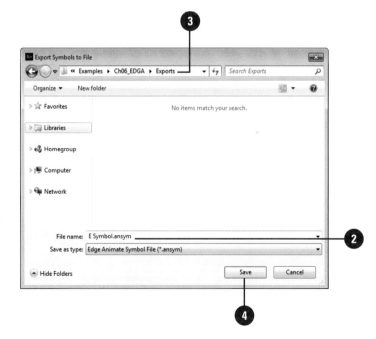

Creating an Instance from a Symbol

An **instance** is a copy of a symbol. When you use a symbol on the Stage or in the Timeline you are using an instance of it. You can animate an instance of a symbol and apply a variety of effects to it without affecting the original symbol in the Library. You can use multiple instances of the same symbol. When you change the properties of an instance in the Timeline or Properties panel, you are only applying these changes to that copy, or instance, of the symbol. In this way, you keep the file size down because Edge Animate only keeps track of the changes you've made while preserving the symbol in the form you created. If you have several instances of a symbol in your composition and you want to edit the artwork, you can make changes to the master symbol. When you do this, all of the instances of that symbol will be updated with these changes.

Create an Instance from a Symbol

① Click the **Selection Tool** on the Tools panel.

② In the Library panel, drag a symbol on the Stage.

The symbol appears renamed with a number at the end as an instance in the Elements panel.

Instance

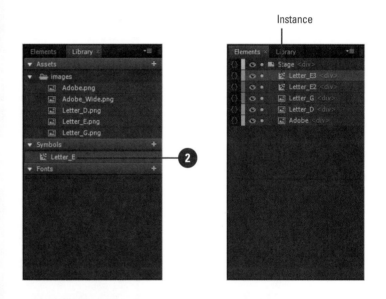

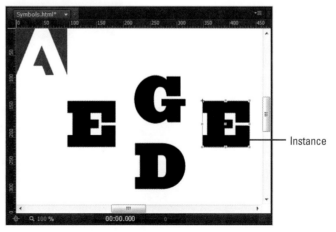

Instance

Modifying an Instance from a Symbol

You can animate an instance of a symbol and apply various effects to it without affecting the original symbol in the Library. When you change the properties of an instance in the Timeline or Properties panel, you are only applying these changes to that copy, or instance, of the symbol. The default setting for an instance is to play all animations on the Timeline, however, you can change the behavior with Playback commands, which allow you to stop, play, play in reverse, or specify exact times. You can set different Playback commands for each instance.

Modify an Instance in the Properties Panel

1. Click the **Selection Tool** on the Tools panel.

2. Select an instance of the symbol on the Stage or in the Elements panel.

3. Use the Properties and Timeline panels, modify the settings to change the instance or add an animation.

   ◆ Display. Change the display of the instance.

   ◆ Overflow. Change the off Stage setting for the instance.

   ◆ Opacity. Change the transparency of the instance.

   ◆ Position and Size. Change settings to specify the position and size of the instance.

   ◆ Transform. Change settings to scale, skew, or rotate the instance.

   ◆ Playback. Specify how and when to play or stop an instance. Select the **Scrub** check box to play the instance animation when you scrub the Playhead in the Timeline.

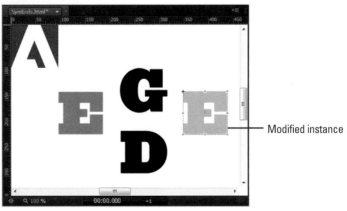

Modified instance

Modify an Instance with Playback Commands

1 Click the **Selection Tool** on the Tools panel.

2 Select an instance of the symbol on the Stage or in the Elements panel.

3 In the Timeline, drag the Playhead to where you want to add the Playback command.

4 In the Properties panel under Playback or in the Timeline next to Playback, click the **Playback Actions** button, and then select a Playback option:

◆ **Play.** Sets the instance to play.

◆ **Play From.** Sets the instance to play at a specific time or label.

◆ **Play Reverse.** Sets the instance to play in reverse.

◆ **Play Reverse From.** Sets the instance to play in reverse at a specific time or label.

◆ **Stop.** Sets the instance to stop.

◆ **Stop At.** Sets the instance to stop at a specific time or label.

A play or stop icon appears on the Timeline.

5 In the Properties panel, select the **Scrub** check box to play the instance animation when you scrub the Playhead in the Timeline.

6 To delete the Playback command, select the icon in the Timeline, and then press **Delete**.

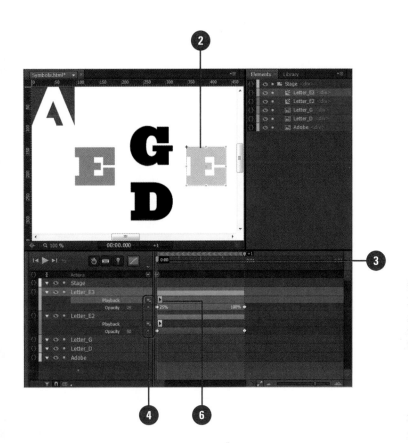

Editing Symbols

When you need to change or modify a symbol, you must enter a special symbol editing mode. Entering this mode allows you to view and edit the symbol. Any changes you make are stored in the Library, and all other instances of the symbol are updated with these changes. You can think of it like a master symbol. When you enter symbol editing mode, the window only displays elements associated with the symbol. It's like a mini composition with its own Timeline, Elements, and Properties panels. You can modify an element in symbol editing mode just like in the main composition. Above the Stage is a Back button and Stage button along with the name of the symbol that you can use to exit symbol editing mode and return back to the main composition.

Edit a Symbol

1. Click the **Selection Tool** on the Tools panel.

2. Select an instance of the symbol on the Stage or in the Elements panel.

3. Click the **Modify** menu, and then click **Edit Symbol**.

   TIMESAVER *Double-click a symbol instance on the Stage or in the Elements panel.*

   Symbol editing mode opens, displaying its own Stage and Timeline. The Stage grays out with all the elements viewable for perspective purposes.

4. Select an element on the Stage or in the Elements panel.

5. Modify the symbol in the Properties panel or in the Timeline.

6. Click the **Back** button or **Stage** on the Edit bar to exit symbol editing mode.

Did You Know?

You can edit a symbol without the Stage elements. In the Library panel, double-click the Symbol icon, or right-click (Win) or control-click (Mac) the symbol element, and then click Edit.

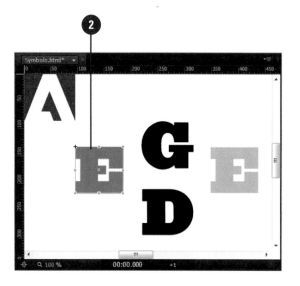

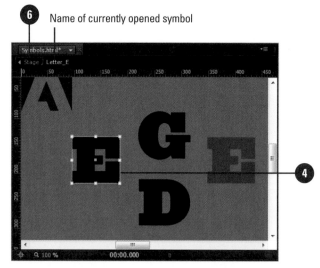

Name of currently opened symbol

Edit Symbol Stage Properties

1. Click the **Selection Tool** on the Tools panel.

2. Select an instance of the symbol on the Stage or in the Elements panel.

3. Click the **Modify** menu, and then click **Edit Symbol**.

   The Properties panel appears, displaying Stage properties.

4. View and change settings in the Properties panel:

   ◆ **Width and Height Size.** The current size of the Stage. Point to the width (w) and height (h) and drag the scrub or click and enter a size in pixels (px) (fixed position) or percentage (%) (relative position).

   ◆ **Overflow.** The area outside of the Stage. Click the **Overflow** list arrow, and then select an option: **visible**, **hidden**, **scroll** (adds right and bottom scroll bars), or **auto** (adds scroll bars as needed).

   ◆ **Autoplay.** Select to start playing the animation when it is ready in your browser.

   ◆ **Instance.** Select to have the instance scale or resize.

   ◆ **Min W and Max W.** The settings specify the CSS minimum and maximum width for the Stage when the screen size changes.

5. Click the **Back** button or **Stage** on the Edit bar to exit symbol editing mode.

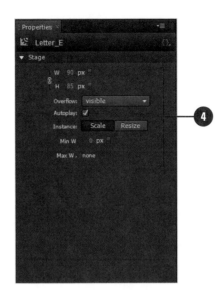

5 Name of currently opened symbol

Nesting Symbols within Symbols

As you have seen, you can create or import a symbol in a composition. However, you can also create or import a symbol in other symbols. This technique is called **nesting**. The nested symbol becomes an element of the parent symbol. For example, you can create a car body symbol that animates across the screen and then create a car wheel symbol with two instances (for front and back) that spin inside the car body symbol. This keeps everything together in the parent symbol. The beauty of this happens when you want to export it for use in another composition, which get stored in a single file.

Nest a Symbol within a Symbol

1. Click the **Selection Tool** on the Tools panel.

2. Select an existing symbol and any other elements you want to include in the nested symbol.

3. Click the **Modify** menu, and then click **Convert to Symbol**.

   TIMESAVER *Press Ctrl+Y (Win) or ⌘+Y (Mac) to convert to symbol.*

4. Enter a name for the symbol.

5. To have the symbol automatically play when you display the symbol in the timeline, select the **Autoplay timeline** check box.

6. Click **OK**.

Did You Know?

You can duplicate a symbol. In the Library panel under Symbols, right-click or control-click the symbol element, and then click Duplicate. This creates a copy of the symbol, not an instance.

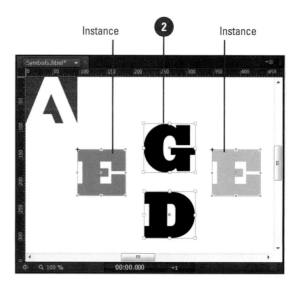

Work with a Nested Symbol

1. Click the **Selection Tool** on the Tools panel.

2. Select an instance of a nested symbol on the Stage or in the Elements panel.

3. Click the **Modify** menu, and then click **Edit Symbol**.

    TIMESAVER *Double-click a symbol instance on the Stage or in the Elements panel.*

4. Select an instance of a symbol on the Stage or in the Elements panel.

5. Click the **Modify** menu, and then click **Edit Symbol**.

6. Modify the nested symbol in the Properties panel or in the Timeline.

7. To exit symbol editing mode, do any of the following:

    ◆ Back. Click the **Back** button to exit the symbol to the parent symbol.

    ◆ Stage. Click **Stage** to exit the symbol to the main composition.

    ◆ Symbol name. Click the symbol name to exit the symbol to the parent symbol.

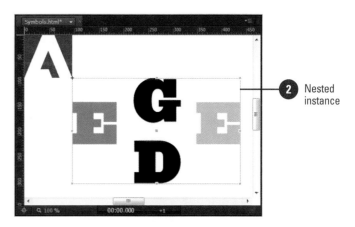

2 Nested instance

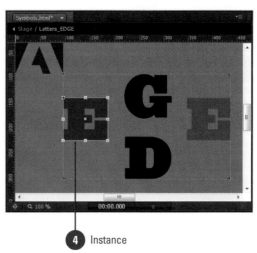

4 Instance

7 Name of currently opened symbol

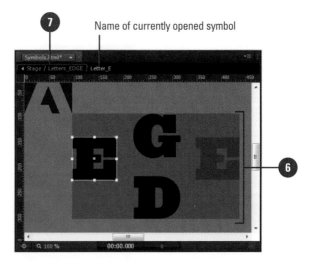

6

Copying or Duplicating Elements

You can copy and move elements from one location to another on the Stage. When you copy elements, a duplicate of the selected elements are placed on the Clipboard. When you move elements, the selected elements are removed and placed on the Clipboard. To complete the copy or move, you must paste the elements stored on the Clipboard in another location. Instead of taking two steps to copy and paste elements, you can complete the same task in one step by duplicating elements. Duplicating elements can be a powerful way of creating geometrical artwork. You can duplicate one or more selected elements by using the Duplicate command. The Duplicate command combines the Copy and Paste commands into one easy to use command.

Copy or Cut and Paste Elements

1. Click the **Selection Tool** on the Tools panel.

2. Select one or more elements on the Stage you want to copy or move (cut).

3. Click the **Edit** menu, and then click **Cut** (move) or **Copy**.

    TIMESAVER *Press Ctrl+V or Ctrl+C (Win) or* ⌘+V *or* ⌘+C *(Mac) to cut or copy.*

4. Click the **Edit** menu, and then click **Paste**.

    TIMESAVER *Press Ctrl+V (Win) or* ⌘+V *(Mac) to paste.*

    The selected elements are copied and pasted directly over the selected elements on the Stage, so you need to move them.

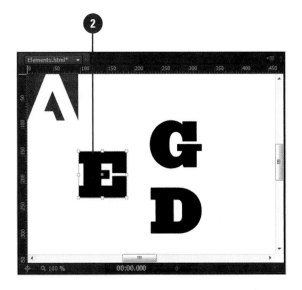

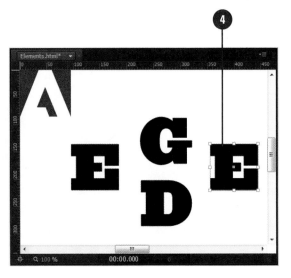

Duplicate Elements

1. Click the **Selection Tool** on the Tools panel.

2. Select one or more elements on the Stage you want to duplicate.

3. Click the **Edit** menu, and then click **Duplicate**, or Ctrl+drag (Win) or Option (Mac)+drag the selected elements.

   TIMESAVER *Press Ctrl+D (Win) or ⌘+D (Mac).*

   The selected elements are copied and pasted directly over the selected elements on the Stage, so you need to move them.

   The new elements appear in the Elements panel with "Copy" appended to the name.

Did You Know?

You can use Copy and Paste Special commands to copy specialized elements in Edge Animate. With the Paste Special submenu on the Edit menu, you can paste transitions, inverted animations, and actions.

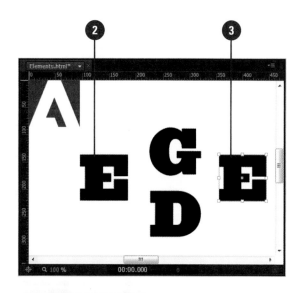

Copied element in the Elements panel

Deleting Elements

If you no longer need one or more elements, you can quickly delete them from your composition. This is important when you want to reduce the size of your project files. When you delete an element from a composition, the element is removed from the Elements panel, however, if there is a file, such as a graphic, associated with it, the file is not removed from your composition unless you manually delete it from the folder.

Delete Elements

1. Click the **Selection Tool** on the Tools panel.

2. Select one or more elements on the Stage you want to remove.

3. Click the **Edit** menu, and then click **Delete**.

   TIMESAVER *Press Backspace (Win) or delete (Mac).*

   The selected elements are removed from the Stage and Elements panel. However, they remain in the Library panel under Assets in the Images folder.

   You'll need to remove it manually in the Windows or File Explorer (Win) or Finder (Mac).

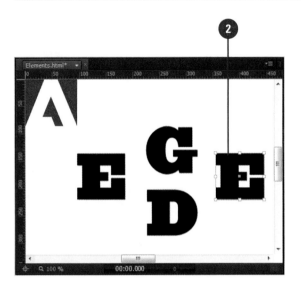

Delete Files of Elements

1. In the Library panel under Assets, right-click (Win) or control-click the element file, and then click **Reveal in Explorer** (Win) or **Reveal in Finder** (Mac).

   Windows Explorer or Finder window opens, displaying the folder with the file selected.

2. Delete the selected file using either of the following:

   ◆ **Windows.** Press **Delete**, and then click **Yes**.

   ◆ **Mac.** Drag the file to the Trash on the Dock.

   The file is moved to the Recycle Bin (Win) or Trash (Mac), where you can permanently remove it.

3. Switch back to Edge Animate, and then click **Yes** to update your composition with the change.

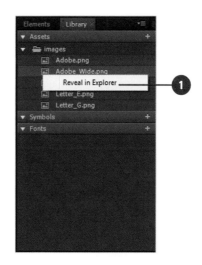

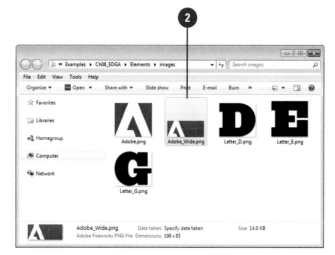

Displaying Rulers

Ruler bars are located on the top and left sides of the Stage and serve several purposes. They help you measure the width and height of Edge Animate elements and they let you place guides on the screen to control the placement of elements on the Stage. In all, rulers serve a very important role. When you display rulers, you can use guides to help you correctly align elements with other elements. By using guides, you have access to precise alignment systems. To create guides, the ruler must first be visible. When you change the width or height of the Stage to percentage units to create a responsive (resizeable) design, the ruler displays an adjustment handle (pin) that you can drag to see how the Stage and its content respond to the sizing change. It also includes a marker above the adjustment handle to indicate the original location. When you no longer need the rulers, you can hide the rulers to free up more workspace.

Show and Hide Rulers

① Click the **View** menu, and then click **Rulers**.

    TIMESAVER *Press Ctrl+R (Win) or ⌘+R (Mac) to show or hide the ruler.*

    A check mark appears next to the menu command to show the ruler.

② To hide rulers, click the **View** menu, and then click **Rulers**.

    The check mark next to the menu command disappears to hide the rulers.

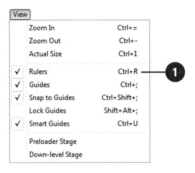

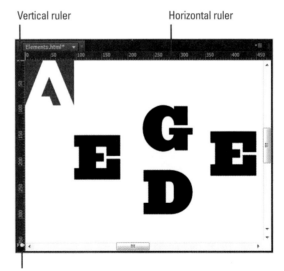

Vertical ruler   Horizontal ruler

Marker and adjustment handle (pin)

Displaying Guides

Edge Animate comes with guides and rulers to help you lay out artwork, text, and other elements with precision. A guide is a line that aids in aligning elements on the Stage. Guides are modifiable; you can show or hide them, lock them in place, have elements snap to them as they get close, and change the guide type to pixels or percentage. Guides appear in two colors, either purple for a pixel-based or teal for a percentage-based guide type. Though you see guides on the Stage during development, they are invisible when published.

Show and Hide Guides

1. Click the **View** menu, and then click **Guides**.

   A check mark appears next to the menu command to show the guides.

2. To hide the guide, click the **View** menu, and then click **Guides**.

   The check mark next to the menu command disappears to hide the guides.

   TIMESAVER *Press Ctrl+'
   (apostrophe) (Win) or ⌘+'
   (apostrophe) (Mac) to show
   or hide guides.*

See Also

See "Using Guides with Elements" on page 160 for more information on creating and working with guides.

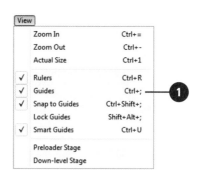

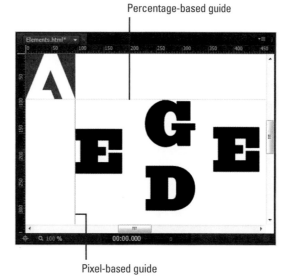

Percentage-based guide

Pixel-based guide

Using Guides with Elements

A guide is a line that aids in aligning elements on the Stage. Use guides to align elements along a vertical or horizontal path. You can add multiple guides to the Stage. Before you can add a guide, you need to display guides and rulers, which you use to create them. Guides are modifiable; you can show or hide them, lock them in place, have elements snap to them as they get close, and change the guide type to pixels or percentage. Guides appear in two colors, either purple for a pixel-based or teal for a percentage-based guide type. Though you see guides on the Stage during development, they are invisible when published.

Create and Work with Guides

1. Click the **View** menu, and then click **Rulers** to display rulers.

2. Click the **Selection Tool** on the Tools panel.

3. To create a vertical guide, click on the vertical ruler and drag to the right to place the guide.

4. To create a horizontal guide, click on the horizontal ruler and drag down to place the guide.

5. To move a guide, point to the guide (cursor changes to a double-line with arrows), and then drag to reposition it.

6. To remove a guide, point to the guide (cursor changes to a double-line with arrows), and then drag it off the Stage to the ruler.

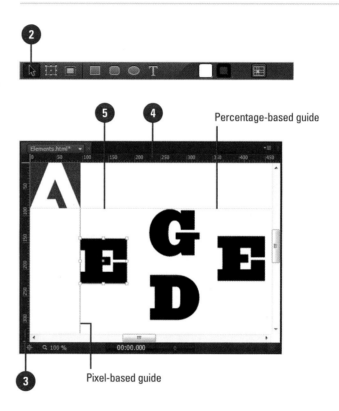

Percentage-based guide

Pixel-based guide

Did You Know?

You can lock or unlock guides on the Stage. Click the View menu, and then click Lock Guide to toggle on and off. You can also press Shift+Alt+; (Win) or Shift+Option+; (Mac).

See Also

See "Displaying Guides" on page 159 for information on viewing guides.

Snap Elements to Guides

1. Click the **View** menu, and then click **Guides** to display guides.

2. Click the **View** menu, and then click **Snap to Guide** to turn on (enable).

    TIMESAVER *Press Ctrl+Shift+; (Win) or* ⌘*+Shift+; (Mac) to turn Snap to Guide on or off.*

3. Click the **Selection Tool** on the Tools panel.

4. Drag an element close to a guide.

    As you drag close to the guide, the element snaps to the guide.

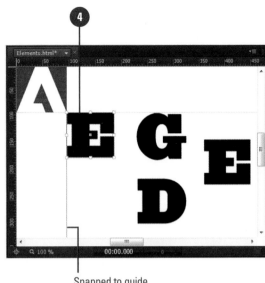

Snapped to guide

View Position and Change Type

1. Click the **View** menu, and then click **Guides** to display guides.

2. Point to the guide you want to view its position or change its type.

3. Right-click (Win) or Control-click (Mac) the guide.

    The position of the guides appears on the context menu. For example, "Vertical guide at 96px"

4. To convert the guide type to pixels or percentage, click **Convert Guide to Pixels** or **Convert Guide to Percentage**.

    Pixel-based guides appear in purple and percentage-based guides appear in teal.

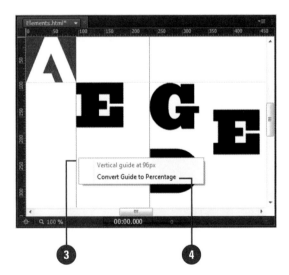

Aligning and Distributing Elements

Edge Animate provides two ways to align elements on the Stage. You can use Smart Guides or individual guides, or Align commands on the Modify menu. Smart Guides allow you to automatically display horizontal and vertical guides to help you move and align the edge or middle of selected element(s) with other elements on the Stage or to the center of the Stage. Smart Guides are automatically turned on by default. The Align commands, on the other hand, allow you to align two or more elements relative to each other vertically to the left, center, or right, or horizontally from the top, center, or bottom. To evenly space, or distribute, several elements relative to each other across the Stage, either horizontally or vertically, select them and then use Distribution commands on the Modify menu.

Align Elements with Smart Guides

1. Click the **Modify** menu, and then click **Smart Guides** to turn it on (displays a check mark).

2. Click the **Selection Tool** on the Tools panel.

3. Select one or more elements you want to move and align.

4. Drag the selected element(s).

   As you move the element(s), Smart Guides appear to help you align it to the edge or middle of other elements on the Stage or to the center of the Stage.

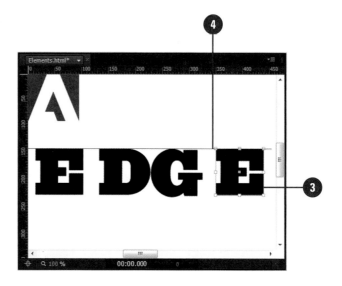

See Also

See "Using Smart Guides with Elements" on page 90 for more information on working with Smart Guides.

See "Using Guides with Elements" on page 160 for more information on creating and working with guides.

Align Elements to Each Other

1. Click the **Selection Tool** on the Tools panel.

2. Select one or more elements you want to align with other elements.

3. Click the **Modify** menu, point to **Align**, and then click an option:

   ◆ **Left.** Aligns all left edges to the left most element.

   ◆ **Horizontal Center.** Aligns all element centers to the horizontal center of the Stage.

   ◆ **Right.** Aligns all right edges to the right most element.

   ◆ **Top.** Aligns all top edges to the left top element.

   ◆ **Vertical Center.** Aligns all element centers to the vertical center of the Stage.

   ◆ **Bottom.** Aligns all bottom edges to the bottom most element.

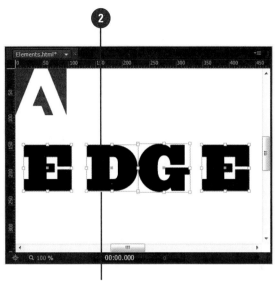

Align Vertical Center

Distribute Elements

1. Click the **Selection Tool** on the Tools panel.

2. Select two or more elements you want to evenly space.

3. Click the **Modify** menu, point to **Distribute**, and then click a distribution option: **Left**, **Horizontal Center**, **Right**, **Top**, **Vertical Center**, or **Bottom**.

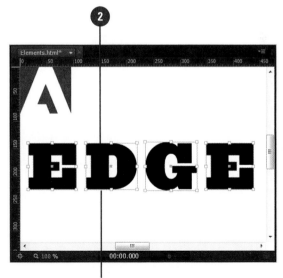

Distribute Vertical Center

Stacking Elements

As you create or import elements on the Stage, each one appears in a stacking order, like layers of transparencies. Stacking is the placement of elements one on top of another. In other words, the first element that you create or import is on the bottom and the last element that you create or import is on top. The stacking order of the elements on the Stage appears in the Elements panel. The first element in the list is at the top of the stacking order and the last element is at the bottom. You can change the stacking order of elements by dragging elements in the Elements panel or using Arrange commands—Bring to Front, Bring Forward, Send Backward, and Send to Back—on the Modify menu.

Arrange Elements in Stacking Order

1. Click the **Selection Tool** on the Tools panel.

2. Select one or more elements on the Stage or in the Elements panel you want to arrange.

3. Do any of the following:

   ◆ **Stage.** Click the **Modify** menu, point to **Arrange**, and then click a stacking option:

      ◆ **Bring to Front.** Brings the element to the top of the stacking list.

      ◆ **Bring Forward.** Brings the element up one level in the stacking list.

      ◆ **Send Backward.** Brings the element down one level in the stacking list.

      ◆ **Send to Back.** Brings the element to the bottom of the stacking list.

   TIMESAVER *Press Ctrl+Shift+], Ctrl+], Ctrl+[, or Ctrl+Shift+[(Win) or ⌘+Shift+], ⌘+], ⌘+[, or ⌘+Shift+[(Mac).*

   ◆ **Elements Panel.** Click a selected element name, and then drag it to the position you want (a thick black line appears to indicate the location).

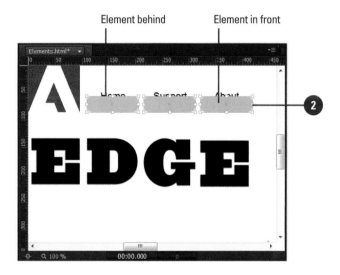

Element behind   Element in front

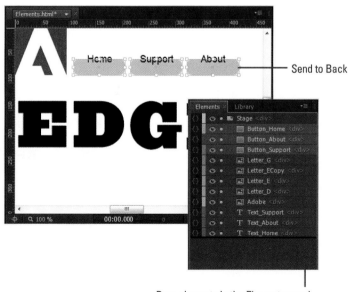

Send to Back

Drag elements in the Elements panel

Hiding and Showing Elements

When you have a lot of elements on the Stage, especially when you open an existing HTML document, it's hard to work with the ones you want without the other ones getting in the way. By temporarily hiding the elements that are in the way, it unclutters the Stage to allow you to focus on and work with the ones you want to change and animate. The Elements and Timeline panels include controls that you can click to quickly hide and show (toggle off and on) elements on the Stage. When you show or hide an element, an Eye icon (show) or grey dot (hide) appears in the Visibility column in the Elements and Timeline panels. When you save, close, and reopen your composition, any hidden elements remain hidden until you show them.

Hide and Show Elements

1 In the Elements or Timeline panel, do the following:

◆ **Hide.** Click the **Eye** icon (changes to the grey dot) in the Visibility column to hide the element.

◆ **Show.** Click the **grey dot** (changes to the Eye icon) in the Visibility column to show the element.

Hide element

Show element

Hidden button   Hidden text

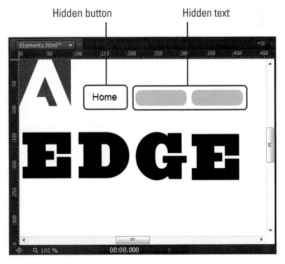

Grouping Elements

Grouping elements together allows you to work with multiple elements as a single unit. When you group elements together, they are stored as individual elements in the same container, known as a DIV. Grouping elements together is useful when you want to use or move them around as one element. Groups have properties like any other element. You can give groups ID names, adjust properties, such as opacity, size, and rotate, and apply triggers and actions to them. If you want to break up a group into individual elements, you can ungroup it.

Group and Ungroup Elements

1. Click the **Selection Tool** on the Tools panel.

2. Select one or more elements on the Stage or in the Elements panel you want to arrange.

3. Click the **Modify** menu, and then click **Group Elements in DIV**.

   TIMESAVER *Press Ctrl+G (Win) or ⌘+G to group elements.*

   In the Elements panel, a group is created, and then elements are indented below it.

4. To ungroup elements, select the grouped elements on the Stage or in the Elements panel you want to arrange, click the **Modify** menu, and then click **Ungroup Elements**.

   TIMESAVER *Press Ctrl+Shift+G (Win) or ⌘+Shift+G to ungroup elements.*

   In the Elements panel, a group is removed, and then elements are independent.

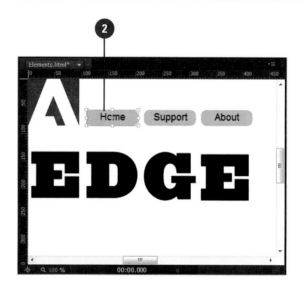

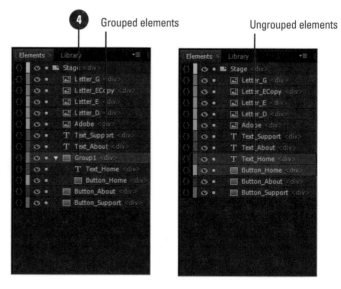

Grouped elements   Ungrouped elements

Reparenting Elements

In the Elements panel, you'll notice that the Stage is at the top of the list, and all the other elements in your composition are indented below it. The Stag is the parent and all the elements below it are the children. The children take on the properties of the parent, unless they are uniquely changed. In addition to the Stage parent/child relationship, you can also create your own parent/child relationships. You can create new relationships by moving (dragging) an element (becomes the child) on top of another element (becomes the parent) in the Elements or Timeline panel.

Reparent Elements

1. In the Elements panel, do the following:

   ◆ **Reparent.** Drag an element (child) on top of another element (parent). When the parent element highlights, release the mouse to complete the process.

   ◆ **Unparent.** Drag the child element outside the parent element (a thick black line appears to indicate the location).

Did You Know?

You can unparent elements with Ungroup. In the Elements or Timeline panel, select the parent element, click the Modify menu, and then click Ungroup.

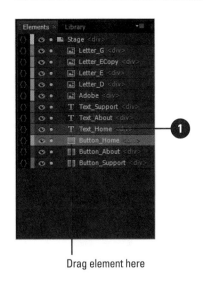

Drag element here

Parent

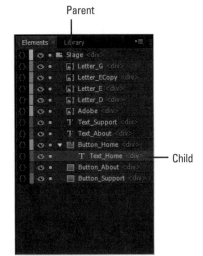

Child

Locking and Unlocking Elements

The Elements and Timeline panels include controls that you can click to quickly lock and unlock (toggle on and off) elements on the Stage. When you lock or unlock an element, a padlock (lock) or grey dot (unlock) appears in the Lock column in the Elements and Timeline panels. Locking an element in place is useful when you don't want it to move. For example, if you don't want a background image to move while you work on other elements, you can lock the background image in place. If you want to move or modify a locked element, you need to unlock it first.

Lock and Unlock Elements

1. In the Elements or Timeline panel, do the following:

   ◆ **Lock.** Click the **grey dot** (changes to the Lock icon) in the Lock column to lock the element.

   ◆ **Unlock.** Click the **Lock** icon (changes to the grey dot) in the Lock column to unlock the element.

Unlocked element

Locked element

Unlocked elements

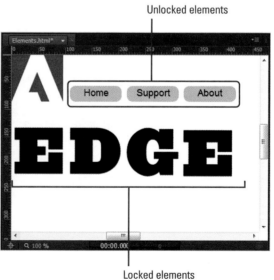

Locked elements

Renaming Elements

When you create an element in Edge Animate, the program automatically assigns a distinct name, such as Rectangle1, RoundRect3, or Ellipse2, or uses the file name from an import. To make it easier to identify and use in animations, you can rename element names in the Elements and Timeline panels. Renaming an element in Edge Animate is similar to editing a file name in your operating system.

Rename Elements

1. In the Elements or Timeline panel, double-click the element name.

   The existing element name is selected in an edit box.

2. Type to replace the existing name with a new one, or click to place the insertion point, and then edit the name.

3. Press Enter (Win) or Return (Mac).

See Also

See "Naming Element IDs or Classes" on page 94 for more information on naming an element.

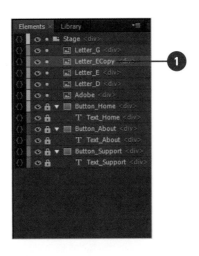

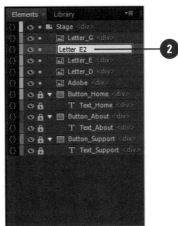

Creating Motion Animations

7

Introduction

Edge Animate is a property based animation system using keyframes to mark changes in properties. This means that keyframes mark the start and end points of an animation based on changes in element properties, such as location, size, color, border size, border style, border radius, rotation, skew, or scale. Keyframes appear as diamonds in the Timeline. The Timeline displays content in sequential order from 0:00 seconds to the end of the animation. As you play an animation, the playhead moves through the Timeline displaying the current content on the Stage.

There are three main ways to create animations in Edge Animate. The first is an automatic method with the pin, the second is an automatic method with keyframes, and the third is a manual method with keyframes. Each method creates an animation using keyframes. The Pin method provides the fastest way to create an animation, while the manual Keyframe method gives you the most control. You can pick the method that best works for you.

As you create an animation, you can develop the design to respond to changes in the screen size. This allows you to deliver your animation on different screens sizes on a variety of devices, such as desktops, laptops, tablets, and mobile devices. You can make the Stage and individual elements responsive to the screen size by changing their units from pixels (fixed) to percentage (adjustable). By using percentages, the design can respond to any size screen.

What You'll Do

Create an Animation with the Pin

Create an Animation with Auto Keyframes

Create an Animation with Keyframes

Create an Animation with a Transition

Play Animations

Make Adjustments to an Animation

Adjust Time in an Animation

Insert Time in an Animation

Make a Resizable Animation

Test a Resizable Animation

Creating an Animation with the Pin

With the Pin, you can minimize the amount of time it takes to a create an animation in Edge Animate. You create an animation by setting keyframes at specific times in the Timeline and changing property values between them. Keyframes appear as diamonds in the Timeline. Instead of creating individual keyframes one at a time, you can use the Pin to create *from* and *to* keyframes with a single edit. So, the Pin can be a time saver. To help make the process even easier, you can also use Auto Keyframe Mode, which automatically creates keyframes when a property is modified, and Auto Transition Mode, which automatically creates a transition as needed.

Create an Animation with the Pin

1. In the Timeline, drag the **Playhead** to the place where you want to start the animation.

2. Double-click the **Playhead** to display a blue pin on top.

   The Auto-Keyframe Mode, Auto-Transition Mode, and the Toggle Pin button are turned on in the Timeline.

3. Drag the **Pin** (blue) to the ending place of the animation.

   The Playhead remains in place while the Pin moves to display a blue region for the animation.

4. Select and position the elements where you want them to start (this can be on or off the Stage) and/or adjust the properties you want for the start in the Properties panel.

   This automatically adds keyframes for each property change.

5. Click the **Play** button or press Space to play back the animation.

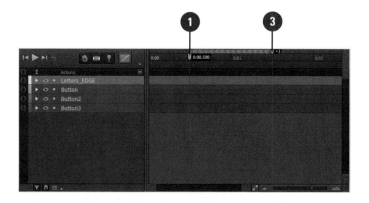

Project: Create an Animation with the Pin

① Open the *Pin_start.html* file in the chapter folder, and then save it in a new folder.

② In the Timeline, drag the **Playhead** to 0:00.500 (0.5 seconds).

③ Double-click the **Playhead** to display a blue pin on top.

The Auto-Keyframe Mode, Auto-Transition Mode, and the Toggle Pin button are turned on in the Timeline.

④ Drag the **Pin** (blue) to 0:01.500 (1.5 seconds).

The Playhead remains in place while the Pin moves to display a blue region for the animation.

⑤ Shift-drag the *Letters_EDGE* element off the Stage to the right.

This automatically adds keyframes for each property change.

⑥ Click the **Play** button or press Space to play back the animation.

The Edge letters animate in from the left.

Did You Know?

You can flip the position of the Playhead and the Pin. Click the Timeline menu, and then click Flip Playhead And Pin or press Shift+P.

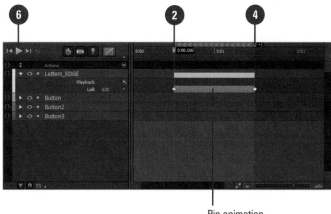

Pin animation

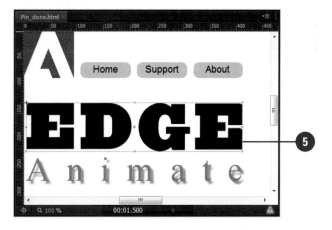

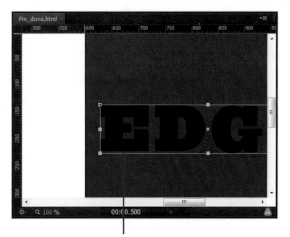

Letters_EDGE element off the Stage

Creating an Animation with Auto Keyframes

You create an animation by setting keyframes at specific times in the Timeline and changing property values between them. Keyframes mark the start and end points of an animation based on changes in element properties, such as location, size, color, border size, border style, border radius, rotation, skew, or scale. Keyframes appear as diamonds in the Timeline. You can set keyframes manually one at a time, or you can use Auto-Keyframe Mode, which automatically creates keyframes when a property is modified. It makes the process a little easier, however, it can also add keyframes for property changes you may not want. If this happens, you can delete the keyframes.

Create a Animation with Auto Keyframes

1. Click the **Auto-Keyframe Mode** button and the **Auto-Transition Mode** button to turn them on (highlighted), and then click the **Toggle Pin** button to turn it off (non-highlighted).

2. In the Timeline, drag the **Playhead** to the place where you want to start the animation.

3. Select and position the elements where you want them to start (this can be on or off the Stage) and/or adjust the properties you want for the start in the Properties panel.

   This automatically adds keyframes for each property change.

4. In the Timeline, drag the **Playhead** to the place where you want to end the animation.

5. Select and position the elements where you want them to end (this can be on or off the Stage) and/or adjust the properties you want for the end in the Properties panel.

   This automatically adds keyframes for each property change.

6. Click the **Play** button or press Space to play back the animation.

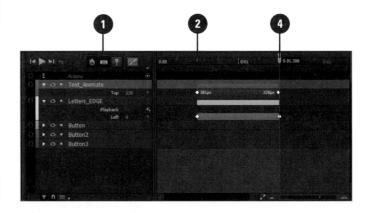

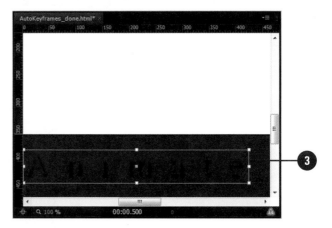

Project: Create an Animation with Auto Keyframes

1 Open the *Keyframes_start.html* file in the chapter folder, and then save it in a new folder.

2 Click the **Auto-Keyframe Mode** button and the **Auto-Transition Mode** button to turn them on (highlighted), and then click the **Toggle Pin** button to turn it off (non-highlighted).

3 In the Timeline, drag the **Playhead** to 0:00.500 (0.5 seconds).

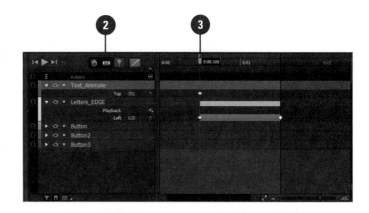

4 Shift-drag the *Text_Animate* element off the Stage to the bottom to Y = 381 px in the Properties panel.

This automatically adds keyframes for the property change.

5 In the Timeline, drag the **Playhead** to 0:01.500 (1.5 seconds).

6 Shift-drag the *Text_Animate* element on the Stage from the bottom to Y = 228 px in the Properties panel.

This automatically adds keyframes for the property change. Auto-Transition Mode adds a transition between the keyframes.

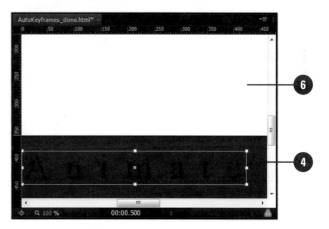

7 Click the **Play** button or press Space to play back the animation.

The Edge letters animate in from the left and the Animate text animates in from the bottom.

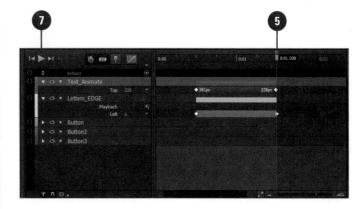

Creating an Animation with Keyframes

With the Add Keyframe diamonds in the Properties panel, you can manually add keyframes to the Timeline to create an animation. Manually adding keyframes is more time consuming, however, you have more control over the results. Keyframes mark the start and end points of an animation based on changes in element properties, such as location, size, color, border size, border style, border radius, rotation, skew, or scale. If a keyframe appears hollow (not filled in), it means that it has a different value than the previous keyframe. When a keyframe is hollow, it displays a jump between the keyframes instead of a transition.

Create a Manual Animation with Keyframes

1. Click the **Auto-Keyframe Mode** button and the **Toggle Pin** button to turn them off (non-highlighted), and then click the **Auto-Transition Mode** button to turn it on (highlighted).

2. In the Timeline, drag the **Playhead** to the place where you want to start the animation.

3. Select and position the elements where you want them to start (this can be on or off the Stage) and/or adjust the properties you want for the start in the Properties panel.

4. In the Properties panel, click the **Add Keyframe** diamond for the properties you want to animate.

5. In the Timeline, drag the **Playhead** to the place where you want to end the animation.

6. Select and position the elements where you want them to end (this can be on or off the Stage) and/or adjust the properties you want for the end in the Properties panel.

7. In the Properties panel, click the **Add Keyframe** diamond for the properties you want to animate.

8. Click the **Play** button or press Space to play back the animation.

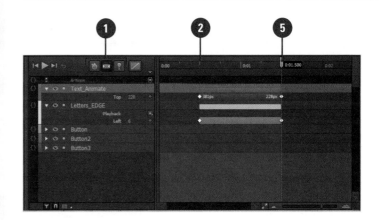

Keyframe diamond

Project: Create an Animation with Keyframes

1. Open the *Keyframes_start.html* file in the chapter folder, and then save it in a new folder.

2. Click the **Auto-Keyframe Mode** button and the **Toggle Pin** button to turn them off (non-highlighted), and then click the **Auto-Transition Mode** button to turn it on (highlighted).

3. In the Timeline, drag the **Playhead** to 0:00.500 (0.5 seconds).

4. Shift-drag the *Text_Animate* element off the Stage to the bottom. Set **Y** = 381 px in the Properties panel.

5. Click the **Add Keyframe** diamond next to Y (under Position and Size).

   This adds a keyframe for the element for the property change.

6. In the Timeline, drag the **Playhead** to 0:01.500 (1.50 seconds).

7. Shift-drag the *Text_Animate* element on the Stage. Set **Y** = 228 px in the Properties panel.

8. Click the **Add Keyframe** diamond next to Y (under Position and Size).

   This adds another keyframe for the element for the property change.

9. Click the **Play** button or press Space to play back the animation.

   The Edge letters animate in from the left and the Animate text animates in from the bottom.

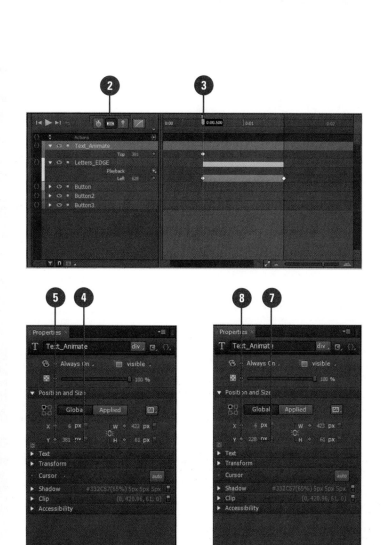

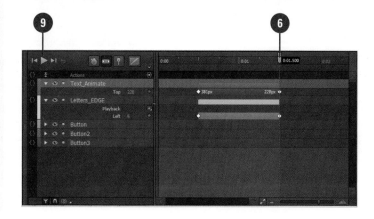

Creating an Animation with a Transition

When you create an animation with Auto-Transition Mode turned on (highlighted), Edge Animate applies a smooth transition between the keyframes. Edge Animate uses the current transition selected with the Easing button, which displays a graph of the transition path to provide a visual perspective. If you create an animation with Auto-Transition Mode turned off, no transition is applied between the keyframes. Instead, the animation displays a jump between the keyframes. Without a transition, one of the keyframes appears hollow (not filled in). When a keyframe is hollow, it means that it has a different value than the previous keyframe. In this situation, you can manually create a transition. After you apply and select a transition, you can copy and paste it to another location in the Timeline or invert it to display in the opposite direction. If you no longer want to use a transition, you can remove it at any time.

Create a Animation with a Transition

1. Click the **Auto-Transition Mode** button to turn it on (highlighted).

2. Click the **Easing** button, click a transition type (first column), and then click a transition (second column).

    The selected transition will be applied to any animation.

    TIMESAVER *Point to the Easing button to display a tooltip with the currently selected transition.*

3. Create an animation using the Pin or Auto-Keyframe Mode method.

    See topics earlier in this chapter for step-by-step instructions to create an animation.

4. Click the **Play** button or press Space to play back the animation.

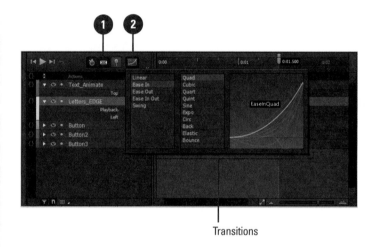

Transitions

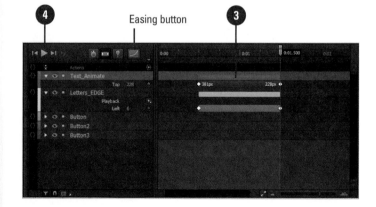

Easing button

Work with Transitions

◆ **Invert a Transition.** Select the animation layer in the Timeline, click the **Timeline** menu, and then click **Invert Transitions**.

◆ **Remove a Transition.** Select the animation layer in the Timeline, click the **Timeline** menu, and then click **Remove Transitions**.

   TIMESAVER *Press Shift+Del to remove a transition.*

◆ **Change a Transition.** Select the animation layer in the Timeline, click the **Easing** button, click a transition type (first column), and then click a transition (second column).

◆ **Copy and Paste a Transition.** Select the animation layer, press Ctrl+C (Win) or ⌃⌘+C (Mac), position the Playhead, click the **Edit** menu, point to **Paste Special**, and then click **Paste Transitions To Location** or **Paste Transitions From Location**.

   TIMESAVER *Press Ctrl+Shift+V (Win) or ⌃⌘+Shift+V (Mac) to paste transitions from location.*

◆ **Create a Transition (Manually).** Select the two keyframes without a transition in between. One of the keyframes should be hollow. Click the **Timeline** menu, and then click **Create Transitions**.

   TIMESAVER *Press Ctrl+Shift+T (Win) or ⌃⌘+Shift+T (Mac) to create a transition manually.*

Selected animation layer

Easing button

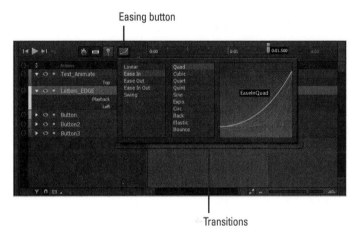

Transitions

Transition commands

Playing Animations

The order in which content appears in the Timeline determines the order in which it appears in the animation. The Timeline displays content in sequential order from 0:00 seconds to the end of the animation. A Playhead appears in the header (with the timecode) with a red line going down the Timeline to indicate the current position in the animation. As you play an animation, the Playhead moves through the Timeline displaying the current content on the Stage. If you want to display specific content on the Stage or review the animation, you can move (drag) the Playhead, known as scrubbing, across the Timeline to a specific position or through a section to display it. Playhead and Timeline commands are available on the Timeline panel and Timeline menu as well as with keyboard shortcuts.

Work with the Playhead

◆ **Play Animation.** Click the **Play/Pause** button or press Space to play or pause the animation.

◆ **Move Playhead.** Do any of the following:

  ◆ **Move Playhead to Start.** Click the **Rewind** button (left of Play/Pause) or press Home.

  ◆ **Move Playhead to End.** Click the **Forward** button (right of Play/Pause) or press End.

  ◆ **Move Playhead to Last Play Position.** Click the **Return** button (right of Forward) or press Enter (Win) or Return (Mac).

  ◆ **Move Playhead to Exact Time.** Click and enter a time value or point to the time value and drag.

  ◆ **Move/Scrub Playhead.** Drag the **Playhead**.

  ◆ **Move/Scrub Playhead without Snapping.** Ctrl (Win) or ⌘ (Mac)+drag the **Playhead**.

  ◆ **Go to Previous Keyframe.** Press Ctrl+Left Arrow (Win) or ⌘+Left Arrow (Mac).

  ◆ **Go to Next Keyframe.** Press Ctrl+Right Arrow (Win) or ⌘+Right Arrow (Mac).

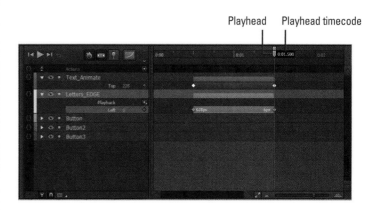

Playhead   Playhead timecode

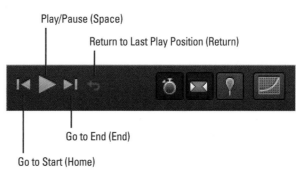

Play/Pause (Space)

Return to Last Play Position (Return)

Go to End (End)

Go to Start (Home)

Use the Timeline Panel

- **Show or Hide the Timeline Panel.** Click the **Window** menu, and then click **Timeline** to select (show) or deselect (hide) the check mark.

- **Zoom In or Out the Timecode.** Drag the slider to the right to zoom in and to the left to zoom out.

  TIMESAVER Press = (equal) to Zoom In. Press - (minus) to Zoom Out.

- **Zoom Timeline to Fit.** Click the **Zoom Timeline to Fit** button to display the animation to fit in the Timeline view.

  TIMESAVER Press \ (back slash) to Zoom to Fit.

- **Show the Grid.** Click the **Show Grid** button to toggle on or off.

- **Change the Grid Size.** Click the **Grid Size** button, and then select a grid size.

- **Filter Animated Elements.** Click the **Only Show Animated Elements** button to toggle on (highlighted) and off (non-highlighted). When turned on, only animated elements show in the Timeline, which helps reduce the Timeline clutter.

  When the light bar is grey, the element is not animated; when it's a color, the element is animated using keyframes.

- **Timeline Snapping.** Click the **Timeline Snapping** button to toggle on (highlighted) and off (non-highlighted). You can set **Snap To** options on the Timeline menu. When turned on, Timeline items snap to the **Grid**, **Playhead**, or **Keyframes, Labels, Triggers**.

  TIMESAVER Press Alt+; (Win) or Option+; (Mac) to toggle on or off timeline snapping.

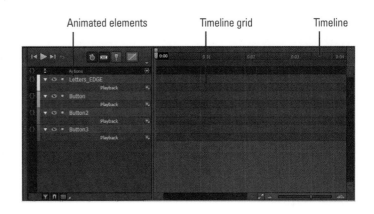

Animated elements   Timeline grid   Timeline

Zoom Timeline to Fit button   Zoom Timeline In

Zoom Timeline Out   Zoom slider

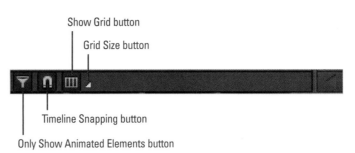

Show Grid button

Grid Size button

Timeline Snapping button

Only Show Animated Elements button

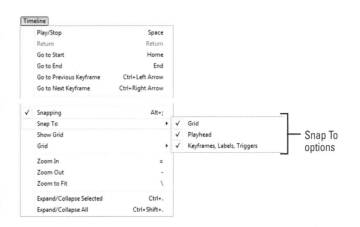

Making Adjustments to Animations

Elements along with their properties appear on the left side of the Timeline while layers (denoted as bars) along with their keyframes (denoted as diamonds) appear on the right. A keyframe defines a point in time where an element property changes in an animation. A layer defines the animation between the keyframes. After you create an animation in the Timeline, you can adjust one or more keyframes or the layer to achieve the result that you want. You can click to select a keyframe (turns orange) or use the Shift key or drag to select multiple keyframes. Once you select a keyframe, you can drag it to adjust the length of an animation or delete it. You can also click to select a layer to change its position, adjust its length, copy and paste it, or delete it.

Work with Keyframes in the Timeline Panel

◆ **Select a Keyframe.** Click a keyframe diamond (turns orange) in the Timeline.

◆ **Select Multiple Keyframes.** Press and hold the Shift key, and then click individual keyframe diamonds (turns orange) in the Timeline.

◆ **Select Keyframes in a Layer.** Click the bar in the property row of an element. The layer and its keyframes are selected.

◆ **Deselect Keyframes.** Click a blank area in the Timeline.

◆ **Adjust the Length of a Keyframe.** Select the keyframe, and then drag it to adjust the length.

◆ **Delete Keyframes.** Select the keyframes you want to remove, and then press Delete.

◆ **Go to Previous Keyframe.** Click the **Timeline** menu, and then click **Go to Previous Keyframe**, or press Ctrl+Left Arrow (Win) or ⌘+Left Arrow (Mac).

◆ **Go to Next Keyframe.** Click the **Timeline** menu, and then click **Go to Next Keyframe**, or press Ctrl+Right Arrow (Win) or ⌘+Right Arrow (Mac).

Not selected keyframes   Selected keyframes

Selected keyframes in a layer

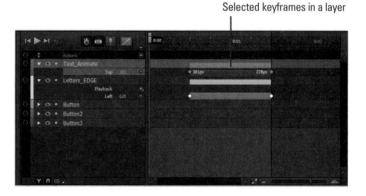

Work with Animations in the Timeline Panel

- ◆ **Select an Animation Layer.** Click the bar in the name row of an element. All layers for the element are selected.

- ◆ **Select an Animation Property Layer.** Click the bar in the property row of an element. The layer and its keyframes are selected.

- ◆ **Move an Animation Layer.** Point to the bar in the name row of an element, and then drag it. All layers for the element are moved.

- ◆ **Move an Animation Property Layer.** Point to the bar in the property row of an element, and then drag it. Only the property layer for the element is moved.

- ◆ **Adjust the Length of an Animation Layer.** Select the animation layer, point to the edge (cursor changes to a double-arrow), and then drag.

- ◆ **Delete an Animation Layer.** Select the animation layer you want to remove, and then press Delete.

- ◆ **Copy and Paste an Animation Layer.** Select the animation layer, press Ctrl+C (Win) or ⌘+C (Mac), position the Playhead, click the **Edit** menu, point to **Paste Special**, and then click **Paste All**.

- ◆ **Copy and Paste Inverted an Animation Layer.** Select the animation layer, press Ctrl+C (Win) or ⌘+C (Mac), position the Playhead, click the **Edit** menu, point to **Paste Special**, and then click **Paste Inverted**.

Drag to adjust the length

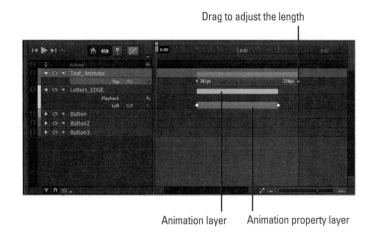

Animation layer   Animation property layer

Drag to move

Adjusting Time in an Animation

If you want an animation to last longer, all you need to do is extend the animation layer in the Timeline to the amount of time you want it to last. The more you extend an animation layer in the Timeline, the more time is added to it. To adjust one or more animation layers, select the layers, and then drag an edge keyframe. As you drag a keyframe, the animation displays on the Stage with the adjustment. You can also change the starting position of an animation by moving the animation layer to a different position. To move one or more animation layers, select the layers, and then drag them.

Adjust Time in an Animation

1 In the Timeline, click the bar in the name row of an element to select the animation layer you want to change. All layers for the element are selected.

2 To extend the animation time, drag an edge keyframe to the position you want.

3 To move an animation, point to the bar in the name row of an element, and then drag it. All layers for the element are moved.

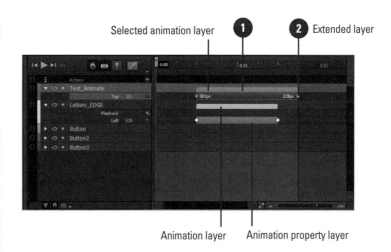

Selected animation layer **1**   **2** Extended layer

Animation layer   Animation property layer

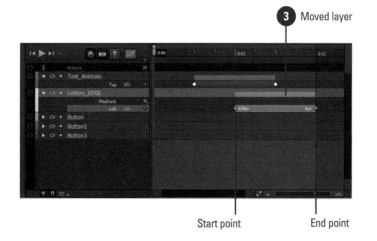

3 Moved layer

Start point   End point

Inserting Time in an Animation

Sometimes you want an animation to last longer. When this is the case, you can insert time to extend it. Instead of adjusting each individual animation layer, you can extend them all with the Insert Time command on the Timeline menu. In the Insert Time dialog box, you can specify the amount of time you want to insert from the Playhead position. You can enter a time or scrub to adjust it.

Insert Time in an Animation

1 In the Timeline, drag the **Playhead** to the place where you want to insert a specific amount of time.

2 Click the **Timeline** menu, and then click **Insert Time**.

3 Click the time, enter a time, and then press Enter (Win) or Return (Mac), or drag the scrub to the time to adjust it.

4 Click **Insert Time**.

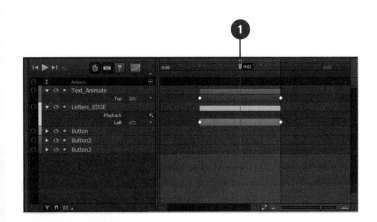

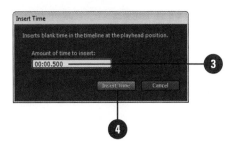

Making a Resizable Animation

As you create an animation, you can develop the design to automatically respond (resize) to changes in the screen size. This allows you to deliver your animation on different screen sizes on a variety of devices, such as desktops, laptops, tablets, and mobile devices. You can make the Stage and individual elements responsive to the screen size by changing their units from pixels (fixed) to percentage (adjustable). By using percentages, the design can respond to any size screen. For individual elements, you can also modify the relative change position to any corner, either relative to the Stage (Global) or to its parent (Applied), for better control over where elements display. By default, elements are positions relative to the upper-left corner of their parent. You can change the relative position to any corner in the Properties panel. Instead of changing individual values to make an element adjustable, you can apply a layout preset.

Set the Stage for Adjustability

① In the Elements panel, select the **Stage <div>** element.

② In the Properties panel, point to the units for **W** and/or **H** , and then drag the slider from pixels (px) to percentage (%).

The percentage is set 100%. This allows the Stage to adjust to screen size changes. The Stage fills the width of the browser with its background to the right of the animation.

③ To set a minimum and maximum width, do any of the following:

◆ **Min W.** Point to the units for **Min W**, and then drag the slider from pixels (px) to percentage (%).

◆ **Max W.** Click **Max W** label, and then click **None** to deselect it. Point to the units for **Max W**, and then drag the slider from pixels (px) to percentage (%).

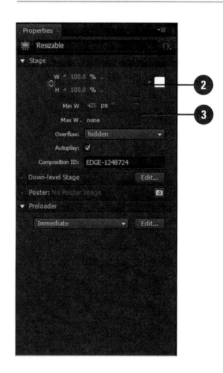

Set Elements for Adjustability

1 Click the **Selection Tool** on the Tools panel.

2 Select the element you want to change.

3 To use preset options, click the **Layout Preset** button, select a preset and view its settings, and then click **Apply**.

- ◆ **Scale Position (X and Y).** Sets the X and Y position to %.

- ◆ **Scale Size (W and H).** Sets the W and H position to %.

- ◆ **Scale Background Image.** Sets the W and H position to %, image position to %, background width to %, and background height to auto.

- ◆ **Center Background Image.** Sets the W and H position to %, background position to 50%, and background size to pixels.

- ◆ **Clip Background Image.** Sets the W and H position to %, background position to 0%, and background size to pixels.

- ◆ **Static Background Image.** Sets the W and H position to pixels, background position to pixels, and background size to pixels.

4 To set individual adjustable options, point to units for the position (**X** and **Y**) and size (**W** and **H**), and then drag the slider from px (pixels) to % (percentage).

5 To set the relative position (upper-left, upper-right, lower-left or lower-right) of the element on the screen, click the corner square in the Coordinate Space Picker, and then click **Global** or **Applied**.

Global calculates the position relative to the Stage, while Applied calculates it relative to its parent.

Layout Preset options

Apply Layout Preset

Continue from Previous Page

Project: Make a Resizable Animation

① Open the *Resizable_start.html* file in the chapter folder, and then save it in a new folder.

② Click the **File** menu, and then click **Preview In Browser** or press Ctrl+Enter (Win) or ⌘+Return (Mac).

③ Resize the browser window to see how it responds, and then click the **Close** button to exit.

The animation doesn't respond to changes in the windows size.

④ In the Elements panel, select the **Stage <div>** element.

⑤ In the Properties panel, point to the units for **W** and **H**, and then drag the slider from pixels (px) to percentage (%).

⑥ Click the **File** menu, and then click **Preview In Browser** or press Ctrl+Enter (Win) or ⌘+Return (Mac).

⑦ Resize the browser window to see how it responds, and then click the **Close** button to exit.

The Stage fills the width of the browser with its background to the right of the animation.

⑧ In the Elements panel, select the **Text_Animate <div>** element.

⑨ In the Properties panel, click the **Layout Presets** button, click the **Scale Position** preset, and then click **Apply**.

⑩ In the Properties panel, select the **Bottom Right** square in the Coordinate Space Picker.

Continue Next Page

11 Move the Stage adjustment handle on the top ruler back and forth to preview, and then return it to its original position at 600 px.

This makes the element resize on both X and Y axis while keeping it relative to the bottom right.

12 In the Elements panel, select the **Letters_EDGE <div>** element.

13 In the Properties panel, point to the units for **X** and **Y** separately, and then change from pixels (px) to percentage (%).

14 In the Properties panel, select the **Bottom Left** square in the Coordinate Space Picker.

15 Move the Stage adjustment handle on the top ruler back and forth to preview, and then return it to its original position at 600 px.

This makes the element resize on both X and Y axis while keeping it relative to the bottom left.

16 In the Properties panel, set the **Min W** value to 600 px.

17 Click **Max W**, deselect **None**, and then set the **Max W** value to 1280 px.

18 In the Properties panel, point to the units for **H**, and then drag the slider from percentage (%) to pixels (px).

This keeps the width size range between 600 px and 1280 px, and the height to 350 px.

19 Click the **File** menu, and then click **Preview In Browser** or press Ctrl+Enter (Win) or ⌘+Return (Mac).

20 Resize the browser window to see how it responds, and then click the **Close** button to exit.

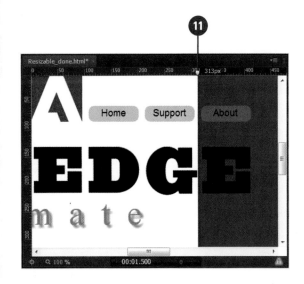

Testing a Resizable Animation

After you create a resizable animation in Edge Animation, you can test the layout by previewing screen size changes in a browser or on the Stage. When you set the Stage width and height units property to percentage (relative position) to create a responsive design, an adjustable pin and nonadjustable marker appear on the right (width) or bottom (height) Stage edge of the ruler, where you can reposition the pin to preview how the design layout responds to Stage size changes. The marker (small down arrow) remains in place to indicate the original width and height. To test your design in a browser, you use the Preview In Browser command, where you can resize the browser window to see how your design responds.

Test a Resizable Animation on the Stage

1. Open the composition with the resizable animation you want to test; display the ruler, if needed, Ctrl+R (Win) or ⌘+R (Mac).

2. To preview the results on the Stage, move the Stage adjustment handle (pin) on a ruler back and forth.

    The elements on the Stage respond to the size change based on the attributes set to percentage (%).

3. Move the Stage adjustment handle (pin) back to its original position marker.

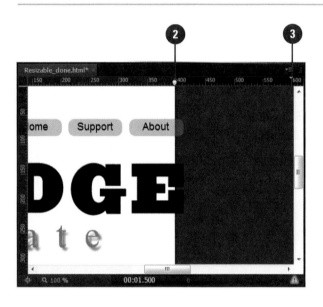

Did You Know?

You can drag an adjustment handle for the width or height. When you change the Stage width or height to %, you can drag the adjustment handle on the horizontal or vertical ruler.

See Also

See "Making a Resizable Animation" on page 186 for more information on creating a resizable animation.

Test a Resizable Animation in a Web Browser

1. Open the composition with the resizable animation you want to test.

2. Click the **File** menu, and then click **Preview In Browser** or press Ctrl+Enter (Win) or ⌘+Return (Mac).

3. Resize the browser window to see how it responds.

   The Stage fills the width of the browser with its background to the right of the animation.

4. Click the **Close** button to exit your web browser.

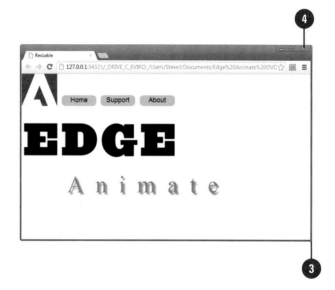

Creating Interactive Animations

8

Introduction

JavaScript is a scripting language that adds functionality to a web page. Many elements that you find on a web page, such as menus, are created with JavaScript code. Since JavaScript is so common in web page development, Edge Animate uses JavaScript as part of the structure behind a composition. When you save a composition, Edge Animate creates and includes JavaScript files (denoted by a .js extension) in the project folder.

Within Edge Animate, you can use JavaScript as a way to add interactivity and animation effects to a composition. If you're not very comfortable working with JavaScript code, you can use code snippets to help get started. A code snippet is a predefined segment of JavaScript code. In Edge Animate, you can insert and work with code snippets in any of the script panels, either Trigger, Open Actions, or Code.

You can create interactivity in a composition by adding actions to elements or triggers to the Timeline. An action or trigger enables you to invoke a script with JavaScript code to perform a function. The script is invoked when a certain "event" occurs, such as the click of the mouse or the position of the Playhead. For example, you can attach the Click event action script to a button that runs whenever the user clicks the button.

Inserting Labels

Creating a label in the Timeline allows to reference a specific timeline location in a script. For example, you can label the beginning of an animation "start," and then create an action to send the animation back to the label (which is the start in this case) when it's done, thus creating a loop. After you create a label, you can move it to another place in the Timeline, and not have to make any changes to the script. You can also quickly rename a label, and if you no longer need it, you can delete it too.

Insert a Label

1. Position the playhead where you want to insert a label.

2. Click the **Insert Label** button in the Timeline or click the **Timeline** menu, and then click **Insert Label**.

   TIMESAVER Press ⌃⌘+L (Mac).

3. Type the label text you want, and then press Enter (Win) or Return (Mac).

   An arrow and black line going down the Timeline appear to the left of the label name.

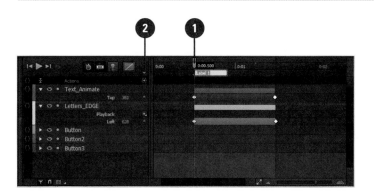

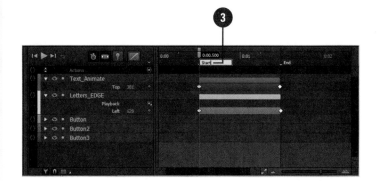

Did You Know?

You can use a label to create a loop. A loop allows you to repeat all or part of an animation. Create a start label at the Playhead start of the loop. Create a trigger at the Playhead location where you want to loop (jump) back, and then use the script .sym.play(start);

Work with Labels in the Timeline Panel

◆ **Select a Label.** Click the label to highlight and select it.

◆ **Delete a Label.** Click the label, and then press Delete.

◆ **Rename a Label.** Double-click the label, type label text, and then press Enter (Win) or Return (Mac).

◆ **Move a Label.** Point to the label (cursor changes to a hand), and then drag it.

Select a label

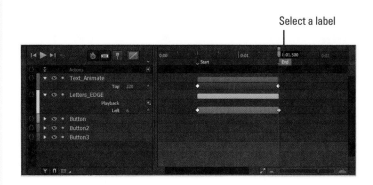

Rename a label

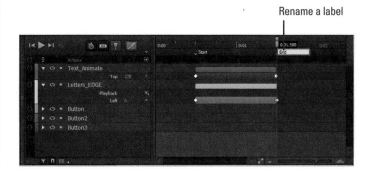

Move a label

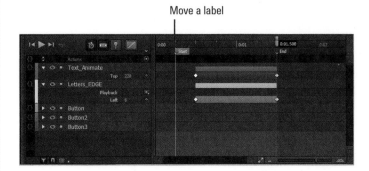

Inserting and Editing Triggers

A trigger enables you to invoke a script to perform a function. The script is invoked when a certain "trigger" occurs. You attach a trigger to the Timeline. When the Playhead reaches the trigger, the script executes the code. You can enter in your own JavaScript code or insert predefined snippet code. For example, you can attach a trigger in the Timeline with the Stop snippet code. When the Playhead reaches the trigger, it stops the Playhead in the Timeline. A trigger appears on the Timeline under Actions (at the top) as a keyframe diamond between brackets. You can drag a trigger in the Timeline to change its position. If you want to use the same trigger in another place, you can copy and paste it. If you no longer need a trigger, you can delete it.

Insert a Trigger

1. In the Timeline, drag the **Playhead** to the place where you want to insert a trigger.

2. Click the **Insert Trigger** button in the Timeline or click the **Timeline** menu, and then click **Insert Trigger**.

    TIMESAVER *Press Ctrl+T (Win) or ⌘+T (Mac).*

    A script panel appears for the trigger with a code editor and snippet buttons.

3. Click to place the insertion point where you want to insert code.

4. Type in your own code or click a snippet button to insert predefined snippet code.

5. For a code snippet, select the red code (placeholder), and then replace it with your own.

6. Click the **Close** button to exit the script panel.

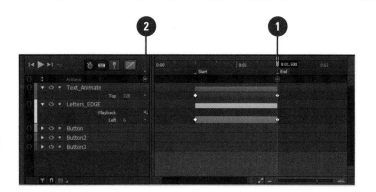

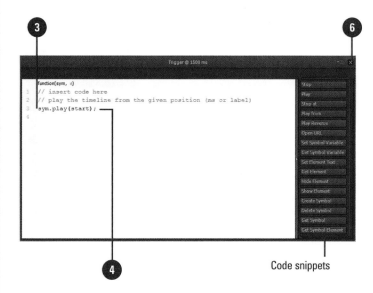

Code snippets

Work with Triggers in the Timeline Panel

◆ **Edit a Trigger.** Double-click a trigger in the Timeline to open the script panel. Edit the script code. When you're done, click the **Close** button.

◆ **Select a Trigger.** Click the trigger in the Timeline to select it. The keyframe diamond turns orange.

◆ **Move a Trigger.** Point to the trigger under Actions in the Timeline (cursor changes to a hand), and then drag it.

◆ **Delete a Trigger.** Click the trigger in the Timeline to select it, and then press Delete.

◆ **Copy and Paste a Trigger.** Click the trigger in the Timeline to select it, click the **Edit** menu, click **Copy**, position the **Playhead** where you want, click the **Edit** menu, and then click **Paste**.

Select a trigger

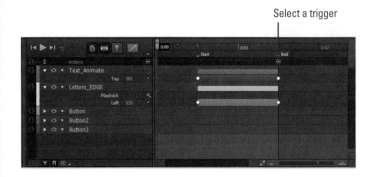

Move a trigger

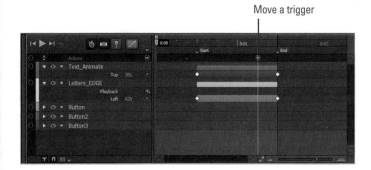

Did You Know?

You can change the code font size in a script panel. In a script panel, click the Options button, point to Font Size, and then click Small, Medium, or Large to select (show) the check mark.

You can show or hide code line numbers in a script panel. In a script panel, click the Options button, and then click Show Line Numbers to select (show) the check mark.

You can include or not include snippet comments in a script panel. In a script panel, click the Options button, and then click Include Snippet Comments to select (show) the check mark.

Inserting and Editing Action Events

An action enables you to invoke a script to perform a function. The script is invoked when a certain "event" occurs, such as the click of the mouse. You can attach an action script to an element (including the Stage and Timeline) that responds when a specific event occurs. For example, you can attach the Click event action script to a button that runs whenever the user clicks the button. You can attach a script to an element by using the Actions panel by using an Open Actions button (appears with brackets) for an element in the Elements, Properties, or Timeline panels. You can enter in your own JavaScript code or insert predefined snippet code. When an element contains an action event, it appears with a square between the brackets. You can attach multiple actions to the same element.

Insert an Action

1. In the Elements, Properties (with a selected element), or Timeline panel, click the **Open Actions** button for an element.

   A script panel appears with a code editor and snippet buttons. For a new action, a menu appears.

2. To add another action, click the **Add** button (+).

3. Click an event action on the menu.

   An event action tab appears where you can enter code to respond to the action.

4. Click to place the insertion point where you want to insert code.

5. Type in your own code or click a snippet button to insert predefined snippet code.

6. For a code snippet, select the red code (placeholder), and then replace it with your own.

7. Click the **Close** button to exit the script panel.

> ### See Also
> See "Listing of Action Events" on page 200 for a list of available action events.

Element with an action

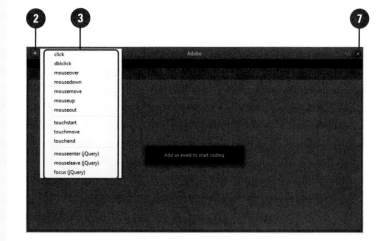

Edit an Action

1. In the Elements, Properties (with a selected element), or Timeline panel, click the **Open Actions** button for the element (a square appears between the brackets).

2. Click an action tab.

3. Click to place the insertion point where you want to insert code.

4. Edit the code or click a snippet button to insert predefined snippet code.

5. For a code snippet, select the red code (placeholder), and then replace it with your own.

6. Click the **Close** button to exit the script panel.

Delete an Action

1. In the Elements, Properties (with a selected element), or Timeline panel, click the **Open Actions** button for the element (a square appears between the brackets).

2. Click an action tab for the action you want to delete (if more than one).

3. Click the **Delete** button (-).

4. Click the **Close** button to exit the script panel.

Listing of Action Events

An action enables you to invoke a script to perform a function that responds when a specific event occurs. You can attach an action script to an element (including the Stage and Timeline) that responds when a specific event occurs. For example, you can attach the Click event action script to a button that runs whenever the user clicks the button.

There are a variety of different action events available in Edge Animate. The most common ones are probably click or mouseover, for a computer, however, you can also use events—such as touchstart,

touchend, or orientationchange—for a touch-based tablet or mobile device.

In addition to attaching events to an element, such as a shape or graphic, you can also attach an event to the Stage or Timeline. For example, you can attach a keyboard event, such as keydown, to the Stage. When you press a specified key on the keyboard, an event can take place. If you need to load one or more time consuming graphics, you can use the compositionReady event to start an animation when the composition is fully loaded.

Element Action Events

Event	Executes when the user ...
Element	
click	clicks an element.
dblclick	double-clicks an element.
mouseover	points to (hover over) an element.
mousedown	clicks down on an element without needing to release the mouse on it.
mousemove	moves the pointer over an element.
mouseup	releases a click on an element (don't need to click on the element).
mouseout	moves the pointer off an element.
touchstart	touches an element (for touch devices only).
touchmove	drags an element (for touch devices only).
touchend	stops touching an element (for touch devices only).
mouseenter (jQuery) *	enters an element with the pointer.
mouseleave (jQuery) *	leaves an element with the pointer.
focus (jQuery) *	gains focus for an element.

* jQuery is a JavaScript library that provides functionality to Edge Animate and web browsers.

Stage and Timeline Action Events

Event	Executes when ...
Stage **	
creationComplete	the symbol is created.
beforeDeletion	before a symbol is deleted.
compositionReady	the composition is fully loaded.
scroll	the page scrolls.
keydown	the user presses down a specified key down.
keyup	the user releases a specified key down.
orientationchange	the orientation of the screen changes.
resize	the Stage resizes.
onError	a JavaScript error occurs.
Stage for a Symbol	
creationComplete	the symbol is created.
beforeDeletion	before a symbol is deleted.
Main Timeline	
update	the Playhead reaches every tick on the Timeline.
play	the Timeline plays.
complete	the Timeline completes.
stop	the Timeline stops.

** The Stage also includes all the events for elements.

Inserting Code Snippets

A code snippet is a predefined segment of JavaScript code. In Edge Animate, you can insert and work with code snippets in any of the script panels, either Trigger, Open Actions, or Code. You can open the Trigger panel when you insert or edit a trigger in the Timeline. You can open the Open Actions panel when you create or edit an action for an element. And finally, you can open the Code panel from the Windows menu. In the Code panel, you may need to use the Toggle Display of Code Snippets button to show the snippet. You can insert JavaScript code by clicking a snippet button. You can insert as many code snippets as you want into the script. After you insert a code snippet, you can edit it. Code in red is placeholder text that you can modify to suit your own needs.

Insert a Code Snippet

1. Open a script panel, either Trigger, Open Actions, or Code.

   ◆ **Trigger Panel.** Position the **Playhead** in the Timeline, and then click the **Insert Trigger** button, or double-click an existing trigger in the Timeline.

   ◆ **Open Actions Panel.** Click an **Open Actions** button in the Timeline, Elements or Properties panel. For a new action, click an event on the menu.

   ◆ **Code Panel.** Click the **Window** menu, click **Code**, and then click the **Toggle Display of Code Snippets** button to show the snippet buttons.

2. To include or not include snippet comments, click the **Options** button, and then click **Include Snippet Comments**.

3. Click to place the insertion point where you want to insert the snippet code.

4. Click the snippet button with the code you want to insert.

5. Select the red code (placeholder), and then replace it with your own.

6. Click the **Close** button to exit the script panel.

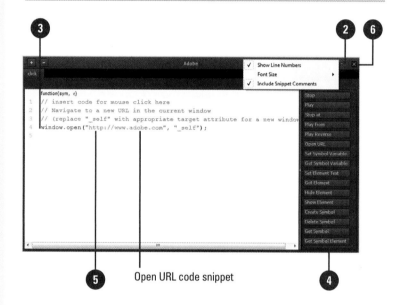

Open URL code snippet

Listing of Code Snippets

A code snippet is a predefined segment of JavaScript code. You can access code snippets in a script panel, either Trigger, Open Actions, or Code. You can access the Trigger panel when you insert or edit a trigger; click the Insert Trigger button or double-click an existing trigger. You can access the Open Actions panel when you create or edit an action for an element; click an Open Actions button in the Timeline, Elements, or Properties panel. You can access the Code panel from the Windows menu; click the Window menu, and then click Code. In the Code panel, click the Toggle Display of Code Snippets button to show or hide it. You can insert code by clicking a snippet button. For example, the Open URL snippet button inserts the following code:

window.open("http://www.adobe.com","_self");

After you insert a code snippet, you can edit it. Code in red is placeholder text that you can modify to suit your own needs.

Code Snippets	
Snippet	**Description**
Stop	Stops the Timeline.
Play	Plays the Timeline.
Stop at	Stops the Timeline at a specified in time (milliseconds) or label.
Play from	Plays the Timeline from a specified in time (milliseconds) or label.
Play Reverse	Plays the Timeline in reverse.
Open URL	Opens the specified web address location.
Set Symbol Variable	Sets the value of a symbol variable.
Get Symbol Variable	Gets the value of a symbol variable.
Set Element Text	Changes an element's contents.
Get Element	Gets an element by name.
Hide Element	Hides an element.
Show Element	Shows a hidden element.
Create Symbol	Creates an instance element of a symbol as a child of the given parent element.
Delete Symbol	Deletes an instance element of a symbol.
Get Symbol	Get an instance element of a symbol for use in a function.
Get Symbol Element	Gets the jQuery handle for an element.

Working with JavaScript Code

JavaScript code is made up of individual statements. Each statement follows a basic syntax, which is the grammar of a programming language. For example, when you insert the Play code snippet, the following statement is inserted into a script panel:

sym.play(0);

When you insert the Show Element code snippet, the following statement is inserted into a script panel:

sym.$("Text1").show();

The word sym stands for symbol and represents the element (including the Stage and Timeline). The **dot** (.) is a separator between elements, functions, and attributes. The **dollar sign** ($) is the jQuery selector that looks up the element in the parenthesis (in this case, Text1) by name (ID). The word play or show represent the function command, and the value or variable in the parenthesis represents attributes for the command. The statement ends with a **semicolon** (;). If a statement becomes too long to fit on a line, you can add a **backward slash** (\) to continue the statement on the next line.

JavaScript is **case sensitive**, which means that capitalization matters when you write code. For example, the following names are different: "addvideo," "Addvideo," or "AddVideo." JavaScript **ignores whitespace**, including spaces, tabs, and new lines. This allows you to add whitespace to your code in order to make it easier to read. JavaScript includes reserved word or keywords that have special meaning and functionality to the programming language. For example, JavaScript uses the following common reserve words: var, function, new, if, else, and while. You can't use these in your code.

Working with Comments

When you insert a snippet, the code also includes a comment at the top by default. A comment appears after **two forward slashes** (//). A comment can start anywhere on the line, like after a statement. When you want to make a comment block (multiple lines), JavaScript uses /* at the beginning and */ a the end. Comments are ignored by JavaScript. If you don't want a snippet to include comments, you can set an option to do so. In a script panel, click the Options button, and then click Include Snippet Comments to deselect (hide) the check mark.

Working with Variables

When you insert some snippets—such as Get Element, Create Symbol, Get Symbol, Get Symbol Variable or Get Symbol Element—the JavaScript code includes a variable. A variable is a container for storing information. A **variable** can hold data, such as a number or text, known as a **string**. A string appears inside quotes, either single or double. You declare a variable in JavaScript with the var keyword. Variable names must begin with a letter, $, or _ (no numbers). The characters that follow can only be letters, $, _, or numbers. After you specify a variable name, you can assign it a value. To assign a value to a variable, you use an equal sign followed by a value or element.

For example, when you insert the Get Element code snippet, the following statement is inserted into a script panel:

var element = sym.$("Text1");

The word var stands for variable. The word element is the variable name, which you can change. The equal sign makes the assignment. The assignment value is sym.$("Text1"), which is the contents of the Text1 element.

After declaring the variable, you can use JavaScript code to modify it. For example, you can modify the Text1 element by using the following statements:

element.hide();

element.animate('opacity', 0.25);

element.attr('src, 'images/trees.jpg');

Using HTML and CSS Code

JavaScript gives you the ability to use HTML and CSS code in Edge Animate. When you create a shape, add text, or import a graphic, Edge Animate automatically assigns the element an HTML ID name and division (DIV) tag, and creates CSS based on the attributes set in the Properties panel. A tag is HTML's basic way to identify items. An ID name creates a unique identifier for an element. If you want to work with multiple elements for a similar purpose, you can assign them a common class name. You can access and change these options in the Properties panel.

Adding HTML Code

HTML is the code behind a web page. In a script panel, you can add HTML in JavaScript code. When you view HTML code, tags always appear with **angle brackets** (< >), such as <div>. Here are a few HTML examples:

sym.$("Text1").html("NewText");

sym.$("Text1").html("<a href='http://www.adobe.com'>Adobe</a>");

If you want to add straight HTML code (no JavaScript) to your composition, you can open the HTML document in an external editor, such as Adobe Edge Code.

Adding CSS Code

CSS (Cascading Style Sheets) is an industry standard method for formatting and positioning HTML content on a web page. Edge Animate uses CSS behind the scenes. Here are a few CSS examples:

sym.$("Text1").css('cursor','pointer');

sym.$("RoundRec").css('width','640px');

sym.$("RoundRec").css('height','360px');

sym.$("RoundRec").css('backgroundColor','blue');

If you want to add multiple CSS attributes, you can use **curly brackets** ({ }). Here is an example:

```
sym.$("RoundRec").css({
       "width" : "640px",
       "height" : "360px"
       "backgroundColor" : "blue"
});
```

If you want to add straight CSS code (no JavaScript) to your composition, you can open the HTML document in an external editor, such as Adobe Edge Code, or create an external .css file. For more information, see "Working with CSS," on page 254.

Getting JavaScript Help

If you need more detailed information about JavaScript in Edge Animate, you can find out on the web. Edge Animate JavaScript API provides information on how Edge Animate uses JavaScript and how you can too. To access the online help, click the Help menu, click Edge Animate JavaScript API, and then click a link to the topic you want to find out more about. If you like to learn by example, the online JavaScript resource provides example code throughout the site to give you perspective on how to use it.

Using Show and Hide Element Snippets

The Show Element and Hide Element snippets allow you to show or hide an element on the Stage. It's a simple function, however it's very useful for showing and hiding elements on the screen. After you insert the Show Element or Hide Element snippet, you can specify the element that you want to change, as well as indicate how long you want to wait before the action takes place. For example, the Hide Element JavaScript code sym.$("RoundRec").hide(1000); hides the RoundRec element after a one second (or 1000 milliseconds) delay. In addition to the code snippets, you can also use other JavaScript code to show and hide elements with an added fade in and out or slide up and down. You can also use JavaScript code to toggle that shows or hides an element based on its current state. If the element is currently shown, toggle hides it; if its currently hidden, toggle shows it.

Use Show and Hide Element Snippets

1. In the Elements, Properties (with a selected element), or Timeline panel, click the **Open Actions** button for an element.

    For a new action, a menu appears. If not, click the **Add** button (+).

2. Click an event action on the menu.

3. Click to place the insertion point where you want to insert code.

4. Click **Show Element** or **Hide Element**.

    Either of the following statements gets inserted in the script panel.

    sym.$("Text1").show();

    sym.$("Text1").hide();

5. Replace Text1 with the name of the element you want to show or hide.

6. If you want to add a delay, enter a time in milliseconds in the parenthesis after show or hide.

7. Click the **Close** button to exit the script panel.

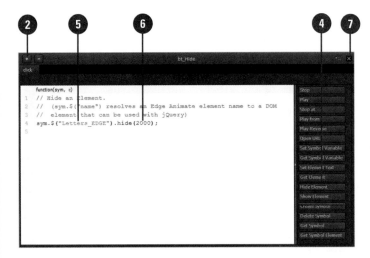

Use Fade, Slide, and Toggle Element Code

1. In the Elements, Properties (with a selected element), or Timeline panel, click the **Open Actions** button for an element.

   For a new action, a menu appears. If not, click the **Add** button (+).

2. Click an event action on the menu.

3. Click to place the insertion point where you want to insert code.

4. Enter any of the following code statements:

   sym.$("Element").toggle();

   sym.$("Element").fadeIn();

   sym.$("Element").fadeOut();

   sym.$("Element").fadeToggle();

   sym.$("Element").slideUp();

   sym.$("Element").slideDown();

   sym.$("Element").slideToggle();

5. If you want to add a delay, enter a time in milliseconds or the attributes 'slow', 'normal', or 'fast' in the parenthesis.

   sym.$("Element").fadeIn(2000);

   sym.$("Element").fadeIn('slow');

6. Click the **Close** button to exit the script panel.

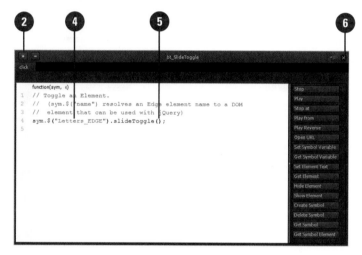

Using Element Text Snippets

Sometimes you want to change the text as part of an action. For example, you can point to a text box and have the text change from one message to another or from one style to another. You can accomplish the text change by using the Get Element or Set Element Text snippets. The Get Element snippet creates a variable (a container) where you can store information and then modify it using additional JavaScript code. The Set Element Text snippet replaces the current contents of an element with HTML text (by default). However, you can integrate HTML tags, such as a URL web address, in the code.

Use the Get Element Snippet

1. In the Elements, Properties (with a selected element), or Timeline panel, click the **Open Actions** button for an element.

   For a new action, a menu appears. If not, click the **Add** button (+).

2. Click an event action on the menu.

3. Click to place the insertion point where you want to insert code.

4. Click **Get Element**.

   var element = sym.$("Text1");

5. Replace Text1 with the name of the element you want assign to the variable.

6. Click to place the insertion point on the next line.

7. Type the following code:

   element.html("NewText");

   This assigns the variable element to the HTML text NewText.

   This example replicates the functionality of the Set Element Text snippet. You can use the variable with other attributes.

8. Click the **Close** button to exit the script panel.

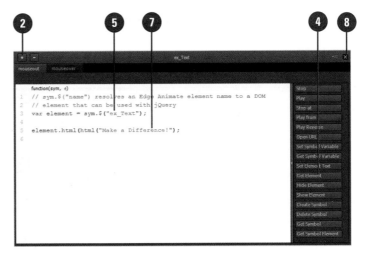

Use the Set Element Text Snippet

1 In the Elements, Properties (with a selected element), or Timeline panel, click the **Open Actions** button for an element.

For a new action, a menu appears. If not, click the **Add** button (+).

2 Click an event action on the menu.

3 Click to place the insertion point where you want to insert code.

4 Click **Set Element Text**.

sym.$("Text").html("NewText");

5 Replace Text with the name of the element you want to use, and then replace NewText with the HTML text you want to exchange it with.

The .html("") code uses text in the default case. However, you can insert HTML tags.

6 Click the **Close** button to exit the script panel.

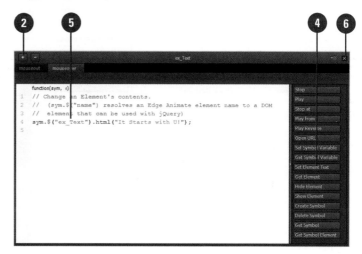

Using the Open URL Snippet

The Open URL snippet makes it quick and easy to add a URL (a web address) link to an element in Edge Animate. The URL link allows a user to open a web page from within your animation. For example, you can click a button or image to open a web address. The Open URL snippet provides a default URL for Adobe (*http://www.adobe.com*), however, you can change it to anyone you want. You can also specify a target attributes that indicates how the URL opens. The Open URL snippet doesn't display with the pointing finger or as an underlined text link. You can add a pointing finger with the Cursor button in the Properties panel or with JavaScript code. If you want the URL to have an underlined text link, you can create a URL link using HTML code.

Use the Open URL Snippet

1. In the Elements, Properties (with a selected element), or Timeline panel, click the **Open Actions** button for an element.

   For a new action, a menu appears. If not, click the **Add** button (+).

2. Click an event action on the menu.

3. Click to place the insertion point where you want to insert code.

4. Click **Open URL**.

   window.open("http://www.adobe.com","_self");

5. Replace the URL in red, and then keep the _self target attribute or replace it with another one:

   ◆ **_blank.** Loads the URL into a new window.

   ◆ **_parent.** Loads the URL into the parent frame.

   ◆ **_self.** Replaces the URL with the current page.

   ◆ **_top.** Replaces the URL with any frameset that may be loaded.

   ◆ **name.** Names the window.

6. Click the **Close** button to exit the script panel.

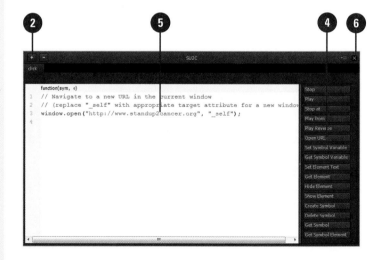

Open a URL with HTML Code

1. In the Elements, Properties (with a selected element), or Timeline panel, click the **Open Actions** button for the Stage.

   For a new action, a menu appears. If not, click the **Add** button (+).

2. Click **compositionReady** on the menu.

   This attaches the action to the Stage which plays when the composition starts in a web browser.

3. Click to place the insertion point where you want to insert code.

4. Click **Get Element**.

   var element = sym.$("Text1");

5. Replace element with your own variable name, and then replace Text1 with the name of the element you want to assign to the variable.

6. Click to place the insertion point on the next line.

7. Type the following code:

   element.html("<a href='http:// www.standup2cancer.org'>SU2C </a>");

   Replace the web address and link text in red.

8. Click the **Close** button to exit the script panel.

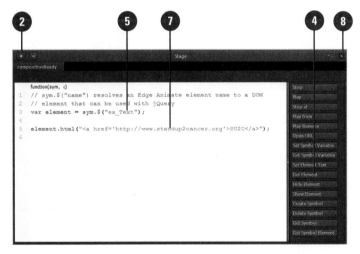

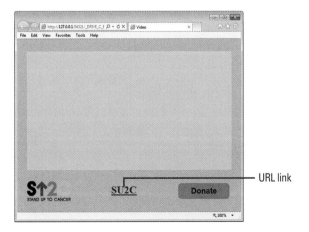

URL link

Using Get Symbol Snippets

Edge Animate provides several snippets that allow you to work with symbol instances. The snippets include Create Symbol, Delete Symbol, Get Symbol, and Get Symbol Element. With the Create Symbol snippet, you can create an instance element of a symbol as a child of the given parent (an existing symbol). After you create an instance of an element, either with a snippet using JavaScript code or manually using Edge Animate tools, you can modify it using the Get Symbol and Get Symbol Element snippets. Both Get Symbol snippets create a variable that you can use to modify elements within an instance.

Use the Get Symbol Snippets

1 In the Elements, Properties (with a selected element), or Timeline panel, click the **Open Actions** button for an element.

For a new action, a menu appears. If not, click the **Add** button (+).

2 Click an event action on the menu.

3 Click to place the insertion point where you want to insert code.

4 Click **Get Symbol**.

var mySymbolObject = sym.getsymbol("Symbol1");

5 Replace mySymbolObject with your own variable name, and then replace Symbol1 with the name of the symbol instance you want to assign to the variable.

6 Click to place the insertion point on the next line.

7 Type a statement that references the symbol variable. Here are some examples:

mySymbolObject.play();

mySymbolObject.stop();

mySymbolObject.$("Square")
.css("backgroundColor","blue");

This changes the Square element in the symbol instance to a blue background color.

8 Click the **Close** button to exit the script panel.

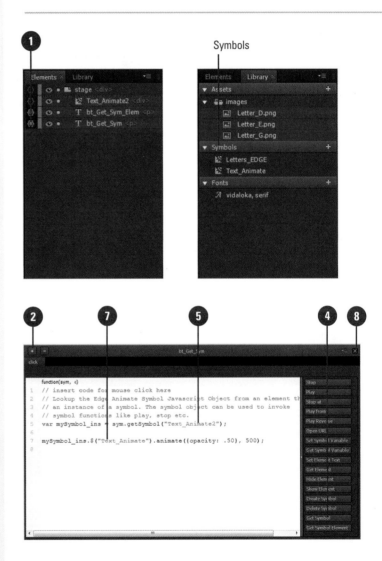

Use the Get Symbol Element Snippet

1 In the Elements, Properties (with a selected element), or Timeline panel, click the **Open Actions** button for an element.

For a new action, a menu appears. If not, click the **Add** button (+).

2 Click an event action on the menu.

3 Click to place the insertion point where you want to insert code.

4 Click **Get Symbol Element**.

var symbolElement = sym.getsymbolElement();

5 Replace symbolElement with your own variable name.

6 Click to place the insertion point on the next line.

7 Type a statement that references the symbol variable. Here are some examples:

symbolElement.play();

symbolElement.animate({opacity: 0}, 5000);

This animates the symbol instance to the opacity of 0 after a 5000 millisecond delay.

8 Click the **Close** button to exit the script panel.

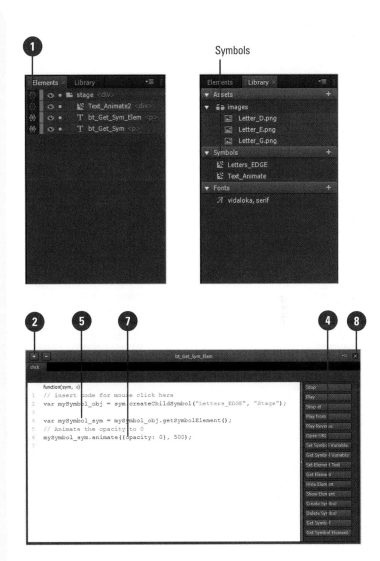

Symbols

For Your Information

Accessing a Nested Symbol

If you have a nested symbol, a symbol within a symbol, you can access the nested symbol using JavaScript code. The code is similar to the Get Symbol snippet, yet with an added function. Here is an example:

sym.getSymbol("symbolName").getSymbol("nestedElementName").play();

Using Create and Delete Symbol Snippets

You can create a symbol in Edge Animate by converting an existing element or importing external ones. However, you if you need to create a symbol on the fly during an animation, you can do it using JavaScript code. With the Create Symbol snippet, you can create an instance element of a symbol as a child of the given parent (an existing symbol). After you create an instance of an element, either manually or with JavaScript code, you can use the Delete Symbol snippet to remove it. If you want to modify a symbol instance element, you can use the Get Symbol and Get Symbol Element snippets.

Use the Create Symbol Snippet

1. In the Elements, Properties (with a selected element), or Timeline panel, click the **Open Actions** button for an element.

   For a new action, a menu appears. If not, click the **Add** button (+).

2. Click an event action on the menu.

3. Click to place the insertion point where you want to insert code.

4. Click **Create Symbol**.

   var mySymbolObject = sym.createChildSymbol("Symbol_1", "ParentElement1");

5. Replace Symbol_1 with the name of the symbol, and then replace ParentElement1 with the parent element where you want the symbol, such as the Stage.

6. Click to place the insertion point on the next line.

7. Type the following code:

   mySymbolObject.play();

   mySymbolObject.$("Square").css("backgroundColor","blue");

   This creates a new instance from the existing symbol and changes the Square element in the symbol instance to a blue background color.

8. Click the **Close** button to exit the script panel.

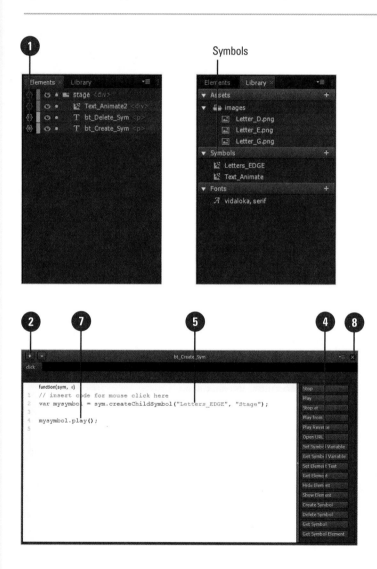

Symbols

Use the Delete Symbol Snippet

1. In the Elements, Properties (with a selected element), or Timeline panel, click the **Open Actions** button for an element.

   For a new action, a menu appears. If not, click the **Add** button (+).

2. Click an event action on the menu.

3. Click to place the insertion point where you want to insert code.

4. Click **Delete Symbol**.

   sym.getSymbol("Symbol1"). deleteSymbol();

5. Replace Symbol1 with the name of the instance of the element you want to delete.

6. Click the **Close** button to exit the script panel.

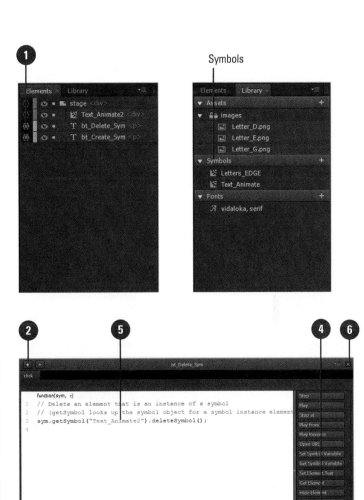

Symbols

Creating a Rollover Button

A rollover button is a button element that changes, or reacts, when a user rolls the cursor over it. A rollover button is a nice way to provide feedback to the user when a button is available. Another way to provide feedback for a user is to change the cursor when it hovers over a button. The cursor is set to auto by default, which lets the web browser set the cursor, which for an element is the black pointer. With the Cursor button in the Properties panel, you can select from 24 different cursors, including pointer and busy.

Project: Create a Rollover Button

1. Open the *RolloverButton_start.html* file in the chapter folder, and then save it in a new folder.

2. Select the *buttonRect* element on the Stage or in the Elements panel.

3. Click the **Modify** menu, click **Convert to Symbol**, type Button, deselect the **Autoplay timeline** check box, and then click **OK**.

4. Double-click the *Button* instance on the Stage.

   The symbol opens, displaying its own Timeline and Stage.

5. With the Playhead at 0:00, click the **Insert Label** button in the Timeline, type normal, and then press Enter (Win) or Return (Mac).

6. Select the *buttonRect* element on the Stage.

7. Click the **Auto-Keyframes Mode** button to select it, and then click the **Auto-Transition Mode** button to deselect it.

8. In the Properties panel, click the keyframe diamond next to **Opacity**, and then change **Opacity** to 65%.

   Use the selected background color and 65% opacity.

9. Move the **Playhead** to 0:01, and then create another label named over.

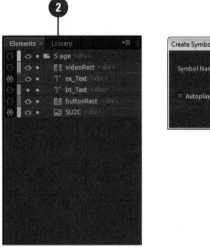
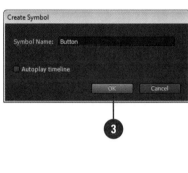
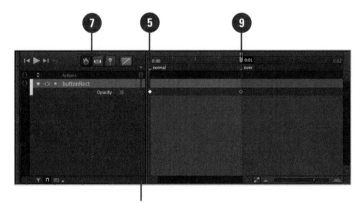

Insert Label button

10 In the Properties panel, click the keyframe diamond next to **Opacity**, and then change **Opacity** to 35%.

11 In the Elements, click the **Open Actions** button for the *buttonRect* element.

12 Click **mouseover** on the menu.

13 Click **Stop at**, and then type **'over'** to replace the selected value.

14 Click the **Add** button (+), and then click **mouseout** on the menu.

15 Click **Stop at**, and then type **'normal'** to replace the selected value.

16 Click the **Close** button to exit the script panel.

17 Click the **Back** button or **Stage** on the Edit bar to exit symbol editing mode.

18 Select the *Button* instance on the Stage or in the Elements panel.

19 In the Properties panel, click the **Cursor** button, and then select the **pointer** cursor (third one top row).

20 In the Elements panel, click the **Visibility** icon next to the *bt_Text* element to display the text.

21 Click the **File** menu, and then click **Preview In Browser** or press Ctrl+Enter (Win) or ⌘+Return (Mac).

22 In the example page, point to the Donate button to display the opacity change for the button.

23 Click the **Close** button to exit your web browser.

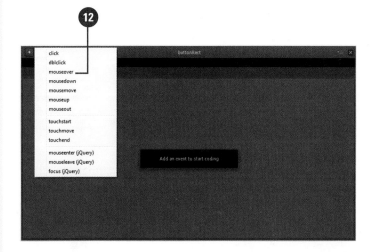

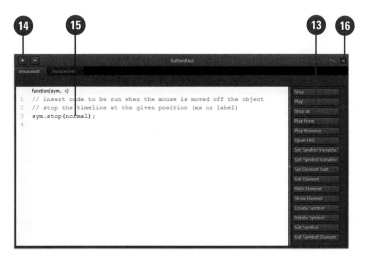

Creating a Shopping Cart Button

PayPal is a popular merchant service provider that allows you to buy and sell products or send money. If you want to provide the ability to use PayPal in a composition, you need to create a PayPal account at www.paypal.com. Once you create an account, you can use the service to create a shopping cart for an item, and then copy the embed code into a selected button (using the Open URL snippet) for use in a composition. When you click the shopping cart button, the PayPal site opens displaying the product information that you created in PayPal.

Project: Get the PayPal Shopping Cart Embed Code

1. In your web browser, go to *www.paypal.com*, and then sign in to your PayPal account.

2. Click **Merchant Services**, and then click **Create payment buttons for your website**.

3. Type information in the form to create a Shopping Cart button.

4. Click **Create Button**.

   Paypal creates the embed needed to access Paypal to purchase the item.

5. Click the **Email** tab, and then select the URL embed code for the Shopping Cart button.

6. Press Ctrl+C (Win) or ⌘+C (Mac) to copy the selected embed code.

7. Click the **Close** button to exit your web browser.

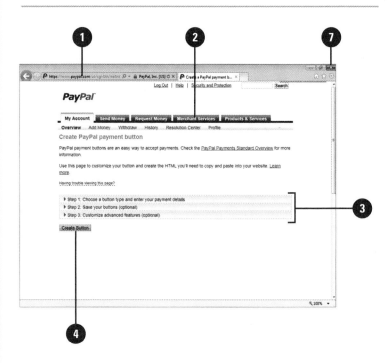

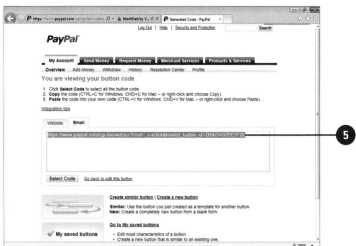

Project: Create a PayPal Shopping Cart Button

① Open the *AddCart_start.html* file in the chapter folder, and then save it in a new folder.

② Select the *Button* instance on the Stage or in the Elements panel.

③ In the Properties panel, click the **Cursor** button, and then select the **pointer** cursor (third one top row).

④ Click **Open Actions** next to Button in the Elements panel.

⑤ Click **click** on the menu, and then click **Open URL**.

⑥ Select the default URL http://www.adobe.com, and then paste in the Paypal embed code.

See the previous page for details to copy the embed code to the Clipboard.

⑦ Change "_self" to "_top".

This allows you to click Continue Shopping on the PayPal page and return to your page.

⑧ Click the **Close** button to exit the script panel.

⑨ Click the **File** menu, and then click **Preview In Browser** or press Ctrl+Enter (Win) or ⌘+Return (Mac).

⑩ In the example page, click the Donate button to open the PayPal page, and then click Continue Shopping to return to your page.

⑪ Click the **Close** button to exit your web browser.

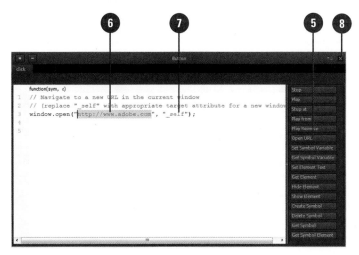

Embedding and Playing a Video

Video is everywhere on the web, so why not add it to your composition in Edge Animate. With JavaScript code, you can embed a video into a composition. You can trigger the video to play when you click an element or when you start the composition. If you want to start the video when you start the composition, you can attach the compositionReady action event to the Stage. Edge Animates waits until the composition and its resources are loaded before executing the script.

Project: Embed and Play a YouTube Video

1. Open the *EmbedVideo_start.html* file in the chapter folder, and then save it in a new folder.

2. Select the **Rectangle Tool** on the Tools panel, and then draw a rectangle shape.

3. In the Properties panel, set the rectangle shape **W** to 640 and **H** to 360.

   This is one of the default sizes for a YouTube video.

4. In the Elements panel, rename the rectangle shape to *videoRect*.

5. In the Elements panel, select the Stage.

6. Click the **Open Actions** button for the Stage element in the Elements panel.

7. Click **compositionReady** on the menu.

8. Type in the code as shown in the illustration.

9. Click the **Close** button to exit the script panel.

10. Click the **File** menu, and then click **Preview In Browser** or press Ctrl+Enter (Win) or ⌘+Return (Mac).

    The video plays in the element.

11. Click the **Close** button to exit your web browser.

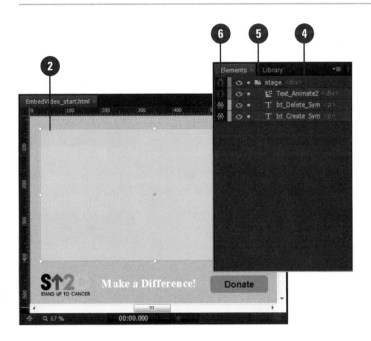

220   Chapter 8

Adding and Playing a Sound

Adding sound to a composition is a nice way to enhance it. Edge Animate doesn't provide a directly solution for sound at this point. However, you can take advantage of HTML5 to do the job. You can use the HTML5 <audio> tag to provide progressive playback for MP3, OGG, or WAV audio files. The audio tag is similar to the <img> or <video> tags that also come with HTML5. It provides attributes to display playback controls, autoplay, loop, and preload. The audio tag is supported by Internet Explorer 9, Firefox, Opera, Chrome, and Safari. However, not all formats are supported by each. So, you can provide multiple format sources and the browser will use the first recognized format. You can add sound by creating a composition in Edge Animate, and then adding HTML5 audio tags in an HTML editor, such as Adobe Edge Code.

Project: Add and Play a Sound

1. Start Adobe Edge Code or another HTML editor.

2. Open the *AddSound_start.html* file in the chapter folder, and then save it in a new folder.

3. Enter the HTML code in the illustration between the <audio> and </audio> tags.

4. Click the **File** menu, and then click **Save**.

5. Click the **Close** button to exit the HTML editor.

6. Start Edge Animate, and then open the *AddSound_done.html* file.

7. Click the **File** menu, and then click **Preview In Browser** or press Ctrl+Enter (Win) or ⌘+Return (Mac).

   The video plays in the element.

8. Click the **Close** button to exit your web browser.

See Also

See *"Getting to Know HTML" on page 248* for more information about HTML.

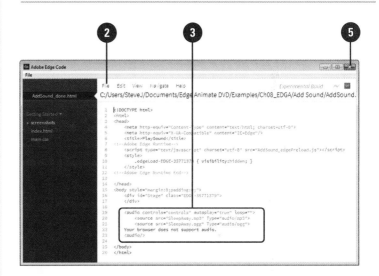

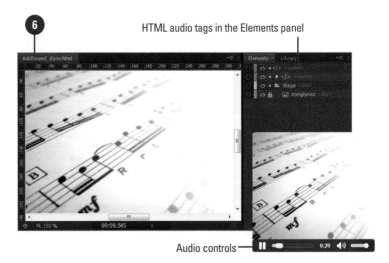

HTML audio tags in the Elements panel

Audio controls

Swapping Images in a Photo Gallery

A photo gallery is a popular feature to have on a web site. In order to create one, you need to swap images. You can swap images on the screen by using JavaScript code that changes the source attribute for an image. You can trigger the image swap by hovering over or clicking an image or button. When you point to the image or button, you can also change the cursor to a pointing finger to let the user know the element contains some interactivity.

Project: Swap an Image in a Photo Gallery

1 Open the *SwapImages_start.html* file in the chapter folder, and then save it in a new folder.

2 Select the *Bg_Photo* element on the Stage or in the Elements panel.

3 In the Properties panel, click the **Tag** button, and then click **img**.

4 Select the *Sm_Bridge* element on the Stage or in the Elements panel.

5 In the Properties panel, click the **Cursor** button, and then select the **pointer** cursor (third one top row).

6 Click the **Open Actions** button for the *Sm_Bridge* element in the Elements panel.

7 Click **mouseover** on the menu.

8 Type in the following code:

sym.$("Bg_Photo").attr('src', 'images/bridge.jpg');

9 Click the **Close** button to exit the script panel.

10 Select each element (*Sm_Trees*, *Sm_Barn*, and *Sm_Farm*), and then repeat Steps 4 thru 9.

11 Click the **File** menu, and then click **Preview In Browser** or press Ctrl+Enter (Win) or ⌘+Return (Mac).

12 Move the mouse over each thumbnail to view the image swap.

13 Click the **Close** button to exit your web browser.

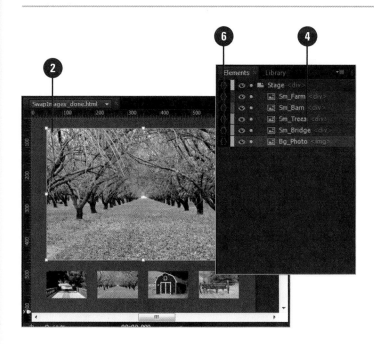

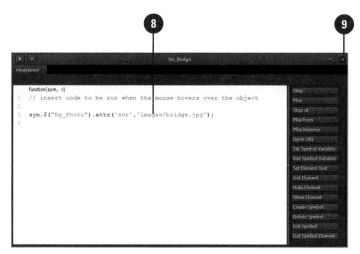

Publishing Animations

9

Introduction

After you finish creating your animation in Edge Animate, you can publish your composition for use in different applications. Edge Animate provides three publishing options: Web, Animate Deployment Package, and iBooks / OS X. The Web option, the most common, publishes for use on the web as an optimized HTML web page. When you publish a web page, you can view your animation in an HTML5/JavaScript compatible web browser, which includes Mozilla Firefox, Apple Safari, Google Chrome, and Microsoft Internet Explorer 9, and mobile devices. The Animate Deployment Package option publishes for use in other Adobe programs, such as InDesign, Digital Publishing Suite (DPS), and Muse. And finally, the iBooks / OS X option publishes for use in Apple iBooks Author on OS X systems as an OS X Dashboard Widget.

Before you publish a composition, you need to do a few things first. You need to specify the publish settings you want, and define the optional use of the Down-level Stage and Preloader Stage. The Down-level Stage allows you to create an information display screen, known as a poster image, for users who don't have a compatible web browser to view your Edge Animate composition. The Preloader Stage allows you to create a progress bar for display when your Edge Animate composition loads in a web browser.

What You'll Do

Publish Considerations

Publish a Composition

Publish for the Web

Publish to the Web for IE 6, 7, or 8

Publish to the Web Using CDN

Publish to the Web as Static HTML

Publish for Adobe Programs

Publish for iBooks Author

Capture a Poster Image

Create a Down-level Stage

Create a Preloader Stage

Publishing Considerations

You may be asking yourself, what is the difference between saving a composition and publishing one. When you save a composition, Edge Animate saves the HTML, Edge Animate (.an), JavaScript (.js), and related files for development purposes. Edge Animate manages the internal structure of the files for organization and development, not for optimization and distribution. That's where publishing comes in.

Preparing to Publish a Composition

Before you publish a composition, you need to do a few things first. You need to specify the publish settings you want, and define the optional use of the Down-level Stage and Preloader Stage. The Down-level Stage allows you to create an information display screen for users who don't have a compatible web browser to view your composition. The Preloader Stage allows you to create a progress bar for display when your composition loads in a web browser.

You can specify publish settings in the Publish Settings dialog box in Edge Animate, which you can access on the File menu. Edge Animate provides three publishing options: Web, Animate Deployment Package, and iBooks / OS X.

Publish for the Web

The Web option allows you to publish a composition for use on the web as an optimized HTML web page. In addition, you can specify options to publish for use with the Google Chrome Frame plug-in for IE 6, 7, and 8, for distribution with CDN (Content Delivery Network), or for use as static HTML content.

Publish for Adobe Programs

The Animate Deployment Package (.oam) option allows you to publish a composition for use with other Adobe programs, such as Muse, InDesign CS6, and Digital Publishing Suite (DPS).

Adobe Muse is a program built upon Adobe AIR (Flash Platform) that allows you to design and publish web sites. Muse takes advantage of other Adobe services, much like Edge Animate does, such as TypeKit to integrate fonts, and Business Catalyst for creating web sites.

Adobe InDesign is a program that allows you to design and pre-flight page layouts for print or digital distribution.

Adobe Digital Publishing Suite (DPS) is an online service that allows you to create, optimize, and distribute content produced in Adobe InDesign for tablet devices. Once imported into InDesign, you can use DPS tools to publish content to the online service.

Publish for Apple iBooks Author

The IBooks / OS X option allows you to publish a composition for use with Apple iBooks Author, which is only available on OS X (not for use on the Windows platform). Apple iBooks Author is a free application on the Mac App Store that allows you to create a multi-touch book for iPad tablet devices. Edge Animate publishes a Dashboard Widget (.wdgt) file, which is a compressed folder of files compatible for use in iBooks Author.

Publishing the Files

When you publish a composition, Edge Animate puts the files in a target folder named *publish* within your project folder by default, however you can change it. Edge Animate integrates the content from the Edge Animate file (.an) into the other files and doesn't include it in the publish folder.

Publishing a Composition

Before you publish a composition, you need to do a few things first. You need to specify the publish settings you want, and define the optional use of the Down-level Stage and Preloader Stage. Edge Animate provides three publishing options: Web, Animate Deployment Package, and iBooks / OS X. The Web option publishes for use on the web as an optimized HTML web page. The Animate Deployment Package option (.oam) publishes for use in other Adobe programs, such as InDesign, Digital Publishing Suite (DPS), and Muse. The iBooks / OS X option publishes for use in Apple iBooks Author as an OS X Dashboard Widget (.wdgt) on OS X systems. When you publish a composition, Edge Animate puts the files in a target folder named publish within your project folder by default, however you can change it. However, it's not recommended.

Publish a Composition

1. Open the composition you want to publish.

2. Define the use of the Down-level Stage or Preloader Stage.

   ◆ Click the **View** menu, and then click **Preloader Stage** or **Down-level Stage.**

3. Click the **File** menu, and then click **Publish Settings**.

4. Specify any of the following publishing options:

   ◆ **Web.** Creates optimized HTML and related JavaScript files.

   ◆ **Animate Deployment Package.** Creates an OAM file for use in Adobe Muse, Adobe InDesign, or Adobe DPS.

   ◆ **iBooks / OS X.** Creates a WDGT file for use in Apple iBooks Author (only on OS X systems).

5. Click **Publish** to publish the composition or click **Save** to save the settings and publish later.

   ◆ If you save your publishing settings, you can click the **File** menu, and then click **Publish** to publish the composition.

   TIMESAVER *Press Ctrl+Alt+S (Win) or ⌘+Option+S (Mac) to publish a composition.*

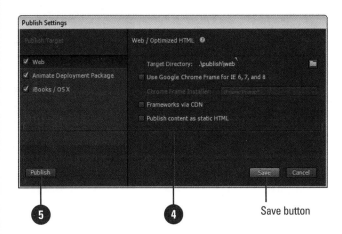

Save button

Publishing for the Web

When you publish a composition for the Web, Edge Animate takes all saved files in the project folder and optimizes them for use on the web. When you publish a composition, Edge Animate integrates the content from the Edge Animate file (.an) into the other files and doesn't include it in the publish folder. In addition for the web, you can specify options to publish with the Google Chrome Frame plug-in for use with IE 6, 7, and 8, for distribution with CDN (Content Delivery Network), or for use as static HTML content.

Publish to the Web

1. Open the composition you want to publish.

2. Click the **File** menu, and then click **Publish Settings**.

3. Click the **Web** category, and then select the **Web** check box.

4. Use the default Target Directory or click the **Browse** folder icon, select a folder location, and then click **Select Folder**.

5. Select or deselect the check boxes for the publishing options:

   ◆ **Use Google Chrome Frame for IE 6, 7, and 8.** Adds HTML code to use a plugin for Microsoft Internet Explorer versions 6, 7, or 8.

   ◆ **Frameworks via CDN.** Uses a link to use jQuery using the content distribution network.

   ◆ **Publish content as static HTML.** Uses HTML instead of some JavaScript into the composition at runtime.

6. Click **Save** to save the settings to publish later or click **Publish** to publish the composition.

   ◆ If you save your publishing settings, you can click the **File** menu, and then click **Publish** to publish the composition.

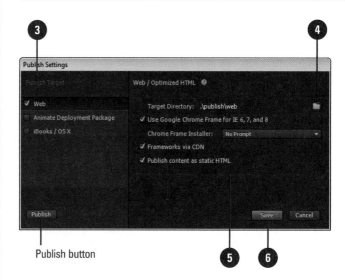

Publish button

Publishing to the Web for IE 6, 7, and 8

When you publish for the web, Edge Animate uses the latest HTML5 and JavaScript technology to create animation for web browsers on desktops, tablets, and mobile devices. If a user is not using the latest web browser, your animation might not work properly. You can help with web browser compatibility by selecting the Web option to make the free Google Chrome Frame plug-in available for Microsoft Internet Explorer (IE) version 6, 7, or 8 users to install on Windows. When the user of an older version of IE tries to view your Edge Animate composition, it prompts them to install the Google Chrome Frame plug-in, which renders your animation as if it was viewed in Google's Chrome browser. This option adds code to the <head> section of the HTML file.

Publish to the Web Using Google Chrome Frame Plug-in

1 Open the composition you want to publish.

2 Click the **File** menu, and then click **Publish Settings**.

3 Click the **Web** category, and then select the **Web** check box.

4 Use the default Target Directory or click the **Browse** folder icon, select a folder location, and then click **Select Folder**.

5 Select the **Use Google Chrome Frame for IE 6, 7, and 8** check box.

6 Click the **Chrome Frame Installer** list arrow, and then select an installer prompt option:

◆ **No Prompt.** Don't prompt the user to install the plug-in.

◆ **IFrame Prompt.** Prompts the user to install using iFrame.

◆ **Overlay Prompt.** Prompts the user to install using an overlay.

7 Click **Save** to save the settings to publish later or click **Publish** to publish the composition.

◆ If you save your publishing settings, you can click the **File** menu, and then click **Publish** to publish the composition.

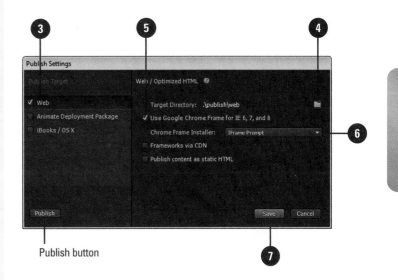

Publish button

Click to install Google Chrome Frame

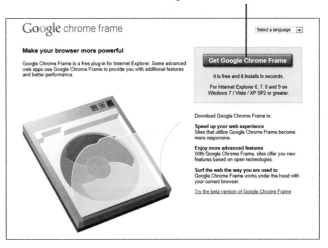

Publishing to the Web Using CDN

The Content Distribution Network (CDN) makes the JavaScript and jQuery library files, known as the Adobe Edge Animate Runtime, needed for an Edge Animate composition available online so you don't have to. The Adobe Edge Animate Runtime libraries are static files required for Edge Animate composition to run properly. The files don't contain any of your content, so once they are downloaded on a user's system, they don't need to be downloaded again. This is useful when you want to reduce the overall size of your composition project files for distribution on the web. The Frameworks via CDN option creates a link to the needed jQuery library files, which are cached locally on the user's system ready for use in your composition as needed.

Publish to the Web Using Frameworks via CDN

1. Open the composition you want to publish.

2. Click the **File** menu, and then click **Publish Settings**.

3. Click the **Web** category, and then select the **Web** check box.

4. Use the default Target Directory or click the **Browse** folder icon, select a folder location, and then click **Select Folder**.

5. Select the **Frameworks via CDN** check box.

6. Click **Save** to save the settings to publish later or click **Publish** to publish the composition.

   ◆ If you save your publishing settings, you can click the **File** menu, and then click **Publish** to publish the composition.

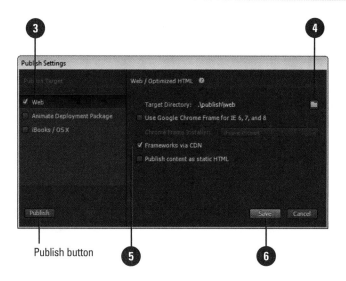

Publish button

Publishing to the Web as Static HTML

The Web option to publish the contents of your composition as a static HTML document takes HTML elements (including the Stage) that are normally created by JavaScript and integrates them into the HTML document. Instead of rendering the elements in your web browser using JavaScript, the elements are rendered using HTML. Since the content is now part of the HTML document, it improves searchability and indexing on the web.

Publish to the Web as Static HTML

1. Open the composition you want to publish.

2. Click the **File** menu, and then click **Publish Settings**.

3. Click the **Web** category, and then select the **Web** check box.

4. Use the default Target Directory or click the **Browse** folder icon, select a folder location, and then click **Select Folder**.

5. Select the **Publish content as static HTML** check box.

6. Click **Save** to save the settings to publish later or click **Publish** to publish the composition.

   ◆ If you save your publishing settings, you can click the **File** menu, and then click **Publish** to publish the composition.

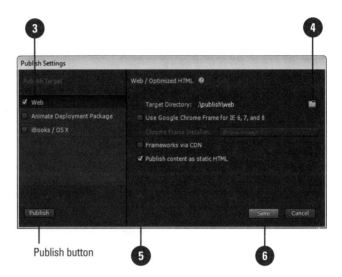

Publish button

Publishing for Adobe Programs

The Animate Deployment Package option allows you to publish a composition for use with other Adobe programs, such as Muse, InDesign CS6, and Digital Publishing Suite (DPS). Adobe Muse is a program built upon Adobe AIR (Flash Platform) that allows you to design and publish web sites. Adobe InDesign is a program that allows you to design and pre-flight page layouts for print or digital distribution. Adobe Digital Publishing Suite (DPS) is an online service that allows you to create, optimize, and distribute content produced in Adobe InDesign for tablet devices. Once imported into InDesign, you can use DPS tools to publish content to the online service. The Animate Deployment Package option publishes a package OAM file that you can drag and drop or import using the Place command in the other Adobe programs. In the published file, you can also include a poster image that gets displayed when the animation first loads. When the user clicks the poster image, the animation starts to play.

Publish as an Edge Animate Deployment Package

1. Open the composition you want to publish.

2. Click the **File** menu, and then click **Publish Settings**.

3. Click the **Animate Deployment Package** category, and then select the **Animate Deployment Package** check box.

4. Use the default Target Directory or click the **Browse** folder icon, select a folder location, and then click **Select Folder**.

5. Use the default Published Name or enter one of your own.

6. To change the poster image, click the **Choose Poster Image** button, and then select an image file from Library assets.

7. Click **Save** to save the settings to publish later or click **Publish** to publish the composition.

   ◆ If you save your publishing settings, you can click the **File** menu, and then click **Publish** to publish the composition.

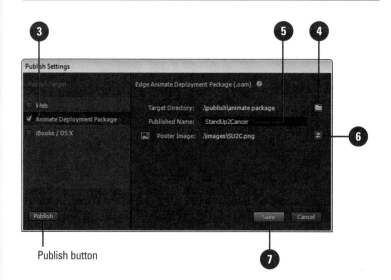

Publish button

Import a Package into Adobe Program

1. Start Adobe program, such as InDesign CS6 or Muse, and then open the file you want to use.

2. Click the **File** menu, and then click **Place**.

3. Click the **Files of type** list arrow, and then click **All Files**.

4. Navigate to and select the Edge Animate Deployment Package **(.oam)** file.

5. Click **Open**.

    For InDesign, a loaded cursor appears with the package.

6. Click or drag in the document where you want to place the composition as you would any other imported file type.

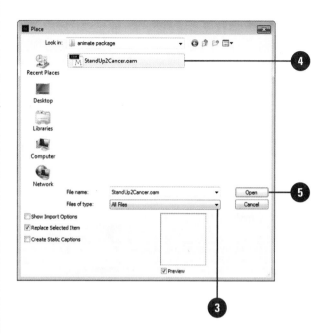

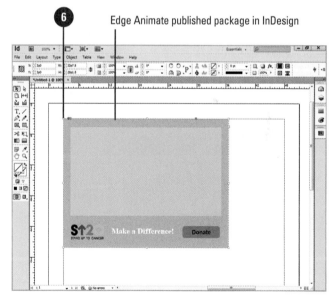

Edge Animate published package in InDesign

Publishing for iBooks Author

The IBooks / OS X option allows you to publish a composition for use with Apple iBooks Author, which is only available on OS X (not for use on the Windows platform). Apple iBooks Author is a free application on the Mac App Store that allows you to create a multi-touch book for iPad tablet devices. Edge Animate publishes a Dashboard Widget (.wdgt) file, which is a compressed folder of files compatible for use in iBooks. Some elements, such as the animated GIF files used for the preloader, cannot be published. You can drag and drop or import using the Insert menu the HTML widget (.wdgt) file into an open iBooks Author file. In the published file, you can also include a poster image that gets displayed when the animation first loads. When the user clicks the poster image, the animation starts to play.

Publish for Apple iBooks / OS X

1. Open the composition you want to publish.

2. Click the **File** menu, and then click **Publish Settings**.

3. Click the **iBooks / OS X** category, and then select the **iBooks / OS X** check box.

4. Use the default Target Directory or click the **Browse** folder icon, select a folder location, and then click **Select Folder**.

5. Use the default Published Name or enter one of your own.

6. To change the poster image, click the **Choose Poster Image** button, and then select an image file from Library assets.

7. Click **Save** to save the settings to publish later or click **Publish** to publish the composition.

   ◆ If you save your publishing settings, you can click the **File** menu, and then click **Publish** to publish the composition.

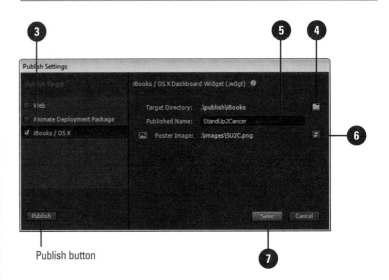

Publish button

Import an Animation into Apple iBooks Author

1 In OS X, start iBooks Author, and then open the file you wan to use.

◆ **Download iBooks Author app.** You can download the free iBooks Author app from the Mac Apple Store.

2 Click the **Insert** menu, point to **Widget**, and then click **HTML**.

An HTML frame appears in the iBooks document. Resize the HTML frame as needed.

3 In the Widget panel under the Interaction tab, click **Choose**.

4 Navigate to and select the Dashboard Widget **(.wdgt)** file.

5 Click **Insert**.

The widget published from Edge Animate appears in the HTML frame.

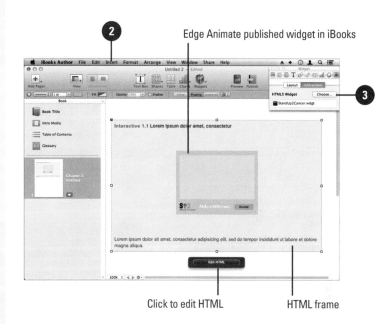

Edge Animate published widget in iBooks

Click to edit HTML   HTML frame

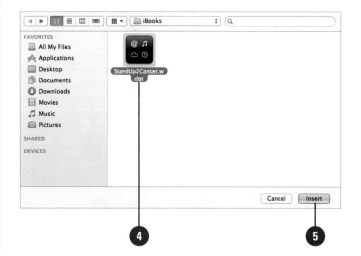

Capturing a Poster Image

If you create a composition that doesn't automatically play the animation (the Autoplay option is deselected) on start up in a web browser or when a web browser is not compatible with Edge Animate, you can set the appearance of a static image, known as a poster image, that gets displayed when the web page first loads. When the user clicks the poster image, the animation starts to play, if compatible. Edge Animate creates a PNG file named Poster.png that gets published along with the composition. The Poster image is used on the Down-level Stage that allows you to create an information display screen for users who don't have a compatible web browser to view your composition. You create a poster image from the Properties panel by capturing a still image of the Stage at a point in the Timeline.

Capture a Poster Image

1 In the Timeline panel, move the **Playhead** to the place where you want to capture a poster image of the Stage.

2 In the Elements panel, click the **Stage**.

3 In the Properties panel, click the **Capture Poster Image** button.

A window appears, displaying options to capture a new poster image or refresh an existing one.

4 Click **Capture** to create a new poster image, or click **Refresh** to overwrite the current poster image.

The captured image named Poster.png is placed in the Library panel under Assets and copied in to your project's images folder.

A window appears, displaying options to access publish settings or the Down-level Stage.

5 Click **Publish Settings** or **Edit Down-level Stage**, or click the **Close** button to exit the window.

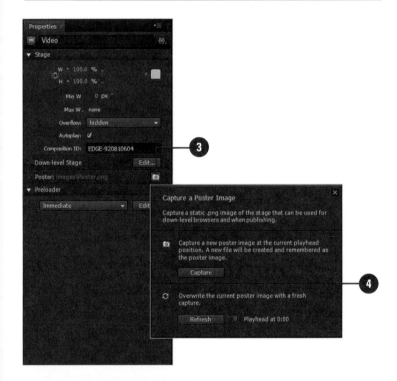

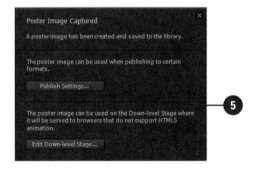

Remove the Poster Image

1 In the Library panel under Assets in the images folder, right-click (Win) or control-click the poster image file, and then click **Reveal in Explorer** (Win) or **Reveal in Finder** (Mac).

Windows Explorer or Finder window opens, displaying the folder with the file selected.

2 Delete the selected file using either of the following:

◆ Windows. Press **Delete**, and then click **Yes**.

◆ Mac. Drag the file to the Trash on the Dock.

The file is moved to the Recycle Bin (Win) or Trash (Mac), where you can permanently remove it.

3 Switch back to Edge Animate, and then click **Yes** to update your composition with the change.

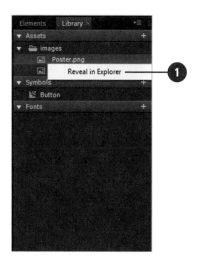

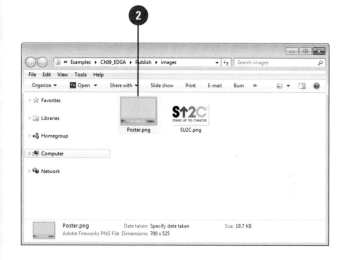

Creating a Down-level Stage

The Down-level Stage allows you to create an information display screen for users who don't have a compatible web browser to view your Edge Animate composition. Instead of displaying a blank screen when the animation can't run, you can display a still screen that gives the user instructions on what to do now. The Down-level Stage opens in a special editing mode with its own Stage. You can capture a poster image from the main Stage in Edge Animate or import an image from another program, such as Adobe Photoshop. In addition to the image, you can also add text with instructions or a link to where the user can download a compatible web browser, such as Google Chrome. The text properties in the Down-level Stage are limited to support low-level browsers. If you want to see the Down-level Stage in action, you need to use a web browser which is not compatible with Edge Animate compositions.

Create a Down-level Stage

1. In the Elements panel, click the **Stage**.

2. In the Properties panel, click the Down-level Stage **Edit** button.

    ◆ **Show and Hide the Down-level Stage.** Click the **View** menu, and then click **Down-level Stage**.

    The Down-level Stage appears with a white fill by default until you change it.

3. To add an image, do any of the following:

    ◆ **Poster Image.** Click the **Insert** button arrow in the Properties panel.

    ◆ **External Image.** Drag an image file from a file system window to the Down-level Stage or click the **File** menu, and then click **Import** to select it.

4. To add text, click the **Text Tool** on the Tools panel, drag a text box, enter text, and then click the **Close** button on the Text window.

5. Click the **Back** button or **Stage** on the Edit bar to exit the Down-level Stage editing mode.

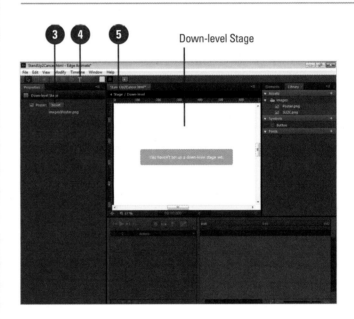

Down-level Stage

Change Properties in the Down-level Stage

1. Click the **View** menu, and then click **Down-level Stage**.

2. Select the element you want to change on the Stage or in the Elements panel; select the Down-level element to set Stage properties.

3. In the Properties panel, select from the available options:

   ◆ **Position and Size.** Specify position **X** and **Y** values or Size **W** and **H** values.

   ◆ **Link.** Select a link target and enter a link URL when the element is clicked.

   You can get Google Chrome at *www.google.com/chromeframe.*

   ◆ **Text.** Select text attributes, such as font-family, size, weight, color, alignment, and spacing.

   ◆ **Image.** Click the **Select Image** button to select an image.

4. Click the **Back** button or **Stage** on the Edit bar to exit the Down-level Stage editing mode.

See Also

See "Saving Images from Photoshop" on page 268 for information on saving an image as a poster image.

See "Using the Open URL Snippet" on page 210 for information on link target options.

Preloader Stage

Poster image

Creating a Preloader Stage

The Preloader Stage allows you to create a progress bar for display when your Edge Animate composition loads in a web browser. The Preloader Stage works in a special editing mode with its own Stage. The Preloader Stage provides built-in loaders with an animated progress bar to make it quick and easy to add one to your composition. However, if you want something more custom, you can create an animated GIF in Adobe Flash Professional and then export it for use in Edge Animate. In addition to the preloader animation, you can also add text with information for the user or a link to access a URL on the web. When you create a preloader be sure to keep it simple and small in size, so it doesn't take a long time to load and defeat its purpose.

Create a Preloader Stage

1. In the Elements panel, click the **Stage**.

2. In the Properties panel, click the **Preloader** list arrow, and then select **Immediate** (right now) or **Polite** (slowly).

3. Click the Preloader **Edit** button.

   ◆ **Show and Hide the Preloader Stage.** Click the **View** menu, and then click **Preloader Stage**.

4. Select a preloader:

   ◆ **Predefined.** Click the **Insert Preloader Clip-Art** list arrow, select a preloader, and then click **Insert**.

   ◆ **External Custom.** Drag an animated GIF file from a file system window to the Preloader Stage or click the **File** menu, and then click **Import** to select it.

   The insert preloader GIF is placed on the Stage, in the Library panel under Assets, and copied in to your project's images folder.

5. To add text, click the **Text Tool** on the Tools panel, drag a text box, enter text, and then click the **Close** button on the Text window.

6. Click the **Back** button or **Stage** on the Edit bar to exit the Preloader Stage editing mode.

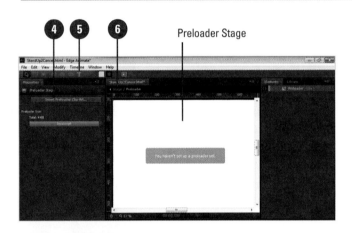
Preloader Stage

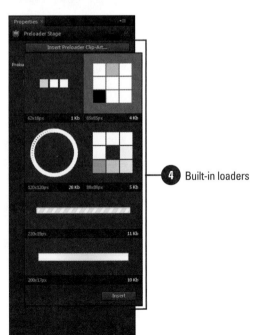
4 Built-in loaders

Change Properties in the Preloader Stage

1 Click the **View** menu, and then click **Preloader Stage**.

2 Select the element you want to change on the Stage or in the Elements panel; select the Preloader element to set Stage properties.

3 In the Properties panel, select from the available options:

- ◆ **Position and Size.** Specify position **X** and **Y** values or Size **W** and **H** values.

- ◆ **Link.** Select a link target and enter a link URL when the element is clicked.

  You can get Google Chrome at *www.google.com/chromeframe.*

- ◆ **Text.** Select text attributes, such as font-family, size, weight, color, alignment, and spacing.

- ◆ **Image.** Click the **Select Image** button to select an image.

4 Click the **Back** button or **Stage** on the Edit bar to exit the Preloader Stage editing mode.

See Also

See "Exporting Animations from Flash" on page 276 for information on creating a custom preloader in Flash Professional.

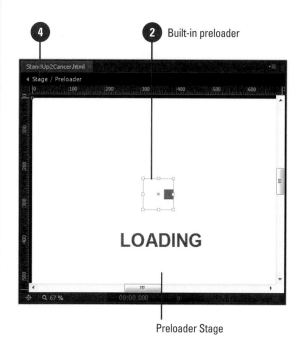

Built-in preloader

LOADING

Preloader Stage

Preloader GIF

Working with HTML, CSS, and JavaScript

Introduction

Edge Animate relies on three related technologies: HTML5, CSS3, and JavaScript. HTML (Hyper Text Markup Language) is the code behind the scenes for web pages. CSS (Cascading Style Sheets) is the code that provides the structure, design, and formatting for web pages. HTML and CSS work hand and hand to display content in a web browser. JavaScript is a scripting language that uses libraries to provide extended functionality for web pages. jQuery is a JavaScript library that provides standard extended functionality so you don't have to develop it. JavaScript and jQuery have become a defacto standard as they continue to be widely used on the web.

The JavaScript libraries used in Edge Animate is collectively referred to as the Adobe Edge Animate Runtime. The Adobe Edge Animate Runtime supports the content defined through the Edge Animate program and provides the code and resources needed for them to run properly in a web browser.

In Edge Animate, you work with JavaScript instead of HTML or CSS code. However, JavaScript gives you the ability to add HTML and CSS code with the html and css functions. If you want to add straight HTML or CSS code (no JavaScript) to your composition, you can open the HTML or CSS document in an HTML editor, such as Adobe Edge Code, add and edit the code, and then save it.

Typically, an animation from Edge Animate, such as a banner, is only part of an existing web page. So, after you create and publish a composition in Edge Animate, you can use an HTML editor to copy/paste HTML code to add the animation to the exiting web page. If you already have an HTML document that was created in another HTML editor, you can open it in Edge Animate and then add an animation or interaction to create a composition.

What You'll Do

Examine Edge Animate Files

View the Code Behind the Scenes

Examine Adobe Edge Animate Runtime

Get to Know HTML

Work with HTML

Get to Know CSS

Work with CSS

Put a Composition in an HTML Document

Add an Animation to an HTML Document

Examining Edge Animate Files

When you save a composition in Edge Animate, the program saves an HTML file and an AN file along with other related files—JS (JavaScript) and Edge Animate includes—needed to display Edge Animate content. The includes folder provides libraries, such as jQuery and JSON (JavaScript Object Notation), with extended functionality that gets used by Edge Animate. For example, Edge Animate uses JSON to store element definitions and attributes. It's critical that you keep all the files together for an Edge Animate composition using the same file and folder structure, otherwise the animation will not run properly, if at all. Let's take a look at the individual files that Edge Animate creates for a new composition, typically named Untitled-1.

Examine the Edge Animate Files

1. In Windows Explorer (Win) or the Finder (Mac), navigate to the main project folder for an Edge Animate composition.

   The folder contains five files (1 HTML, 1 AN, and 3 JS), and a folder.

2. Double-click the **edge_includes** folder.

   The folder contain four JavaScript files, which include jQuery and other libraries.

3. When you're done, close the windows.

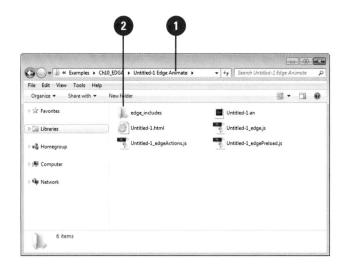

Contents of the edge_includes folder

Did You Know?

You can find out more about jQuery. If you want documentation for jQuery, go to *http://docs.jquery.com*. You can also go to *http://jquery.com*.

You can find out more about JSON. If you want information on JSON, go to *http://www.json.org*.

Edge Animate Files

Format	Description
filename.an	A file that points to and uses HTML and JavaScript files for an Edge Animate composition, not published.
filename.html	A file that stores HTML code used to execute an Edge Animate composition animation in a web browser.
*filename*_edge.js	A separate file with JavaScript that defines the Stage, Timeline, and elements used in an Edge Animate composition.
*filename*_edgePreload.js	A separate file with JavaScript that loads the resources and scripts used in an Edge Animate composition.
*filename*_edgeActions.js	A separate file with JavaScript that executes actions and triggers used in an Edge Animate composition.
edge_includes folder	
edge.1.0.0.min.js	The Edge JavaScript library that refers to methods and functions to create animations and effects.
jquery-1.7.1.min.js	The jQuery library that includes routines for writing code and referring elements.
jquery.easing.1.3.js	A plugin to the jQuery library that handles easing transition effects.
json2_min.js	A specialized JavaScript library (JSON) that serves as a data storage and interchange format used to exchange data from one system to another.
images folder	A folder with the graphics used in the composition. The folder is only available when graphics are used in the composition.

Viewing the Code Behind the Scenes

If you want to view the code behind the scenes for an Edge Animate composition, you can view the HTML code from a web browser or a text or HTML editor, such as Adobe Edge Code or Adobe Dreamweaver. From an HTML editor, you can do more than just view code; you can modify and save it too. HTML editors make it easy to open and edit HTML, CSS, and JavaScript code in order to help speed up the development process. If you want to edit JavaScript, you can also use the Code panel, which provides a central place to view and edit all the JavaScript code in a composition. You can access the Code panel from the Window menu in Edge Animate.

View Source Code from a Web Browser

1. Open the HTML file for the composition you want to view.

2. Click the **File** menu, and then click **Preview In Browser**.

   TIMESAVER *Press Ctrl+Enter (Win) or ⌘+Return (Mac).*

   Your default web browser opens, displaying your content on a web page.

   TROUBLE? *If the web page doesn't open, your web browser, such as Internet Explorer 8 or lower, is not compatible.*

3. Right-click a blank area within the page, and then click **View source** (IE) or **View Page Source** (Firefox or Chrome), or similar command.

   The HTML code for the web page appears in a new window or tab.

4. When you're done, close the web browser.

HTML code from an Edge Animate composition ❹

Microsoft Internet Explorer 9 window

See Also

See "Using the Code Panel" on page 44 for more information on using the Code panel to view and edit code.

For Your Information

Determining HTML5 Browser Compatibility

HTML5 is becoming the new industry standard, however, not all browsers are compatible yet. While most browsers, such as Chrome, Firefox, Internet Explorer 9, and Safari, are ready to go, not all users have the latest version. You can test your browser to make sure it's compatible with HTML5. Go go *http://html5test.com* to see what features are supported by HTML5. You can also find compatibility information at *http://html5please.com*.

View or Edit Source Code from Adobe Edge Code

① Start Adobe Edge Code or another HTML editor.

② Click the **File** menu, and then click **Open**.

③ Navigate to and select the file (HTML, CSS, or JavaScript) that you want to open.

④ Click **Open**.

⑤ View or edit the code just like in a word processing program.

⑥ Click the **File** menu, and then click **Save**.

⑦ Click the **Close** button to exit the HTML editor.

⑧ Start or switch back to Edge Animate.

If the composition that uses the file is already open in Edge Animate, click **Yes** to update and reload it.

⑨ If your composition is not already open, click the **File** menu, click **Open**, select the HTML file, and then click **Open**.

⑩ Work with the composition to add or change content.

See Also

See "Downloading Edge Animate and Tools" on page 282 for information on downloading Adobe Edge Code.

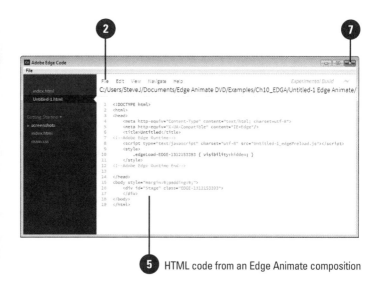

⑤ HTML code from an Edge Animate composition

For Your Information

Working with Adobe Edge Code

With Adobe Edge Code, you can view and work with code content and application with HTML, CSS, and JavaScript. This application allows you to preview CSS, edit code, and use integrated visual design tools to help speed up the development process.

When editing HTML, you can use Ctrl+E (Win) or ⌘+E (Mac) to open a quick inline editor that displays all the related CSS. When you make a tweak to your CSS, press Esc and you're back to editing HTML. No more switching between documents. Instead of going back and forth to review changes, Edge Code creates a live connection to your browser and pushes CSS updates as you type. Your code runs in the browser, but lives in your editor.

Examining the Adobe Edge Animate Runtime

When you create a composition in Edge Animate, it uses JavaScript to animate and work with elements. In addition, it uses JavaScript libraries behind the scenes to manage internal processes and content. The JavaScript libraries used in Edge Animate is collectively referred to as the **Adobe Edge Animate Runtime**. The Adobe Edge Animate Runtime supports the content defined through the Edge Animate program and provides the code and resources needed for them to run properly in a web browser. If you open an HTML document created by Edge Animate, you can see a JavaScript reference to the preloader (JS file), which links all the resources, including jQuery and other runtime libraries, in your composition within the <head> of the HTML document. Edge Animate comes with its own JavaScript API (Application Programming Interface) that you can use to create animation and interaction in your compositions. Code snippets use the APIs to provide added functionality.

Examine the Adobe Edge Animate Runtime

1. Start Adobe Edge Code or another HTML editor.

   ◆ You can can also view the code from a web browser; see the previous topic for details.

2. Click the **File** menu, and then click **Open**.

3. Navigate to and select the HTML file for the composition.

4. Click **Open**.

5. In the program window, you can view and edit the code just like in a word processing program.

   The code to reference JavaScript for the Adobe Edge Animate Runtime appears after the title between the comments.

6. Click the **Close** button to exit the HTML editor.

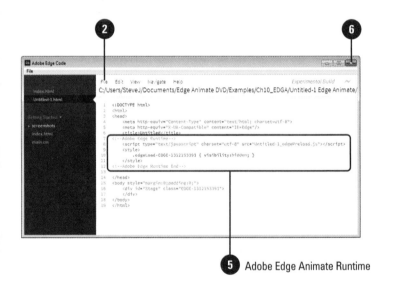

5 Adobe Edge Animate Runtime

> ### See Also
>
> See "Getting to Know HTML" on page 248 for information on understanding and working with HTML.

Get Help for Edge Animate JavaScript API

1. Click the **Help** menu, and then click **Edge Animate JavaScript API**.

   Your web browser opens, displaying the Adobe Edge Animate JavaScript API website.

2. Click a link to the topic you want to find out more about.

   ◆ Adobe Edge Animate overview.

   ◆ Triggers, events and actions.

   ◆ Work with symbols.

   ◆ JavaScript API.

   ◆ Advanced topics.

3. When you're done, close your web browser.

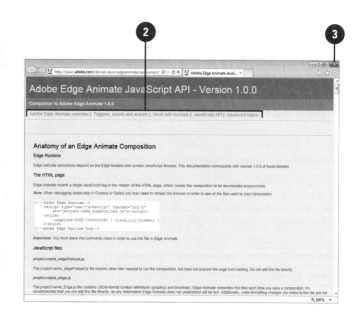

Did You Know?

You can continue a JavaScript statement on the next line. If a statement becomes too long to fit on a line, you can add a backward slash (\) to continue the statement on the next line.

For Your Information

Understanding the Document Object Model (DOM)

The Document Object Model (DOM) is a hierarchical mapping of elements in a web page. The DOM makes elements of a web page available as objects for scripting in JavaScript. DOM works by describing the path from a JavaScript function to an object in an HTML document. When you create an element with an ID and name in Edge Animate, it automatically becomes a DOM element internally with properties like position, background color borders, etc. Edge Animate automatically manipulates DOM elements using JavaScript libraries using the Adobe Edge Animate Runtime, which includes jQuery and JSON.

Getting to Know HTML

HTML (HyperText Markup Language) is a language for describing HTML documents, known as web pages. It's not a programming language, it's a markup language. A markup language is a set of markup tags, known as HTML tags. Tags make up the entire structure of an HTML document. An HTML tag specifies how the document, or a portion of the document, should be formatted. HTML tags are keywords surrounded by angle brackets like <html>. HTML tags normally come in pairs like <div> and </div>. The first tag in a pair is the opening tag and the second tag is the closing tag, which includes the slash (/). The HTML element content is everything between the opening and closing tag. For example, the <b> tag is saying to start bold text, and the </b> tag is saying to stop bold text. Some HTML elements have no content. They are called empty elements.

HTML documents have two parts, the head and the body. The **body** is the larger part of the document, as the body of a letter you would write to a friend. The **head** of the document contains the document's title and similar information, and the body contains most everything else.

HTML documents contain HTML tags and plain text. Here's an example of a basic HTML document:

```
<html>
<head><title>Title goes here</title>
    </head><body>Body goes here</body>
<h1>My First Heading</h1>
    <p>My first paragraph.</p>
</html>
```

You may find it easier to read if you add extra blank lines. With HTML, you cannot change the output by adding extra spaces or extra lines in your HTML code. The web browser will remove extra spaces and extra lines when the page is displayed. Any number of lines count as one line, and any number of spaces count as one space. Here's the example with extra spaces and lines:

```
<html>
<head>
<title>Title goes here</title>
</head>
<body>
<!-- Body goes here -->
<h1>My First Heading</h1>
<p>My first paragraph.</p>
</body>
</html>
```

The text between <html> and </html> describes the web page. The text between <head> and </head> contains the web page

Common Tags

Symbol	Defines
<html>	Start of the HTML document
<head>	The document heading
<body>	The body of the document
<title>	The document title
<div>	A container in a document
<span>	A section in a document
<h1>	Text heading
<p>	A paragraph
<style>	Format of text
<img>	An image placeholder
<a>	A hyperlink
<iframe>	An inline frame
<!-- comment -->	A comment

title. The text between <body> and </body> is the visible page content. The text inside <!-- This is a comment --> the brackets is a comment that is ignored by the web browser and not displayed. The text between <h1> and </h1> is displayed as a heading. The text between <p> and </p> is displayed as a paragraph. HTML tags are not case sensitive, so they can be upper- or lower-case.

HTML elements can have attributes, which provide additional information about them. Attributes are always specified in the opening tag. Attributes come in name/value pairs, such as name = "value". Attribute values should always be enclosed in quotes.

Web browsers, such as Firefox, Chrome, Internet Explorer, and Safari, read HTML documents and display them as web pages. A web browser uses the tags to interpret the content of the page. In your web browser, you can view the HTML markup language to see how the web browser interprets the content. To view the HTML source code, right-click in the page, and then click View Source (IE) or View Page Source (Firefox or Chrome), or other similar command.

HTML files are just plain text files, so they can be composed and edited in any word processing or HTML code editor program; they usually have the extension of .html or .htm.

HTML code in Adobe Edge Code

HTML tags in Elements panel

Same HTML code opened in Edge Animate

Working with HTML

HTML is the code behind a web page. When you view HTML code, tags appear with angle brackets (< >), such as <div>, to define the content on the page. When you create a shape, add text, or import a graphic, Edge Animate automatically assigns the element the division (DIV) tag and an HTML ID name. In Edge Animate, you work with JavaScript instead of HTML code. However, JavaScript/jQuery gives you the ability to add HTML code with the html function method. If you want to add straight HTML code (no JavaScript) to your composition, you can open the HTML document in an HTML editor, such as Adobe Edge Code, add and edit the HTML code, and then save it.

Add HTML to JavaScript

1. Open a script panel, either Trigger, Open Actions, or Code.

   ◆ **Trigger Panel.** Position the **Playhead** in the Timeline, and then click the **Insert Trigger** button, or double-click an existing trigger in the Timeline.

   ◆ **Open Actions Panel.** Click an **Open Actions** button in the Timeline, Elements or Properties panel. For a new action, click an event.

2. Click to place the insertion point where you want to insert the code.

3. Enter JavaScript code that uses the html function method. Here are some examples:

   sym.$("Text1").html("<a href= 'http://www.adobe.com'> Adobe</a>");

   sym.$("Text1").html("NewText");

4. Click the **Close** button to exit the script panel.

See Also

See "Working with JavaScript Code" on page 204 for more information on using JavaScript code.

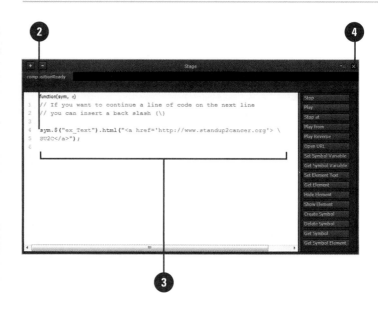

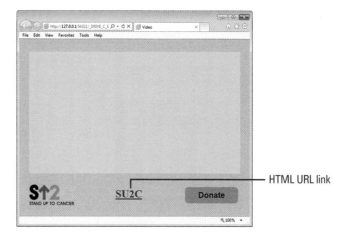

HTML URL link

Work with Straight HTML Code

1. Start Adobe Edge Code or another HTML editor.

2. Click the **File** menu, click **Open**, navigate to and select the HTML file, and then click **Open**.

3. Enter the straight HTML code; see the illustration for an example.

4. Click the **File** menu, and then click **Save**.

5. Click the **Close** button to exit the HTML editor.

6. Start or switch back to Edge Animate.

   If the composition that uses the HTML file is already open in Edge Animate, click **Yes** to update and reload it.

7. If your composition is not already open, click the **File** menu, click **Open**, select the HTML file, and then click **Open**.

8. Work with the composition to add or change content.

See Also

See "Getting to Know HTML" on page 248 for information on understanding and working with HTML.

Did You Know?

You can continue HTML code on the next line. If a line of HTML becomes too long to fit on a line, you can press Enter (Win) or Return (Mac) to continue the statement on the next line. HTML ignores whitespace.

Straight HTML code in Adobe Edge Code

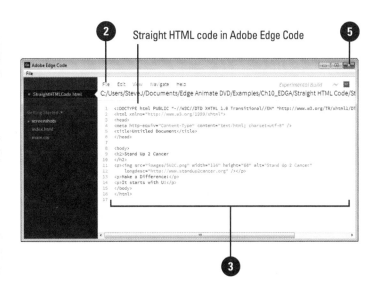

Same HTML code opened in Edge Animate

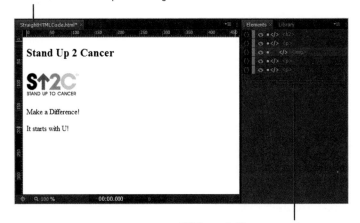

HTML tags in Elements panel

Getting to Know CSS

Cascading Style Sheets (CSS) are a collection of formatting rules that control the appearance of HTML elements in a web page. The term *cascading* relates to the way a web browser displays CSS styles for specific elements on a web page. Using CSS styles to format a page separates content from presentation. This gives you greater flexibility and control over the exact appearance of your web pages.

CSS allow you to define text attributes and give them a style name. This style name, called a selector, can be applied to any implemented text. Each time you need to implement the defined style, you can refer back to the CSS. The styles on a web page come from three different sources: the default styles from the web browser itself, the designer's internal or external style sheet, and any user customized style selections. For example, a web browser may use Times New Roman as the default paragraph font. As the designer, you can create a style to override the paragraph font to be Arial.

CSS Versus HTML

If you wanted to change the color of the background of a web page, the HTML code would look like this:

```
<body bgcolor="#0000FF">
```

To write the same thing using CSS, would look like this:

```
body {background-color: #0000FF;}
```

The code, in both cases, is instructing the browser to paint the background in pure blue.

CSS Breakdown

CSS defines formatting with properties, such as font-family, font-size and color, in a **decla-ration block**, which is contained inside **curly brackets** ({ }). The declaration block is broken down into three sections: a selector, a property, and a value. In our example, body is the selector, background-color is the property, and #0000FF is the value.

Create CSS Styles

There are three ways you can apply CSS to an HTML document: Attributes, Tags, and External Style Sheets.

Attribute Styles

One way to apply CSS to HTML is by using the HTML attribute style. CSS used in this way is coded directly into the HTML document. For example, you can create your own named tags, and use them throughout the active document. Building on the above example, it can be applied like this:

```
<html>
  <head>
    <title>Attribute Style Example<title>
  </head>
  <body style="background-color: #0000FF;">
    <p>This page has a blue background</p>
  </body>
</html>
```

Tag Styles

A second way to include CSS into an HTML document is to use the Tag Style method. In this method you control the formatting of standard HTML tags. For example, you could redefine the <H1> heading tag to always use a specific font, size and justification or, in this example, use the <body> tag to paint the background blue.

```
<html>
  <head>
    <title>Tag Style Example<title>
    <style type="text/css">
        body {background-color: #0000FF;}
    </style>
  </head>
  <body>
    <p>This page has a blue background</p>
  </body>
</html>
```

External Styles

This is the recommended way to create styles. Using this method you create a text document (called a style sheet). This document contains all of the formatting information necessary to drive your web page. This document is then attached to one or more web pages, and when the page loads, it gets its formatting information from the external style sheet. The line of code must be inserted in the header section of the HTML code between the <head> and </head> tags. Like this:

```
<html>
  <head>
    <title>My document</title>
    <link rel="stylesheet" type="text/css"
        href="style/style.css" />
  </head>
  <body>
    <p>This page has a blue background</p>
  </body>
</html>
```

In the example, an external style sheet (basically, a text document) called *style.css* is used to format the active web document. The external *style.css* file contains the following CSS code:

```
// External CSS File: styles.css
headline {
        font-family: Arial, Helvetica, sans-serif;
        font-size: 12 px;
}
body {
        font-family: Arial, Helvetica, sans-serif;
        font-size: 10 px;
}
```

This external CSS file defines two styles, one for a sans-serif headline at 12 pixels, the other a sans-serif body text at 10 pixels. Make sure the CSS file is in the same folder as the HTML document.

Style Types

There are four types of styles, and as you might guess, each one performs a specific function when using Cascading Style Sheets. The four types of Styles are as follows:

- ◆ Class. Creates a custom style that can be applied as a class attribute to a range or block of text. Class names must begin with a **period** (.).
- ◆ ID. Creates a style and attaches it to a current HTML tag that contains a specific ID attribute. ID names must begin with a **pound sign** (#).
- ◆ Tag. Redefines a current style and attaches it to a current HTML tag.
- ◆ Compound. Defines specific formatting for a particular combination of tags or for all tags that contain a specific ID attribute.

Working with CSS

CSS is the formatting rules, known as styles, behind a web page. When you create a shape, add text, or import a graphic, Edge Animate automatically creates internal CSS behind the scenes based on the attributes set in the Properties panel. In Edge Animate, you work with JavaScript. However, JavaScript/jQuery gives you the ability to add CSS. If you want to add CSS (no JavaScript) to your composition, you can open the HTML document in an HTML editor, such as Adobe Edge Code, add and edit code, and then save it. Instead of adding internal CSS, you can also create an external .css file to keep it separate from the HTML document, which makes it easier to manage and make changes. If you create an external .css file, you need to also add code to the <head> of the HTML document to link the external CSS styles to the web page. You can apply a CSS style to a single element ID, which starts with a period (.), or to multiple elements with a class, which starts with a pound sign (#).

Add CSS to JavaScript

1. Open a script panel, either Trigger, Open Actions, or Code.

   ◆ **Trigger Panel.** Position the **Playhead** in the Timeline, and then click the **Insert Trigger** button, or double-click an existing trigger in the Timeline.

   ◆ **Open Actions Panel.** Click an **Open Actions** button in the Timeline, Elements or Properties panel. For a new action, click an event.

2. Click to place the insertion point where you want to insert the code.

3. Enter JavaScript code that uses the css function method. Here are some examples:

   sym.$("RoundRec").css('width', '640px');

   sym.$("RoundRec").css('height', '360px');

   sym.$("RoundRec").css('back groundColor','blue');

4. Click the **Close** button to exit the script panel.

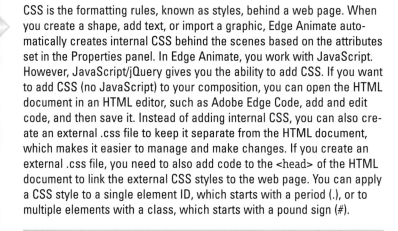

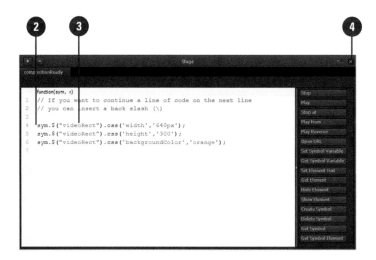

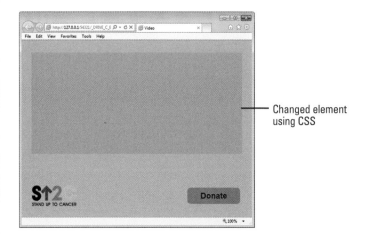

Changed element using CSS

Apply External CSS to Element IDs or Classes

1 Start Adobe Edge Code or another HTML editor.

2 Click the **File** menu, click **Open**, navigate to and select the HTML file, and then click **Open**.

3 Enter the following HTML code between the <head> and </head> tags:

<link rel="stylesheet" href="style.css" />

4 Click the **File** menu, and then click **Save**.

5 Click the **File** menu, click **Open**, navigate to and select the external CSS file (in this case *style.css*) linked to the HTML file, and then click **Open**.

6 Enter the CSS code; see the illustration for an example.

7 Click the **File** menu, and then click **Save**.

8 Click the **Close** button to exit the HTML editor.

See Also

See "Getting to Know CSS" on page 252 for more information about Cascading Style Sheets.

See "Working with JavaScript Code" on page 204 for more information on using JavaScript code.

HTML code with CSS opened in Edge Animate

Putting a Composition in an HTML Document

Typically, an animation from Edge Animate, such as a banner, is only part of an existing web page. So, after you create and publish a composition in Edge Animate, you'll need to do a few things to use it in an existing web page. First, you'll need to copy all the files and folders from your Edge Animate composition folder to the main website folder, and then second, you'll need to copy HTML code from your composition HTML document and then paste it in the existing HTML document. Unfortunately, you cannot do the copy/paste in Edge Animate. You need an HTML editor, such as Adobe Edge Code to do the job. In the HTML editor, you'll need to do three important things. One, copy/paste preloader code from the composition in the head section of the HTML document. Two, add the <div> code that identifies the composition in the body section of the HTML document. And three, edit the <div> code so the composition has a unique ID. You can use the same process to put more than one composition on the same web page.

Put a Composition in an HTML Document

1. In Windows Explorer (Win) or the Finder (Mac), copy all the files and folders from your composition folder to your main website folder with the HTML document.

   ◆ **For Multiple Compositions.** You only need one copy of the edge_includes folder and combine the contents of the images folder into one.

2. Start Adobe Edge Code or another HTML editor.

3. Click the **File** menu, click **Open**, navigate to and select the composition HTML file, and then click **Open**.

4. Select and copy—Ctrl+C (Win) or ⌘+C (Mac)—the HTML code from the following start comment tag to the end comment tag in the head section:

   <!--Adobe Edge Runtime-->

   and

   <!--Adobe Edge Runtime End-->

5. Open the HTML document that you want to put the composition.

6. Place the insertion point between the <head> and <head/> tags; create new lines as needed, and then paste—Ctrl+V (Win) or ⌘+V (Mac)—the code.

7. Switch back or open the composition HTML document.

8. Select and copy—Ctrl+C (Win) or ⌘+C (Mac)—the following <div> code in the body section:

<div id="Stage" class="EDGE-20485945345">

<div

Your number will differ.

9. Switch back or open the HTML document.

10. Place the insertion point between the <body> and <body/> tags; create new lines as needed, and then paste—Ctrl+V (Win) or ⌘+V (Mac)—the code.

The id used in the div is named Stage by default. If you have only one composition on the page, you can leave it alone and you are done. However, if you want to put more than one composition on the page, you need to make the IDs unique.

11. To put more than one composition in the HTML document, repeat Step 3 thru 10.

12. In the div tags, change the id to a unique name, such as "StageOne" and "StageTwo."

13. Click the **File** menu, and then click **Save**.

14. Click the **Close** button to exit the HTML editor.

The composition(s) is now part of the HTML document. Be sure to keep all the Edge Animate related files together with the HTML document.

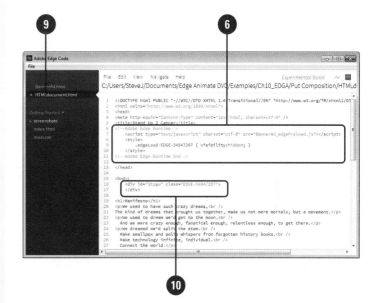

Adding an Animation to an HTML Document

If you already have an HTML document that was created in another HTML editor, such as Adobe Dreamweaver or Adobe Edge Code, you can open it in Edge Animate and then add an animation or interaction. You can open the HTML document using the Open command just as you would with a composition HTML document. When you open an HTML document in Edge Animate, the web page appears on the Stage along with the HTML tags in the Elements panel. Because Edge Animate works with JavaScript, you cannot change the HTML code directly. If you want to edit the HTML code, you need to use an HTML editor. In Edge Animate, you can add animation and interaction just as you would with a new composition. When you add an animation to the HTML document and then save it as a composition, remember that you need to keep all the Edge Animate files together with the HTML document for it to work properly on the web.

Open an HTML Document and Add an Animation

1. Click the **File** menu, and then click **Open**.

   ◆ You can also click **Open File** in the Welcome screen.

2. Navigate to and select the HTML file, and then click **Open**.

   The HTML document appears on the Stage and the associated tags appear in the Elements panel.

3. Use the tools and techniques in Edge Animate to create an animation.

4. Click the **File** menu, and then click **Save**.

   Edge Animate updates the HTML document and creates the normal JavaScript files associated with a composition in the same folder.

5. To publish the composition, click the **File** menu, click **Publish Settings**, select the **Web** check box, and then click **Publish**.

   The composition is now part of the HTML document. Be sure to keep all the Edge Animate related files together with the HTML document.

New animation banner ad

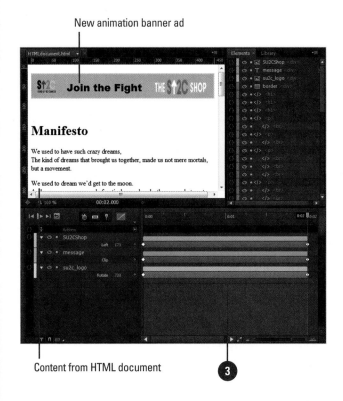

Content from HTML document

Working Together with Adobe Programs

11

Introduction

In addition to Edge Animate, Adobe also produces other programs that create digital media and content for print, mobile, and web-based applications. You can use this content in your compositions in Edge Animate to create a dynamic animation for use on the web or as content you can use back in these programs. It's all a workflow of content in and out of programs to display information in an interactive world. In this chapter, you'll work with several Adobe programs, including Dreamweaver, Muse, InDesign, Photoshop, Fireworks, Illustrator, and Flash Professional.

Dreamweaver creates and works with HTML documents, which means you can take your results from Dreamweaver, and then add animations to them in Edge Animate.

You can import a packaged composition from Edge Animate into a web site using Muse or a print or digital publication using InDesign. After you create a publication, you can use tools in InDesign to work with the Adobe Digital Publishing Suite (DPS), an integrated online service that allows you to create, optimize, and distribute content produced for mobile devices.

Photoshop, Fireworks, and Illustrator are best used for creating and modifying vector and bitmap graphics for website and print-based projects. The web graphics—including JPG/JPEG, PNG, SVG, and GIF files—you create using these Adobe programs can be added to your compositions in Edge Animate.

Flash Professional is a program for developing interactive content, animations, user interfaces, games, and mobile and web applications. Instead of using the built-in preloader assets provided by Edge Animate, you can create a custom animated GIF in Flash Professional and then export it for use in your composition.

What You'll Do

Open Compositions in Adobe Dreamweaver

Import into Adobe Muse

Import into Adobe InDesign

Work with Adobe Digital Publishing Suite

Save Images from Adobe Photoshop

Save Graphics from Adobe Fireworks

Export Images from Adobe Illustrator

Save Artwork from Adobe Illustrator

Export Animations from Adobe Flash

Opening Compositions in Adobe Dreamweaver

Adobe Dreamweaver is a program that allows you to create web site and web programs for desktops, smartphones, and other devices. Dreamweaver uses the latest technologies: HTML/HTML5, CSS, JavaScript, PhoneGap, site management, FTP (File Transfer Protocol), CMS (Content Management Services) frameworks, and SVN (Subversion). Dreamweaver creates and works with HTML documents, which means you can take your results from Dreamweaver, and then add animations to them in Edge Animate, while still preserving the integrity of CSS-based layouts. You can use Dreamweaver to edit the HTML, CSS, and JavaScript code associated with your composition. For example, if you're comfortable working with JavaScript/jQuery, you can open and edit the *filename*_edgeActions.js file that contains the actions and triggers in your composition. In addition, you can preview the animation in Live view and view the animation HTML code in Live Code view. However, you cannot edit the code in Live view; it's read only.

Open an Edge Animate Composition in Dreamweaver

1. Start Adobe Dreamweaver.

2. Click the **File** menu, click **Open**, navigate to and select the composition HTML file, and then click **Open**.

3. Click the **Split** button on the Document toolbar.

   This displays both Code view and Design view.

4. Scroll through Code view.

   You'll notice references to Adobe Edge Runtime in the head section of the HTML code.

5. Scroll through Design view.

   You'll notice the animation doesn't appear at the top of the page.

6. Click the **Live** button on the Document toolbar.

   The animation created in Edge Animate appears in Design view.

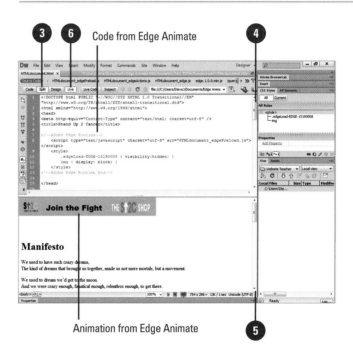

Code from Edge Animate

Animation from Edge Animate

Work with the HTML for an Animation in Dreamweaver

1. Start Adobe Dreamweaver.

2. Click the **File** menu, click **Open**, navigate to and select the composition HTML file, and then click **Open**.

3. Click the **Split** button on the Document toolbar.

4. Click the **Live** button on the Document toolbar.

5. Click the **Live Code** button on the Document toolbar, and then scroll through the code.

   You'll notice the HTML code for your animation. The code is read only in Live Code view. The code doesn't appear in Live view.

6. Click the **Live** button on the Document toolbar to exit Live mode.

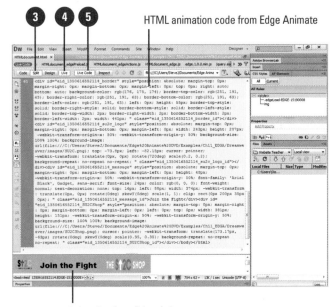

HTML animation code from Edge Animate

Animation from Edge Animate

Importing into Adobe Muse

Adobe Muse is a program that lets you create, design, and publish HTML web sites without writing code. You can design web-standard sites like you design print layouts. Muse takes advantage of Adobe services, much like Edge Animate does, such as TypeKit to integrate fonts, and Business Catalyst for creating and publishing web sites. You can drag and drop or import using the Place command the OAM file into an open Muse web site.

Import and Preview a Package into a Muse Web Site

1. Start Adobe Muse, and then create a new site or open an existing site.

2. In Plan view, double-click the name of the page where you want to add the animation.

3. Click the **File** menu, and then click **Place**.

4. Click the **Save as Type** list arrow (Win) or **Format** popup (Mac), and then click **All Supported Formats**.

5. Navigate to and select the Edge Animate Deployment Package (.oam) file.

6. Click **Open**.

   The cursor loads with the imported content.

7. Click in the document where you want to place the composition as you would a photo or any other imported file type.

8. Click the **Preview Mode** button on the toolbar.

   The animation from Edge Animate plays in Preview Mode.

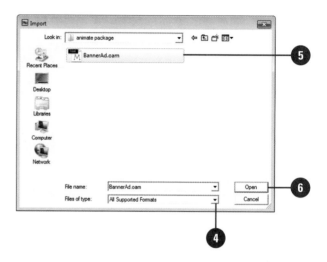

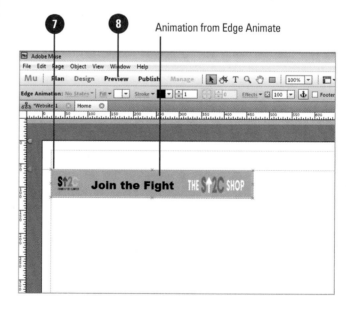

Animation from Edge Animate

Work with the Animation in Muse

① Start Adobe Muse, and then open the existing site with the imported OAM file.

② To view the imported OAM file, click the **Assets** tab.

◆ To view panels, click the **Window** menu, and then click **Show Panels**.

The imported OAM file appears in the Assets panel, where you can relink and update the file, just like any other file.

③ Point to the imported OAM file to display a tooltip with information about the file.

④ To work with the imported OAM file, right-click (Win) or control-click (Mac), and then click an option:

◆ **Relink.** Relinks the OAM file in a different location.

◆ **Update Asset.** Updates the OAM file with any changes; the command appears as needed.

◆ **Go To Asset.** Locates the OAM animation in the site.

◆ **Reveal in Explorer** (Win) or **Reveal in Finder** (Mac). Opens the folder with the OAM file in your operating system.

◆ **Copy Full Path.** Copies the full path location of the OAM file as a link to the Clipboard, where you can paste it in another location.

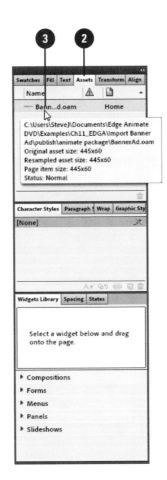

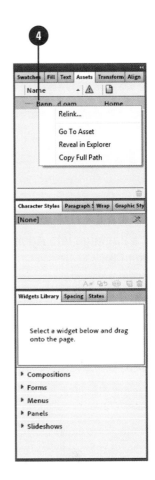

Importing into Adobe InDesign

Adobe InDesign is a program that allows you to design and pre-flight page layouts for print or digital distribution. You can drag and drop or import using the Place command the OAM file into an open InDesign document. In InDesign, you can create interactive documents and digital publication for use on mobile devices, such as an iPad or iPhone, as well as your desktop. You can create alternate layouts, one for print and another for tablet, to leverage the same content on multiple layouts. After you create a layout, you can apply Liquid Layout options to allow page content to adapt to different screen sizes. After you create a digital publication, you can use tools in InDesign, such as Folio Builder and Folio Overlay, to create a Folio publication for use with Adobe Digital Publishing Suite (DPS), an integrated online service that allows you to create, optimize, and distribute content produced for tablet devices.

Import a Package into Adobe InDesign CS6

1. Start Adobe InDesign CS6, and then open the file you want to use.

2. Select the **Selection** Tool in the Tools panel, and then click a blank area off the page to deselect all elements.

3. Click the **File** menu, and then click **Place**.

4. Click the **Save as Type** list arrow (Win) or **Format** popup (Mac), and then click **All Files**.

5. Navigate to and select the Edge Animate Deployment Package (.oam) file.

6. Click **Open**.

   The cursor loads with the imported content.

7. Click in the document where you want to place the composition as you would a photo or any other imported file type.

   The poster image for the animation appears in the document.

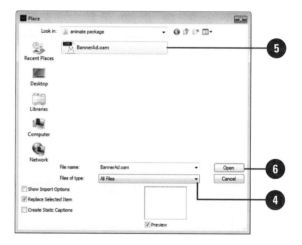

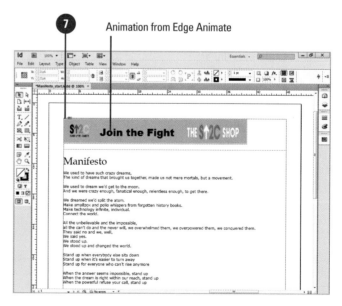

Animation from Edge Animate

Work with Alternate and Liquid Layouts

1. Select the **Pages** panel.

   ◆ Click the **Window** menu, and then click **Pages**.

2. Click the **Options** menu, point to **View Pages**, and then click **By Alternate Layout**.

3. Click the **Layout Options** menu, and then select from the following options:

   ◆ **Create Alternate Layout.** Select to creates a new alternate layout.

   ◆ **Delete Alternate Layout.** Select to delete the selected alternate layout.

   ◆ **Delete Pages.** Select to delete the selected pages in the alternate layout.

   ◆ **HTML5 Pagination Options.** Select to add or remove pages during the creation of folio and EPUB files.

   ◆ **Split Window to Compare Layouts** or **Unsplit Window.** Select to display alternate layouts in side-by-side windows.

4. Select the layout you want to adjust in the Pages panel.

5. Click the **Layout** menu, and then click **Liquid Layout**.

6. Click the **Liquid Page Rule** list arrow, select a rule, and then select other content and object constraint options, if available.

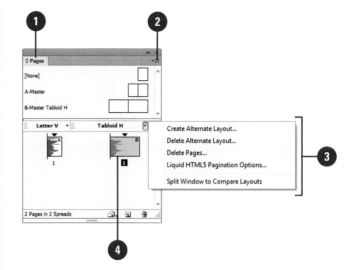

Working with Adobe Digital Publishing Suite

Adobe Digital Publishing Suite (DPS) is a set of tools used by larger publishers to create, distribute, and sell interactive publications for tablet devices. The DPS fee-based solution is available at *www.adobe.com* under Products; the Single Edition allows for publishing to iPad. DPS tools are integrated into InDesign by using the Folio Overlays and Folio Builder panels. The Folio Overlays panel allows you to create the interactive content, while the Folio Builder panel assembles (in a container) all of the necessary files into a format compatible with tablets. You can create local or online publications. For online publications, you need an Adobe ID (available free) to access Adobe DPS and the Adobe Cloud, where documents are stored and distributed to tablets. As an InDesign user, you can use DPS to create one free online publication to try it out and share it with as many people as you want. Before you can get started, you need to download Folio Producer tools (Folio Overlays panel, Digital Publishing plug-in, and Content Viewer for Desktop) and the Folio Builder panel update for InDesign CS6 or later, and install them on your computer. When you sign in to DPS with your Adobe ID on a tablet, it allows you to download and view it.

Get Started with DPS

1. Start Adobe InDesign CS6, and then open the file with the imported Edge Animate Deployment Package (.oam).

2. Click the **Help** menu, and then click **Update**.

3. Update the DPS Tools to get the latest version, and then exit it.

   ◆ You can also download DPS Tools from www.*adobe.com*.

4. Select the **Folio Builder** and **Folio Overlay** panels; click the **Window** menu, and then select a panel.

5. Click **New** on the Folio Builder panel, specify settings, and then click **OK**.

6. To add articles/content, double-click a folio, click **Add**, specify settings, and then click **OK**.

7. To add interactivity, click options on the Folio Overlay panel.

8. To access DPS on the web, click the **Options** menu on the Folio Builder panel, and then click **Folio Producer**.

Preview the Animation with DPS and Adobe Content Viewer

① Start Adobe InDesign CS6, and then open the file with the imported Edge Animate Deployment Package (.oam).

② Select the **Folio Builder** panel.

 ◆ Click the **Window** menu, and then click **Folio Builder**.

③ Select the folio or article you want to preview.

④ Click **Preview** on the Folio Builder panel, and then click **Preview on Desktop**.

 Adobe Content Viewer opens, displaying the folio publication.

 To set folio preview settings, continue.

⑤ Click the **File** menu, and then click **Folio Preview Settings**.

⑥ Specify options:

 ◆ Format. Select Auto to use document setting, Liquid, or Static.

 ◆ Raster Format. Select Auto to use document setting, or a graphic format.

 ◆ JPEG Quality. Select a quality; higher the quality, better the display, bigger the file size.

 ◆ Ignore Object Export Options. Select to ignore option.

 ◆ Resolution. Select a resolution best for the device: OS & web is 72 or 96, tablets are 150, and iPhone is 300.

 ◆ Preview Current Layout. Select to preview the current layout.

⑦ Click **OK**.

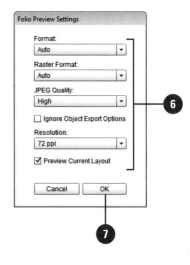

Saving Images from Adobe Photoshop

Adobe Photoshop is a powerful high-end image editor that allows you to create and modify bitmap graphics for print and web-based projects. The Save for Web command in Photoshop is a dream come true for preparing images for the Internet. You can open any Photoshop document, and convert it into a web-friendly format, such as GIF, JPEG, or PNG. In the Save for Web dialog box, you can even try different optimization settings or compare different optimizations using the 2-Up or 4-Up panes. In addition, the dialog area below each image provides optimization information on the size and download time of the file. You can create graphics, such as backgrounds, buttons, or images, which you can import into Edge Animate. For example, you can create and save an image for use as a custom poster image in Edge Animate.

Save an Image from Photoshop in a Web Format

1. Start Adobe Photoshop, and then open or create an image.

   ◆ **Check Image Size.** Before you get started, it's important to check the image size to make sure it's the resolution you want for use on the Stage in Edge Animate. Click the **Image** menu, and then click **Image Size**.

2. Click the **File** menu, and then click **Save for Web**.

3. Click the **Original**, **Optimized**, **2-Up**, or **4-Up** tabs to view the document using different layouts.

4. Click one of the sample images to change its default format.

5. Click the **Preset** list arrow. Use Original or select a template from the available options, if you want to use some timesaving default options.

6. Click the **Optimized File Format** list arrow, and then select from the following options:

   ◆ **GIF.** The Graphics Interchange Format is useful for clip art, text, or images that contain a large amount of solid color. GIF uses lossless compression.

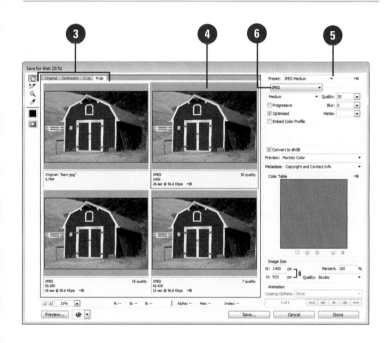

- **JPEG.** The Joint Photographic Experts Group format is useful for images that contain a lot of continuous tones, like photographs. JPEG uses lossy compression.

- **PNG-8.** The Portable Network Graphics 8-bit format functions like the GIF format. PNG uses lossless compression.

- **PNG-24.** The Portable Network Graphics 24-bit format functions like the JPEG format. PNG-24 uses lossless compression.

7 Specify the options you want for the selected format; the options vary depending on the format.

8 To view in the default browser, click the **Preview** button.

- Click the **Browser** list arrow to select another browser.

9 Click **Save**, enter a name, select a location, and then click **Save**.

10 Enter a name, and then select a location to save the file.

11 Click **Save**.

You can now import the image into Edge Animate.

See Also

See "Importing Graphics" on page 85 and "Adding Graphics" on page 86 for information on importing graphics into a composition in Edge Animate.

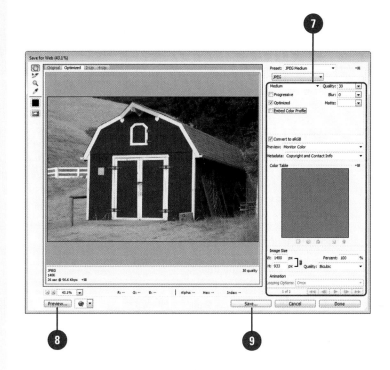

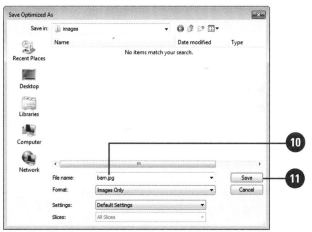

Saving Graphics from Adobe Fireworks

Adobe Fireworks is a powerful high-end image editor that allows you to create, modify and optimize bitmap and vector graphics for web-based projects. You can create web interfaces, effects, and elements—such as rollovers, pop-up menus, and hotspots—image slices, layers, symbols, and optimize graphics to reduce their file size. With the Save As command, you save an image as a PNG, JPG/JPEG, GIF, or Animated GIF, and then import the file into Edge Animate. The default file format for Fireworks is PNG (Portable Network Graphic). You can import PNG files into Edge Animate as bitmap images. When you import a PNG file as a bitmap image, the file, including any vector data, is flattened, or rasterized, and converted to a bitmap. Along with the graphics, you can also save HTML files containing HTML tables and JavaScript code so you can use them on the web, which you can open in Edge Animate.

Save Graphics from Fireworks

1. Start Adobe Fireworks, and then open or create an image.

2. Click the **File** menu, and then click **Save As**.

3. Click the **Save as Type** list arrow (Win) or **Format** popup (Mac), and then select a format:

   ◆ **Fireworks PNG (*.PNG).** PNG format with slices and layers.

   ◆ **Flattend PNG (*.PNG).** PNG with everything flattend into one layer.

   ◆ **GIF (*.GIF).** Bitmap with lossless compression.

   ◆ **Animated GIF (*.GIF).** A sequence of GIF image frames to create an animation.

   ◆ **JPEG (*.JPG, *.JPEG).** Bitmap with lossy compression.

4. Enter a name, and then select a location to save the file.

5. For the default Fireworks PNG file format, select the **Append.fw.png** check box to add .fw to the file name to distinguish it from a flattened PNG file extension.

6. Click **Save**.

   You can now import the image into Edge Animate.

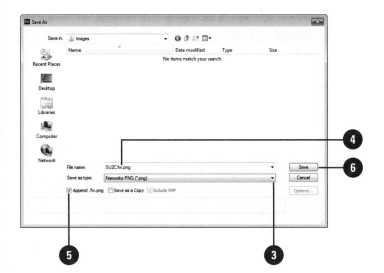

Export as an HTML Document and Images from Fireworks

1. Start Adobe Fireworks, and then open or create an image.

2. Click the **File** menu, and then click **Export**.

3. Click the **Export** list arrow (Win) or **Format** popup (Mac), and then click **HTML and Images**.

4. Click the **HTML** list arrow, and then click **Export HTML File**.

5. Enter a name, and then select a location to save the file.

6. Specify the following options:

   ◆ **Slices.** Select options for any slices in the image.

   ◆ **Pages.** Select the pages you want to include in the HTML file.

7. Click **Options**.

8. Some important options include:

   ◆ **HTML Style.** Select an HTML style for use in Edge Animate: Dreamweaver XHTML or HTML, Generic HTML, or jQuery HTML.

   ◆ **Write CSS to an external file.** Creates an external CSS file for the formatting and positioning of content.

9. Click **OK**.

10. Click **Save**.

    You can now open the HTML file in Edge Animate.

See Also

See "Importing Graphics" on page 85 and "Adding Graphics" on page 86 for information on importing graphics into a composition in Edge Animate.

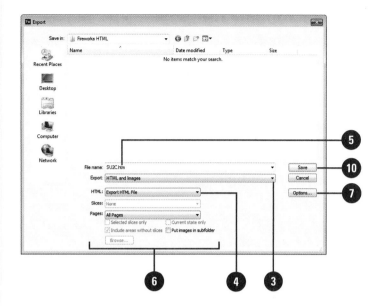

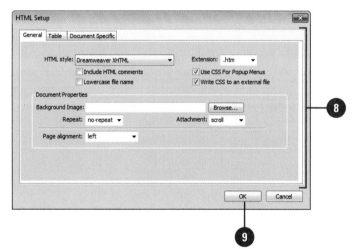

Exporting Images from Adobe Illustrator

Adobe Illustrator is a powerful high-end illustration and image editor that allows you to create and modify vector and bitmap graphics for print and web-based projects. If you have an image that you want to post on the web, you can export it as a PNG or JPEG file. PNG and JPEG are a compressed format with high quality, so it's a common file format for the web. The Export command for PNG and JPEG give you options to specify image resolution and use anti-alias to smooth jagged edges for text and images. For PNG, you can also set options to use a transparent background. For JPEG, you can also set options to specify the color model, quality, and compression as well as embed an ICC color profile.

Export Artwork as a PNG Image from Illustrator

1. Start Adobe Illustrator, and then open or create artwork.

2. Click the **File** menu, and then click **Export**.

3. Click the **Save as Type** list arrow (Win) or **Format** popup (Mac), and then click **PNG (*.PNG)**.

4. Enter a name, and then select a location to save the file.

5. To preserve artboards, select the **Use Artboards** check box (if available), and then select the **All** or **Range** option. If you selected the Range option, enter a range.

6. Click **Save**.

7. Specify the following options:

   - **Resolution.** Select a resolution option in ppi (pixels per inch).

   - **Anti-aliasing.** Select to smooth out the edges of text or artwork.

   - **Interlaced.** Select to load/display the image from top to bottom.

8. Click the **Background Color** list arrow, and then specify an option: **Transparent**, **Black**, **White**, or a custom color.

9. Click **OK**.

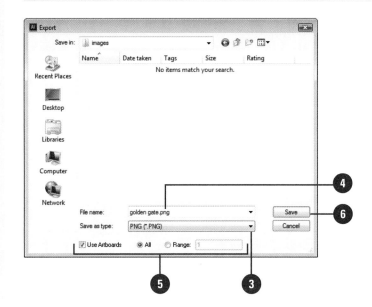

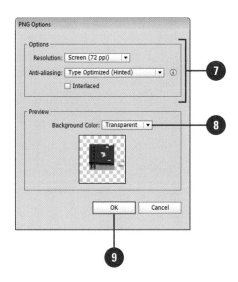

Export Artwork as a JPEG Image from Illustrator

① Start Adobe Illustrator, and then open or create artwork.

② Click the **File** menu, and then click **Export**.

③ Click the **Save as Type** list arrow (Win) or **Format** popup (Mac), and then click **JPEG (*.JPG)**.

④ Enter a name, and then select a location to save the file.

⑤ To preserve artboards, select the **Use Artboards** check box (if available), and then select the **All** or **Range** option. If you selected the Range option, enter a range.

⑥ Click **Save**.

⑦ Specify the following options:

◆ **Color Model.** Select a color mode: RGB, CMYK, or Grayscale.

◆ **Quality.** Select a balance between file size and quality.

⑧ Specify the following options:

◆ **Compression Method.** Select a method: Standard (used by most browsers), Optimized for color and size, and Progressive display for a series of scans.

◆ **Resolution.** Select a resolution option in ppi (pixels per inch).

◆ **Anti-aliasing.** Select to smooth out the edges of text or artwork.

◆ **Imagemap.** Select to generate code for image maps.

⑨ Select the **Embed ICC Profile** check box to attach the color profile of the document to the image.

⑩ Click **OK**.

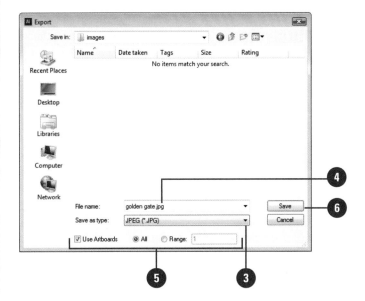

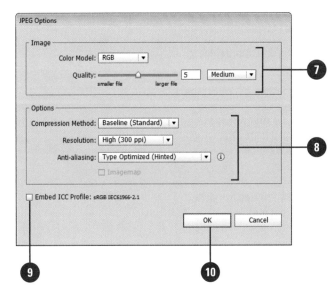

Saving Artwork from Adobe Illustrator

SVG (Scalable Vector Graphics) is a vector based format, like the Illustrator AI format, that describes images as shapes, paths, text and filter effects. Vector images can be resized without sacrificing sharpness and clarity. The SVG format is XML-based, which allows you to add code (XML and JavaScript) so that the web graphic can respond to user actions. Things to remember when you save a document to SVG, each layer is converted to a group (<g>) element, objects appear transparent based on opacity, use slices, image maps, and scripts to add web links, and symbols and paths improve performance.

Save Artwork as a SVG from Illustrator

1. Start Adobe Illustrator, and then open or create artwork.

2. Click the **File** menu, and then click **Save As**.

3. Click the **Save as Type** list arrow (Win) or **Format** popup (Mac), and then click **SVG (*.SVG)** or **SVG Compressed (*.SVGZ)**.

4. Enter a name, and then select a location to save the file.

5. To preserve artboards, select the **Use Artboards** check box, and then select the **All** or **Range** option. If you selected the Range option, enter a range.

6. Click **Save**.

7. Click the **SVG Profiles** list arrow, and then select a SVG specification by version number.

8. Specify the following font options:

   ◆ **Type.** Select a font display option: Adobe CEF has the best display, yet not as widely supported; SVG is the most supported; and Convert to Outline provides the smallest size, yet lowest quality.

   ◆ **Subsetting.** Select the set of font characters you want to include in the file.

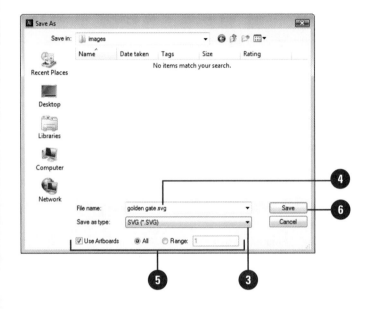

9 Click the **Embed** or **Link** option to specify where you want the image location (embedded in or external), and then select the check box if you want to preserve Illustrator editing capabilities for future revisions.

10 To specify additional options, click **More Options**.

The button changes to Less Options.

11 Specify the following Advanced Options:

- ◆ **CSS Properties.** Select an option to create CSS properties.

- ◆ **Optimize for Adobe SVG Viewer.** Select to optimize for the best performance with the Adobe SVG Viewer.

- ◆ **Include Slicing Data.** Select to include slicing locations and settings.

- ◆ **Include XMP.** Select to include XMP metadata information.

- ◆ **Output fewer <tspan> elements.** Select to reduce the file size by ignoring kerning position.

- ◆ **Use <textPath> element for Text on Path.** Select to use <textPath> tag for path text, which creates more compact XML; deselect to use <text> tag.

12 If you want to view the SVG code in a web browser, click **SVG Code**.

13 Click **OK**.

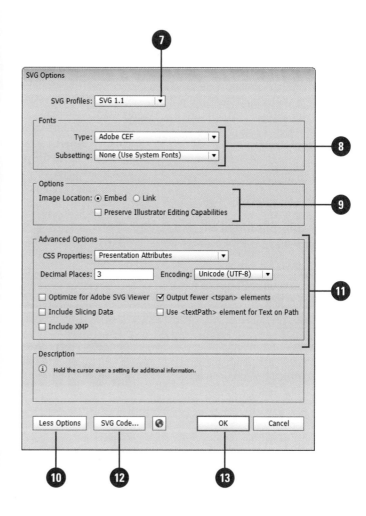

Exporting Animations from Adobe Flash

Adobe Flash Professional is a program for developing interactive content, animations, user interfaces, games, and mobile and web applications that allow designers and developers to integrate video, text, audio, and graphics into rich experiences. Flash Professional uses the following technologies: ActionScript, Flash Player, AIR for desktop and mobile devices. Instead of using the built-in preloader assets provided by Edge Animate, you can create a custom animated GIF in Flash Professional and then export it for use in your composition. The preloader assets are simple animated GIF files. When you create a custom animated GIF be sure to keep the animation simple and small in size, so it doesn't take a long time to load and defeat the purpose of the preloader.

Create a Simple Animated GIF as a Custom Preloader

1. Start Adobe Flash Professional, and then click **ActionScript 3.0** to create a new movie.

2. Select the **Text** Tool on the Tools panel.

3. Create a text box, add some text, such as LOADING, and then use the Properties panel to format it.

4. Click the **Window** menu, and then click **Motion Presets** to open the panel.

5. Select a preset, such as pulse, in the Motion Presets panel.

6. Click **Apply**.

7. Click the **File** menu, and then click **Save As**.

8. Click the **Save as Type** list arrow (Win) or **Format** popup (Mac), and then click **Flash CS6 Document (*.fla)**.

9. Enter a name, and then select a location to save the file.

10. Click **Save**.

    You can now export the movie as an animated GIF for use in Edge Animate.

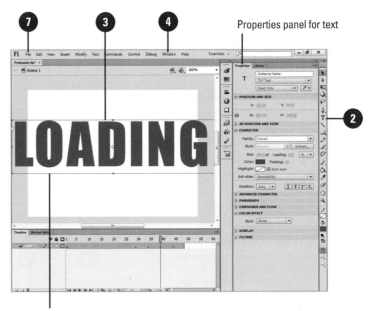

Properties panel for text

Animated GIF as a preloader in Edge Animate

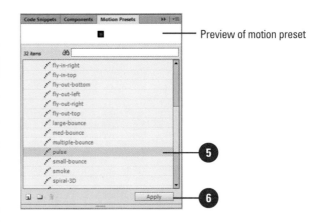

Preview of motion preset

Export an Animated GIF from Flash as a Custom Preloader

1. Start Adobe Flash Professional, and then open or create a movie.

2. Click the **File** menu, point to **Export**, and then click **Export Movie**.

3. Click the **Save as Type** list arrow (Win) or **Format** popup (Mac), and then click **Animated GIF (*.gif)**.

4. Enter a name, and then select a location to save the file.

5. Click **Save**.

6. Specify the following options:

   ◆ **Width and Height.** Specify an image width and height.

   ◆ **Resolution.** Specify a DPI (Dots Per Inch); typically 72.

   ◆ **Colors.** Select a color palette (4 to 256); smaller the better.

   ◆ **Transparent.** Select to output transparent pixels.

   ◆ **Interlace.** Select to interlace horizontal rows.

   ◆ **Smooth.** Select to apply a smoothing effect.

   ◆ **Dither solid Colors.** Select to dither when approximating colors.

   ◆ **Animation.** Specify the number of loops; 0 repeats forever.

7. Click **OK**.

   You can now import the animated GIF into Edge Animate.

   An animated GIF works well as a custom animation on the Preloader Stage.

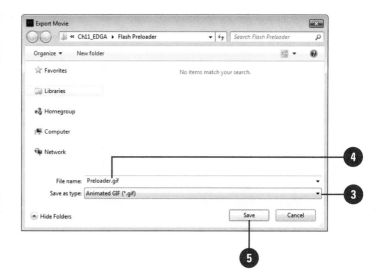

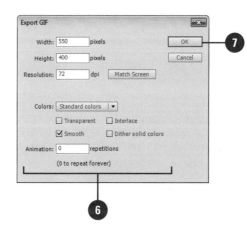

Installing Edge Animate and Edge Tools

A

Introduction

This appendix describes how to prepare and install Adobe Edge Animate and Edge Tools & Services. The temptation is to download the software and start the installation, but you can avoid problems by making sure your system is ready for the software. Before you install Edge Animate and its related tools and services, you need to check your system hardware and software and make several setup decisions that relate to your system. The Adobe Setup wizard walks you through the installation process.

Adobe is continually updating and enhancing Edge Animate and its related tools and services. Instead of releasing multiple updates individually, periodically Adobe releases updates, which provides all-in-one access to the most up-to-date drivers, tools, enhancements, and other critical fixes. Updates are available free for download and installation over the Internet from Adobe Creative Cloud.

What You'll Do

Prepare for Edge Animate and Tools

Download Edge Animate and Tools

Install Edge Animate and Tools

Finish the Edge Inspect Install

Preparing for Edge Animate and Edge Tools

Along with Edge Animate, there are other tools and services you can use to develop content for the web. These tools and services include Edge Reflow, Edge Code, Edge Inspect, Edge Web Fonts, Typekit, and PhoneGap Build.

Edge Animate

With Edge Animate, you can create interactive and animated content using HTML and JavaScript.

Edge Reflow

With Edge Reflow, you can create responsive layouts and visuals with standards-based CSS. This program allows you to use the power of CSS to create designs simultaneously for all screen sizes without sacrificing your design look, quality, or capability.

Edge Code

With Edge Code, you can view and work with code content and application with HTML, CSS, and JavaScript. This program allows you to preview CSS, edit code, and use integrated visual design tools to help speed up the development process.

Edge Inspect

With Edge Inspect, you can preview and inspect your web designs on mobile devices. This program allows you to synchronize browsing in Chrome for wirelessly paired iOS and Android devices, update a device with remote inspection, and capture screenshots from all connected devices.

Edge Web Fonts

With Edge Web Fonts, you can get access to a free web font library from Adobe and Google for use in your site designs.

Adobe Typekit

With Typekit, you can browse commercial fonts by classification, properties, or recommended use, and add them to your site designs.

PhoneGap Build

With PhoneGap Build, you can build mobile apps with HTML, CSS, and JavaScript by reusing existing skills, frameworks, and tools and package mobile apps in the cloud.

Getting Edge Animate and Edge Tools & Services

Adobe Edge Animate and Edge Tools & Services are available for download on the web from Adobe Creative Cloud services at *create.adobe.com* or *html.adobe.com/edge*. After you sign up for a membership, you'll have access to Edge Animate and other Adobe Edge Tools & Services. You can download Edge Animate and its related tools on either the Apple OS X or Windows platforms as separate programs from the site to your hard drive before you install each one on your system. Some tools may be in the development or preview status, so check with Adobe for the latest version available.

Edge Animate System Requirements

Before you can install Adobe Edge Animate and development content, you need to make sure your computer meets the minimum system requirements. You can create Edge Animate content on Windows and Macintosh computers.

For Windows Computers

You need to have a computer with the following minimum configuration:

- Intel Pentium 4 or AMD Athlon 64 processor or equivalent.
- 32-bit and 64-bit computers; the 32-bit application runs on both.
- 1 GB of RAM.
- 200 MB available disk space for installation.
- 1280x800 display resolution with 16-bit video card.

- Microsoft Windows 7 or Windows 8 operating system.
- Internet (broadband connection) required for online services.
- Languages: English, French, German, Japanese, Italian, and Spanish.

For Macintosh Computers

You need to have a computer with the following minimum configuration:

- Multicore Intel-based Macintosh.
- 32-bit and 64-bit computers; the 32-bit application runs on both.
- 1 GB of RAM.
- 200 MB available disk space for installation.
- 1280x800 display resolution with 16-bit video card.
- Mac OS X v10.6, v10.7, or v10.8 operating system.
- Internet (broadband connection) required for online services.
- Languages: English, French, German, Japanese, Italian, and Spanish.

For Browsers and Devices

You can use Edge Animate on Windows and Macintosh computers to create motion content that runs on desktop browsers, such as Mozilla Firefox, Apple Safari, Google Chrome, and Microsoft Internet Explorer 9, and mobile devices, such as Apple iOS and Android. Edge Animate content runs on WebKit enabled devices, such as Chrome, Safari, and Amazon Kindle. WebKit is a layout engine designed to allow web browsers to render web pages.

Downloading Edge Animate and Tools

Adobe Edge Animate and Edge Tools & Services are available for download on the web through Adobe Creative Cloud services at *create.adobe.com* or *html.adobe.com/edge*. After you sign up for a free or purchase plan membership, you'll have access to Edge Animate and other Adobe Edge Tools & Services, such as Edge Inspect and PhoneGap Build. Edge Animate 1.0 is free for a limited time from Adobe; check the Creative Cloud site for the latest details and availability. You can download Edge Animate using Adobe Application Manager and its related tools as separate programs from the site to your hard drive before you install each one on your system. You can download Edge Animate and its related tools on either the Apple OS X or Windows platforms. Along with the Edge tools, you can access Edge Services, such as Edge Web Fonts, Typekit, and PhoneGap Build, which are available online through Creative Cloud.

Download Edge Animate

1. In your web browser, go to *creative.adobe.com*, and then sign in to Creative Cloud or create a new account.

   ◆ You can also access the software from *html.adobe.com/edge*, read the screen, and then click **Get Started**.

2. Click the **Apps** link, and then click the **Download** link for Edge Animate.

3. Read the alert message with download information, and then click **OK**.

   Adobe Application Manager is downloaded to the Downloads folder on your hard disk unless you specify another location.

4. Click **Save** to save the program to the Downloads folder or click **Run** to start the install.

   ◆ To save the download in another folder, click the **Save** list arrow, and then click **Save as**; your browser might differ.

5. Click the **Close** button to exit your web browser.

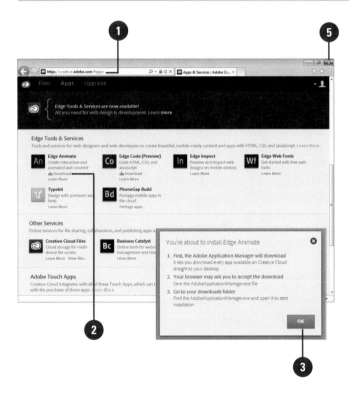

Download Edge Tools and Access Edge Services

1. In your web browser, go to *creative.adobe.com*, and then sign in to Creative Cloud or create a new account.

   ◆ You can also access the software from *html.adobe.com/ edge*, read the screen, and then click **Get Started**.

2. Click the **Apps** link, and then follow the download instructions:

   ◆ **Edge Code.** Click the **Download** link, and then click **OK**.

   ◆ **Edge Inspect.** Click the **Learn More** link, click **Download**, and then click **OK**.

     You also need to download the Google Chrome browser extension and install the mobile client on your devices (iOS, Android, and Kindle Fire).

   ◆ **Edge Web Fonts.** A service with nothing to download. Click the **Learn More** link to find out more and preview Edge Web Fonts.

   ◆ **Typekit.** A service with nothing to download; it comes with Creative Cloud. Click the **Learn More** link to find out more.

   ◆ **PhoneGap Build.** A service with nothing to download; it comes with Creative Cloud. Click the **Package apps** link to access the service.

3. Click **Save** to save the program to the Download folder or click **Run** to start the install.

   ◆ To save the download in another folder, click the **Save** list arrow, and then click **Save as**; your browser might differ.

4. Click the **Close** button to exit your web browser.

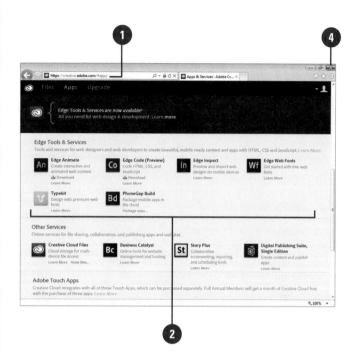

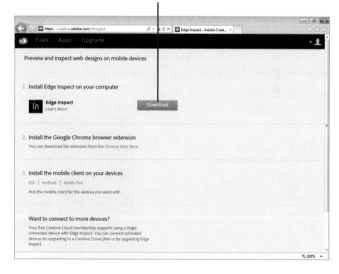

Download Edge Inspect

Installing Edge Animate and Tools

Edge Animate 1.0 is free for a limited time from Adobe; check the Adobe Creative Cloud site (*creative.adobe.com*) for the latest details and availability. To install Adobe Edge Animate, download the installer, Adobe Application Manager, from Creative Cloud to your hard drive, start it, and then follow the on-screen instructions. The installation includes all the required components you need to develop Edge Animate content. With the Adobe Application Manager, you can also install other Adobe programs that come with a Creative Cloud membership. To install Edge Tools, such as Edge Inspect and Edge Code, download the individual installers from Creative Cloud to your hard drive, start each one individually, and then follow the on-screen instructions.

Install Edge Animate

1. Open the Downloads folder or the location where you downloaded the Adobe Application Manager file.

2. Double-click the setup icon.

   ◆ **Windows.** Double-click the **AdobeApplicationManager.exe** file to start the installation of the Edge Animate program.

   ◆ **Macintosh.** Double-click the **AdobeApplicationManager** DMG file to uncompress and start the installation of the Edge Animate program.

3. Follow the on-screen instructions to install the product; the installer asks you to:

   ◆ Read and accept a licensing agreement; click **Accept**.

   ◆ Click **Install** to start the installation process, if necessary.

   ◆ Upon completion, click **Launch App** if you want to start it from Adobe Application Manager.

4. Click the **Close** button to exit Adobe Application Manager.

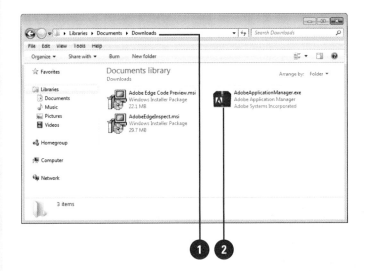

Install Edge Tools

1 Open the Downloads folder or the location where you downloaded the Adobe Application Manager file.

2 Double-click the setup icon.

◆ **Windows.** Double-click the Installer Package file (.msi) to start the installation of the Edge Tool program files.

◆ **Macintosh.** Double-click the Installer DMG file to uncompress and start the installation of the Edge Tool program files.

3 Follow the on-screen instructions to install the product; the installer asks you to:

◆ Read and accept a licensing agreement; click **Next** to continue.

◆ Specify where you want to install the software; typically located in the Program Files/Adobe folder (Win) or Applications folder (Mac); click **Next** to continue.

◆ Click **Install** to start the installation process.

◆ Upon completion, click **Finish**.

Finishing the Edge Inspect Install

Edge Edge Inspect is a tool that allows you to preview and inspect your web designs on mobile devices. This program allows you to synchronize browsing in Chrome for wirelessly paired iOS and Android devices, update a device with remote inspection, and capture screenshots from all connected devices. After you download and install the Edge Inspect program from Adobe Creative Cloud, there are still a couple of things you need to do to start using it. These include installing the Chrome extension, set up Bonjour (which provides auto discovery for devices), and install Edge Inspect device clients (iOS, Android, and Kindle Fire). Google Chrome must be installed as all interactions with devices are controlled from the Edge Inspect Chrome extension.

Finish the Edge Inspect Install

1. Download and install the Adobe Edge Inspect program.

2. Install Google Chrome and the Edge Inspect Chrome extension. In your web browser, go to the following sites.

   ◆ **Google Chrome.** Go to *chrome.google.com.*

   ◆ **Edge Inspect Chrome Extension.** Go to *www.adobe.com/go/ edgeinspect_chrome.*

3. Click the **Close** button to exit your web browser.

4. Install Bonjour, which is available in the folder location where you installed Adobe Edge Inspect.

   ◆ **Windows.** Start the installer at the following default location on your computer:

   Win32: \Program Files\Adobe\ Adobe Edge Inspect\ BonjourPSSetup.exe.

   Win64: \Program Files (x86)\ Adobe\Adobe Edge Inspect\ BonjourPSSetup.exe.

   Follow the on-screen instructions to complete the installation.

   ◆ **Macintosh.** Bonjour is enabled by default; no action required.

Goggle Chrome

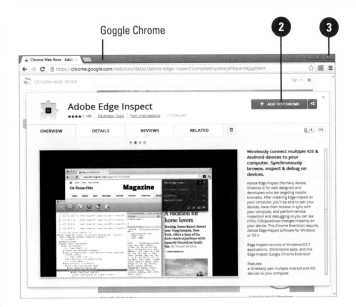

5 For each device you want to use with Edge Inspect, navigate the device to the appropriate store and then download and install the free Edge Inspect app on your devices.

◆ iOS. Go to *www.adobe.com/ go/edgeinspect_ios.*

◆ Android. *www.adobe.com/ go/edgeinspect_android.*

◆ Kindle Fire. *www.adobe.com/ go/edgeinspect_amazon.*

6 Connect your devices to your computer.

◆ Make sure your computer and devices are all on the same network.

◆ Start the Edge Inspect program on your computer and the Edge Inspect apps on each of your devices.

◆ Let the devices discover the computer via Bonjour, or manually connect them by entering the IP address.

◆ Enter the passcode for each device in the Edge Inspect Chrome extension to perform a one-time pairing process.

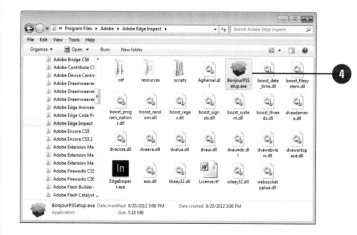

Install Bonjour

Keyboard Shortcuts

Adobe Edge Animate 1.0

If a command on a menu includes a keyboard reference, known as a keyboard shortcut, to the right of the command name, you can perform the action by pressing and holding the first key, and then pressing the second key to perform the command quickly. In some cases, a keyboard shortcut uses three keys. Simply press and hold the first two keys, and then press the third key. Keyboard shortcuts provide an alternative to using the mouse and make it easy to perform repetitive commands.

Edge Animate operates virtually the same on both Macintosh and Windows versions, except for a few keyboard commands that have equivalent functions. You use the [Ctrl] and [Alt] keys in Windows, and the ⌘ and [Option] keys on a Macintosh computer. Also, the term *popup* on the Macintosh and *list arrow* in Windows refer to the same type of option.

If you don't see a keyboard shortcut for a command or want to change an existing one to another keyboard combination, you can define your own in Edge Animate. For detailed steps and instructions, see "Defining Keyboard Shortcuts" on page 52 in this book.

Keyboard Shortcuts		
Menu Command	**Windows**	**Macintosh**
Edge Animate (Mac)		
Quit Edge Animate (Mac only)		⌘+Q
File		
New	Ctrl+N	⌘+N
Open	Ctrl+O	⌘+O
Close	Ctrl+W	⌘+W
Close All	Ctrl+Shift+W	⌘+Shift+W
Save	Ctrl+S	⌘+S
Save As	Ctrl+Shift+S	⌘+Shift+S
Publish	Ctrl+Alt+S	⌘+Option+S

Keyboard Shortcuts *(continued)*

Menu Command	Windows	Macintosh
Preview In Browser	Ctrl+Enter	⌘+Return
Import	Ctrl+I	⌘+I
Exit (Win only)	Ctrl+Q	
Edit		
Undo	Ctrl+Z	⌘+Z
Redo	Ctrl+Shift+Z	⌘+Shift+Z
Cut	Ctrl+X	⌘+X
Copy	Ctrl+C	⌘+C
Paste	Ctrl+V	⌘+V
Paste Special >		
Paste Transitions From Location	Ctrl+Shift+V	⌘+Shift+V
Paste All	Ctrl+Alt+V	⌘+Option+V
Duplicate (Mac only)		⌘+D
Select All	Ctrl+A	⌘+A
Delete	Backspace	delete
Keyboard Shortcuts	Alt+A	Option+A
Special Characters (Mac only)		⌘+Option+T
View		
Zoom In	Ctrl+= (equals)	⌘+= (equals)
Zoom Out	Ctrl+- (minus)	⌘+- (minus)
Actual Size	Ctrl+1	⌘+1
Rulers	Ctrl+R	⌘+R
Guides	Ctrl+; (semi-colon)	⌘+; (semi-colon)
Snap to Guides	Ctrl+Shift+; (semi-colon)	⌘+Shift+; (semi-colon)
Lock Guides	Shift+Alt+; (semi-colon)	Shift+Option+; (semi-colon)
Smart Guides	Ctrl+U	⌘+U
Modify		
Arrange >		
Bring to Front	Ctrl+Shift+]	⌘+Shift+]
Bring Forward	Ctrl+]	⌘+]
Send Backward	Ctrl+[	⌘+[
Send to Back	Ctrl+Shift+[	⌘+Shift+[

Menu Command	Windows	Macintosh
Group Elements in DIV	Ctrl+G	⌘+G
Ungroup Elements	Ctrl+Shift+G	⌘+Shift+G
Convert to Symbol	Ctrl+Y	⌘+Y
Timeline		
Play/Pause	Space	Space
Return (to Play Position)	Enter	Return
Go to Start	Home	Home
Go to End	End	End
Go to Previous Keyframe	Ctrl+Left Arrow	⌘+Left Arrow
Go to Next Keyframe	Ctrl+Right Arrow	⌘+Right Arrow
Auto-Keyframe Mode	K	K
Auto-Transition Mode	X	X
Insert Label (Mac only)		⌘+L
Insert Trigger	Ctrl+T	⌘+T
Create Transition	Ctrl+Shift+T	⌘+Shift+T
Remove Transition	Shift+Del	⌘+
Toggle Pin	P	P
Flip Playhead and Pin	Shift+P	Shift+P
Snapping	Alt+; (semi-colon)	Option+; (semi-colon)
Zoom In	= (equal)	= (equal)
Zoom Out	- (minus)	- (minus)
Zoom Out Fit	\ (backslash)	\ (backslash)
Expand/Collapse Selected	Ctrl+. (period)	⌘+. (period)
Expand/Collapse All	Ctrl+Shift+. (period)	⌘+Shift+. (period)
Window		
Code	Ctrl+E	⌘+E
Lessons (Win only)	Ctrl+F1	

Menu by Menu

m

Adobe Edge Animate 1.0

If you are not sure what a menu does in Edge Animate 1.0, you can refer to this quick reference guide with summary descriptions of every command on every menu.

Menu by Menu	
Menu Command	**Description**
Edge Animate (Mac)	
Quit Edge Animate	Closes all open compositions and exits Edge Animate. Also, prompts to save as needed.
Ctrl+Q (Win), ⌘+Q (Mac)	
File	
New	Creates a new blank composition.
Ctrl+N (Win), ⌘+N (Mac)	
Open	Opens the Open dialog box where you can open an existing com position (AN or HTML) or HTML document.
Ctrl+O (Win), ⌘+O (Mac)	
Open Recent >	Displays a submenus with the last 10 opened compositions or HTML documents that you can reopen.
Clear Recent	Clears the documents on the Open Recent submenu.
Close	Closes the active composition. Also, prompts to save as needed.
Ctrl+W (Win), ⌘+W (Mac)	
Close All	Closes all open compositions. Also, prompts to save as needed.
Ctrl+Shift+W (Win), ⌘+Shift+W (Mac)	
Save	Saves a composition and all of its related files.
Ctrl+S (Win), ⌘+S (Mac)	

Menu Command	Description
Save As	Opens the Save As dialog box where you can save a composition and all of its related files with a new name in a new or separate folder.
Ctrl+Shift+S (Win), ⌘+Shift+S (Mac)	
Revert	Reverts back to the most recently saved composition.
Publish Settings	Opens the Publish Settings dialog box where you can publish a composition to the Web, Adobe programs, or iBooks.
Publish	Publishes the active composition with the options set in the Publish Settings dialog box.
Ctrl+Alt+S (Win), ⌘+Option+S (Mac)	
Preview In Browser	Opens your default web browser and displays your composition.
Ctrl+Enter (Win), ⌘+Return (Mac)	
Import	Opens the Import dialog box where you can select one or more graphics (JPG/JPEG, PNG, SVG, and GIF) to insert into a composition. The graphics are copied to the images folder and appear in the Library panel.
Ctrl+I (Win), ⌘+I (Mac)	
Exit (Win only)	Closes all open compositions and exits Edge Animate. Also, prompts to save as needed.
Ctrl+Q (Win)	
Edit	
Undo	Reverts the last command.
Ctrl+Z (Win), ⌘+Z (Mac)	
Redo	Re-performs the last Undo command.
Ctrl+Shift+Z (Win), ⌘+Shift+Z (Mac)	
Cut	Removes the selection and places it into the Clipboard.
Ctrl+X (Win), ⌘+X (Mac)	
Copy	Copies the selection and places it into the Clipboard.
Ctrl+C (Win), ⌘+C (Mac)	
Paste	Pastes the selection from the Clipboard.
Ctrl+V (Win), ⌘+V (Mac)	

Menu Command	Description
Paste Special >	
Paste Transitions To Location	Pastes the copied or cut keyframes/transitions to the Timeline at the Playhead position.
Paste Transitions From Location	Pastes the copied or cut keyframes/transitions from one element or symbol to another.
Ctrl+Shift+V (Win), ⌘+Shift+V (Mac)	
Paste Inverted	Pastes the copied or cut keyframes/transition to the Timeline in the reverse direction.
Paste Actions	Pastes the copied or cut actions from one element to another.
Paste All	Pastes all properties, transitions, and actions to the target.
Ctrl+Alt+V (Win), ⌘+Option+V (Mac)	
Duplicate	Makes a copy of the selected element.
⌘+D (Mac)	
Select All	Selects everything visible on the Stage.
Ctrl+A (Win), ⌘+A (Mac)	
Transform	Toggles the Transform Tool on and off.
Delete	Removes the selected element.
Backspace (Win), delete (Mac)	
Keyboard Shortcuts	Opens the Keyboard Shortcut dialog box where you can define keyboard shortcuts.
Alt+A (Win), Option+A (Mac)	
Start Dictation (Mac only)	Starts dictation where you can speak text to type in a text box; only available in OS X Mountain Lion (10.8) or later.
Special Characters (Mac only)	Opens the Characters dialog box where you can insert special characters and symbols into a text box.
⌘+Option+T	
View	
Zoom In	Zooms in the Stage.
Ctrl+= (equals) (Win), ⌘+= (equals) (Mac)	

Menu Command	Description
Zoom Out	Zooms out the Stage.
Ctrl+- (minus) (Win), ⌘+- (minus) (Mac)	
Actual Size	Zooms the Stage to 100%
Ctrl+1 (Win), ⌘+1 (Mac)	
Rulers	Toggles the rulers (horizontal and vertical) on and off.
Ctrl+R (Win), ⌘+R (Mac)	
Guides	Toggles guides on and off.
Ctrl+; (semi-colon) (Win), ⌘+; (semi-colon) (Mac)	
Snap to Guides	Snaps elements to guides for alignment as you drag them close.
Ctrl+Shift+; (semi-colon) (Win), ⌘+Shift+; (semi-colon) (Mac)	
Lock Guides	Locks guides in place so they cannot be moved.
Shift+Alt+; (semi-colon) (Win), Shift+Option+; (semi-colon) (Mac)	
Smart Guides	Toggles Smart Guides on and off. Smart Guides display guides as you drag elements on the Stage for alignment.
Ctrl+U (Win), ⌘+U (Mac)	
Preloader Stage	Displays the Stage with a progress bar that gets viewed when a browser loads a composition.
Down-level Stage	Displays the Stage that gets viewed when a browser is not compatible with an Edge Animate composition.
Modify	
Arrange >	
Bring to Front	Brings the selected elements to the top level on the Stage.
Ctrl+Shift+] (Win), ⌘+Shift+] (Mac)	
Bring Forward	Brings the selected elements one level up on the Stage.
Ctrl+] (Win), ⌘+] (Mac)	
Send Backward	Brings the selected elements one level down on the Stage.
Ctrl+[(Win), ⌘+[(Mac)	
Send to Back	Brings the selected elements to the bottom level on the Stage.
Ctrl+Shift+[(Win), ⌘+Shift+[(Mac)	

Menu Command	Description
Align >	
Left	Aligns selected elements along the left edge.
Horizontal Center	Aligns the center of the selected elements to a horizontal position.
Right	Aligns selected elements along the right edge.
Top	Aligns selected elements along the top edge.
Vertical Center	Aligns the center of the selected elements to a vertical position.
Bottom	Aligns selected elements along the bottom edge.
Distribute >	
Left	Distributes the left edge of selected elements to an even distance apart.
Horizontal Center	Distributes the center edge of selected elements to an even distance apart in the horizontal direction.
Right	Distributes the right edge of selected elements to an even distance apart.
Top	Distributes the top edge of selected elements to an even distance apart.
Vertical Center	Distributes the center edge of selected elements to an even distance apart in the vertical direction.
Bottom	Distributes the bottom edge of selected elements to an even distance apart.
Group Elements in DIV Ctrl+G (Win), ⌘+G (Mac)	Groups selected elements together within a div tag.
Ungroup Elements Ctrl+Shift+G (Win), ⌘+Shift+G (Mac)	Ungroups a selected group of elements.
Convert to Symbol Ctrl+Y (Win), ⌘+Y (Mac)	Opens a dialog box to convert the selected element into a symbol.

Menu Command	Description
Edit Symbol	Opens Symbol Editing mode for the selected element.
Timeline	
Play/Pause	Starts and stops the playback of an animation.
Spacebar (Win), Spacebar (Mac)	
Return (to Play Position)	Moves the Playhead back to its previous position before playback.
Enter (Win), Return (Mac)	
Go to Start	Moves the Playhead to the beginning of the Timeline.
Home (Win), Home (Mac)	
Go to End	Moves the Playhead to the end of the Timeline.
End (Win), End (Mac)	
Go to Previous Keyframe	Moves the Playhead to the previous keyframe for the selected element.
Ctrl+Left Arrow (Win), ⌘+Left Arrow (Mac)	
Go to Next Keyframe	Moves the Playhead to the next keyframe for the selected element.
Ctrl+Right Arrow (Win), ⌘+Right Arrow (Mac)	
Auto-Keyframe Mode	Toggles Auto-Keyframes on and off. Auto-Keyframe Mode automatically creates keyframes as you change element properties.
K (Win), K (Mac)	
Auto-Transition Mode	Toggles Auto-Transition Mode on and off. Auto-Transition Mode automatically adds a smooth Transition as you create keyframes.
X (Win), X (Mac)	
Add Keyframe	Adds a keyframe to the Timeline for an element property. A keyframes mark a point on the Timeline as an element property changes to create an animation.
Insert Label (Mac only)	Adds a label marker in the Timeline at the Playhead position.
⌘+L (Mac)	
Insert Trigger	Adds a new trigger to the Actions layer in the Timeline at the Playhead position.
Ctrl+T (Win), ⌘+T (Mac)	

Menu Command	Description
Create Transition Ctrl+Shift+T (Win), ⌘+Shift+T (Mac)	Creates a transition for the selected layer in the Timeline.
Remove Transition Shift+Del (Win), ⌘+Del (Mac)	Removes the transition for the selected layer in the Timeline.
Invert Transition	Inserts the Transition for the selected layer in the Timeline.
Insert Time	Opens a dialog box where you can insert a specific amount of time from the Playhead position to extend it on the Timeline.
Toggle Pin P (Win), P (Mac)	Toggles the Toggle Pin on and off. The Toggle Pin makes it easy to create an animation.
Flip Playhead and Pin Shift+P (Win), Shift+P (Mac)	Toggles the position of the Playhead with that of the Pin.
Snapping Alt+; (semi-colon) (Win), Option+; (semi-colon) (Mac)	Toggles snapping on and off. You can select the snapping options you want to use with the Snap To submenu.
Snap To >	
Grid	Snaps to grid markers on the Timeline.
Playhead	Snaps to the Playhead position.
Keyframes, Labels , Triggers	Snaps to Timeline objects (Keyframes, Labels, and Triggers).
Show Grid	Toggles the Timeline grid on and off.
Grid > 1 /sec to 30 / sec	Selects the incremental gridline display on the Timeline.
Zoom In = (equal) (Win), = (equal) (Mac)	Zooms in the Timeline.
Zoom Out - (minus) (Win), - (minus) (Mac)	Zooms out the Timeline.
Zoom Out Fit \ (backslash) (Win), \ (backslash) (Mac)	Zooms out the Timeline to fit in the Timeline panel

Menu Command	Description
Expand/Collapse Selected Ctrl+. (period) (Win), ⌘+. (period) (Mac)	Expands or collapses selected elements in the Timeline to display or hide individual keyframe properties.
Expand/Collapse All Ctrl+Shift+. (period) (Win), ⌘+Shift+. (period) (Mac)	Expands or collapses all elements in the Timeline to display or hide individual keyframe properties.
Window	
Workspace >	Select, create, delete,or reset a workspace, a custom set of panels.
Timeline	Shows or hides the Timeline panel.
Elements	Shows or hides the Elements panel.
Library	Shows or hides the Library panel (Assets, Symbols, and Fonts).
Tools	Shows or hides the Tools panel.
Properties	Shows or hides the Properties panel.
Code Ctrl+E (Win), ⌘+E (Mac)	Opens or closes the Code panel.
Lessons Ctrl+F1(Win)	Opens or closes the Lessons panel.
Help	
Edge Animate Help	Opens your browser to display online help for Edge Animate.
Edge Animate JavaScript Help	Opens your browser to display online help for JavaScript API.
Edge Animate Community Forums	Opens your browser to display Adobe Community Forums.
Change Language	Opens a dialog box where you can change the language display for Edge Animate.
Adobe Product Improvement	Allows you to participate in Adobe's improvement program.
About Adobe Edge Animate	Displays the current version of the product and credits.

Index